JBoss AS 7 Development

Develop, deploy, and secure Java applications on the new release of this robust, open source application server

Francesco Marchioni

BIRMINGHAM - MUMBAI

JBoss AS 7 Development

First published: December 2009

Second edition: June 2013

Production Reference: 1170613

Published by Packt Publishing Ltd.
Livery Place
35 Livery Street
Birmingham B3 2PB, UK.

ISBN 978-1-78216-134-9

www.packtpub.com

Cover Image by Suresh Mogre (suresh.mogre.99@gmail.com)

Credits

Author
Francesco Marchioni

Reviewers
Peter Johnson
Martin Večeřa

Acquisition Editor
James Jones

Lead Technical Editor
Azharuddin Sheikh

Technical Editors
Vrinda Amberkar Bhosale
Nitee Shetty

Copy Editors
Insiya Morbiwala
Alfida Paiva
Aditya Nair

Project Coordinator
Arshad Sopariwala

Proofreaders
Stephen Copestake
Lucy Henson
Clyde Jenkins

Indexer
Hemangini Bari

Graphics
Ronak Dhruv
Abhinash Sahu

Production Coordinator
Aditi Gajjar

Cover Work
Aditi Gajjar

About the Author

Francesco Marchioni is a Sun Certified Enterprise Architect employed for an Italian company based in Rome. He started learning Java in 1997 and since then has followed the path to the newest application program interfaces released by Sun. He joined the JBoss community in 2000, when the application server was running release 2.x.

He has spent many years as a software consultant, where he has envisioned many successful software migrations from vendor platforms to open source products such as JBoss AS, fulfilling the tight budget requirements of current times.

Over the past 5 years, he has been authoring technical articles for OReilly Media and is running an IT portal focused on JBoss products (`http://www.mastertheboss.com`).

He has authored the following titles:

- *JBoss AS 5 Development, Packt Publishing* (December 2009), which describes how to create and deploy Java Enterprise applications on JBoss AS (`http://www.packtpub.com/jboss-as-5-development/book`)
- *AS 5 Performance Tuning, Packt Publishing* (December 2010), which describes how to deliver fast and efficient applications on JBoss AS (`http://www.packtpub.com/jboss-5-performance-tuning/book`)
- *JBoss AS 7 Configuration, Deployment, and Administration, Packt Publishing* (December 2011), which covers all the aspects of the newest application server release (`http://www.packtpub.com/jboss-as-7-configuration-deployment-administration/book`)

He has also co-authored the book *Infinispan Data Grid Platform, Packt Publishing* (August 2012), with *Manik Surtani*, which covers all the aspects related to the configuration and development of applications using the Infinispan Data Grid Platform (`http://www.packtpub.com/infinispan-data-grid-platform/book`).

I'd like to thank Packt Publishing for sharing the vision of this new book and for all the effort they put into it. I'd like also to thank my family for always being by my side; in particular, I'd like to thank my wife for letting me follow my book author ambitions and my father for buying me a C-64 instead of a motorcycle when I was young.

About the Reviewers

Peter Johnson has over 32 years' enterprise computing experience. He has been working with Java since the past 15 years, and for the last 10 years, has been heavily involved with Java performance tuning. He is a frequent speaker on Java performance topics at various conferences, including the Computer Measurement Group annual conference, JBoss World, and Linux World. He is a moderator for the build tools and JBoss forums at Java Ranch. He is also the co-author of the book *JBoss in Action, First Edition, Manning Publications*, and has been a reviewer on numerous books on topics ranging from Java to Windows PowerShell.

Martin Večeřa is a JBoss Quality Assurance Manager within a division of Red Hat. He is interested in bleeding-edge projects and technologies. His main area of interest is Java middleware and SOA, in which he has almost 10 years' experience. Previously, he has developed information systems for power plants and medical companies. He publishes articles on Java middleware to various international and local web magazines.

He is the co-author of a blog on the PerfCake Performance Testing Framework.

www.PacktPub.com

Support files, eBooks, discount offers and more

You might want to visit www.PacktPub.com for support files and downloads related to your book.

Did you know that Packt offers eBook versions of every book published, with PDF and ePub files available? You can upgrade to the eBook version at www.PacktPub.com and as a print book customer, you are entitled to a discount on the eBook copy. Get in touch with us at service@packtpub.com for more details.

At www.PacktPub.com, you can also read a collection of free technical articles, sign up for a range of free newsletters and receive exclusive discounts and offers on Packt books and eBooks.

http://PacktLib.PacktPub.com

Do you need instant solutions to your IT questions? PacktLib is Packt's online digital book library. Here, you can access, read and search across Packt's entire library of books.

Why Subscribe?

- Fully searchable across every book published by Packt
- Copy and paste, print and bookmark content
- On demand and accessible via web browser

Free Access for Packt account holders

If you have an account with Packt at www.PacktPub.com, you can use this to access PacktLib today and view nine entirely free books. Simply use your login credentials for immediate access.

A thought to my loving family, who care about me, and to all the people who are striving to make our country a better place for our children. As somebody said, "If you have time to whine and complain about something, you have the time to do something about it."

Table of Contents

Preface

The JBoss Application Server is a certified platform for Java EE for developing and deploying Java Enterprise applications. The JBoss Application Server provides the full range of Java EE 1.6 features as well as extended Enterprise services, including clustering, caching, and persistence. This book will show Java EE developers how to develop their applications using the JBoss Application Server and the widely used Eclipse environment combined with the Maven framework, which will greatly increase your productivity. The whole learning process is arranged through a common theme application, the Ticket Booking application, that progressively increases in complexity as new topics are introduced.

What this book covers

Chapter 1, Getting Started with JBoss AS 7, discusses installing the core application server distribution and all the required tools for running it and for developing Java EE applications (JVM, Eclipse, and Maven).

Chapter 2, What's New in JBoss AS 7, provides a crash course on JBoss AS 7. It introduces the new filesystem structure, the application's configuration, and the dichotomy between standalone servers and domain servers.

Chapter 3, Beginning Java EE 6 – EJBs, discusses the new features introduced by EJB 3.1, including Singleton EJB, Asynchronous EJB, and EJB Timer Service. We will develop our Ticket Booking application, which will be the main theme of the book.

Chapter 4, Learning Context Dependency Injection, introduces Context Dependency Injection, comparing its features with the older EJB and JSF programming models. We will show how to enhance out ticket system using CDI annotations.

Chapter 5, Combining Persistence with CDI, discusses the Java Persistence API, showing how we can persist data on a relational database. We will then combine the JPA API with the example developed in the earlier chapters.

Chapter 6, Testing Your Applications, introduces Arquillian, showing how to use it for testing your application using a running application server instance or by managing its own server instance.

Chapter 7, Developing Applications with JBoss JMS Provider, discusses the Java Message Service, showing how you can configure some core JMS elements (such as factories and destinations) on your server. Next, we will enhance our Ticket example by adding a JMS producer and consumer. The last part of this chapter deals with advanced concepts, such as consuming messages from an external JMS provider.

Chapter 8, Adding Web Services to Your Applications, talks about the two core web services stacks: SOAP-based web services and RESTful web services; it provides concrete examples and highlights the differences between the two approaches.

Chapter 9, Managing the Application Server, talks about the core concepts of the Command Line Interface and how it can improve your productivity. The next part of this chapter dives deep into writing CLI scripts using other languages such as Jython.

Chapter 10, Clustering JBoss AS 7 Applications, is all about the world of clustered applications. We will learn how to use the robust clustering features of JBoss AS applied to some of the examples discussed in this book.

Chapter 11, Securing JBoss AS 7 Applications, will show how to use security domains to perform required authorization and authentication checks. The next part of this chapter discusses securing the data that is transmitted from the client to the server and vice versa.

Appendix, Rapid Development Using JBoss Forge, is the last section of this book; it is about the JBoss Forge framework. It shows how you can use this framework to generate a basic CRUD (Create/Read/Update/Delete) application.

What you need for this book

This is a developer's guide; for this reason, it is highly recommended that you read this book with a computer beside you, where you can try the examples and open, compile, and test the provided projects. Besides this, it's also required that you have an Internet connection where you can download the core server and additional libraries used in the examples.

Good programming skills are required to easily understand the examples presented in this book. Most of the chapters complement the covered topics with a set of executable Maven projects. A basic understanding of Maven, Java, and JUnit is also required.

Who this book is for

If you are a Java architect or a developer who wants to get the most out of the latest release of the JBoss Application Server, this book is for you. You are not expected to have accumulated a lot of experience on the application server, though you must know the basic concepts of Java EE.

Conventions

In this book, you will find a number of styles of text that distinguish between different kinds of information. Here are some examples of these styles and an explanation of their meaning.

Code words in text are shown as follows: "The users are stored in a properties file called `mgmt-users.properties` under `standalone/configuration` or `domain/configuration` depending on the running mode of the server."

A block of code is set as follows:

```
@WebServlet("/test")
public class TestServlet extends HttpServlet {
  protected void doGet(HttpServletRequest request,
    HttpServletResponse response) throws ServletException,
    IOException {
    PrintWriter out = response.getWriter();
    out.println("Hello World JBoss AS 7");
    out.close();
  }
  protected void doPost(HttpServletRequest request,
    HttpServletResponse response) throws ServletException,
    IOException {
  }
```

When we wish to draw your attention to a particular part of a code block, the relevant lines or items are set in bold:

```
@SessionScoped
@Named
public class TheatreBookerBean implements Serializable {
}
```

Any command-line input or output is written as follows:

```
mvn install jboss-as:deploy -Dhostname=localhost -Dport=9999
```

New terms and **important words** are shown in bold. Words that you see on the screen, in menus or dialog boxes for example, appear in the text like this: "Click on **Finish** to continue."

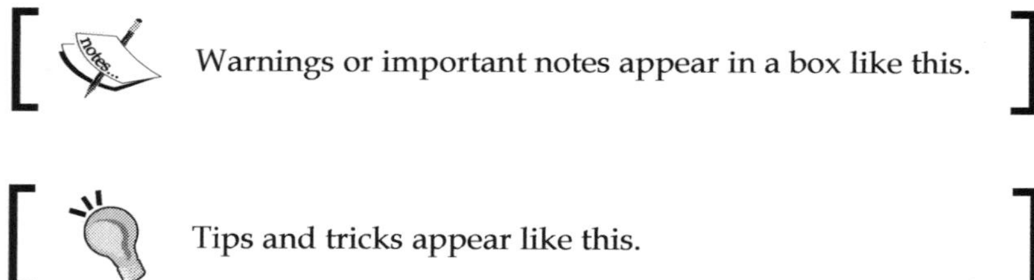

Warnings or important notes appear in a box like this.

Tips and tricks appear like this.

Reader feedback

Feedback from our readers is always welcome. Let us know what you think about this book—what you liked or may have disliked. Reader feedback is important for us to develop titles that you really get the most out of.

To send us general feedback, simply send an e-mail to `feedback@packtpub.com`, and mention the book title via the subject of your message.

If there is a topic that you have expertise in and you are interested in either writing or contributing to a book, see our author guide on `www.packtpub.com/authors`.

Customer support

Now that you are the proud owner of a Packt book, we have a number of things to help you to get the most from your purchase.

Downloading the example code

You can download the example code files for all Packt books you have purchased from your account at `http://www.packtpub.com`. If you purchased this book elsewhere, you can visit `http://www.packtpub.com/support` and register to have the files e-mailed directly to you.

Errata

Although we have taken every care to ensure the accuracy of our content, mistakes do happen. If you find a mistake in one of our books—maybe a mistake in the text or the code—we would be grateful if you would report this to us. By doing so, you can save other readers from frustration and help us improve subsequent versions of this book. If you find any errata, please report them by visiting `http://www.packtpub.com/submit-errata`, selecting your book, clicking on the **errata submission form** link, and entering the details of your errata. Once your errata are verified, your submission will be accepted and the errata will be uploaded on our website, or added to any list of existing errata, under the Errata section of that title. Any existing errata can be viewed by selecting your title from `http://www.packtpub.com/support`.

Piracy

Piracy of copyright material on the Internet is an ongoing problem across all media. At Packt, we take the protection of our copyright and licenses very seriously. If you come across any illegal copies of our works, in any form, on the Internet, please provide us with the location address or website name immediately so that we can pursue a remedy.

Please contact us at `copyright@packtpub.com` with a link to the suspected pirated material.

We appreciate your help in protecting our authors, and our ability to bring you valuable content.

Questions

You can contact us at `questions@packtpub.com` if you are having a problem with any aspect of the book, and we will do our best to address it.

1
Getting Started with JBoss AS 7

In this book, we will learn how to develop applications on the JBoss Application Server Release 7, which marks a giant leap from previous application server releases. The new application server features a truly modular, blazingly fast container that can be managed either as a standalone process or as part of a domain of servers.

The focus of this book is on application development; therefore, we will need at first to gather all resources required for delivering our applications. More in detail, in this chapter we will cover the following topics:

- An overview of Java EE and JBoss AS 7
- Preparing your environment for the installation
- Downloading and installing JBoss AS 7
- Verifying the JBoss AS installation
- Installing other resources needed for development

An overview of Java EE and JBoss AS 7

Java EE (formerly called J2EE) embraces a standard set of technologies for server-side Java development. Java EE technologies include servlets, **Java Server Pages (JSPs)**, **Java Server Faces (JSF)**, **Enterprise JavaBeans (EJBs)**, **Context Dependency Injection (CDI)**, **Java Messaging Service (JMS)**, **Java Persistence API (JPA)**, **Java API for XML Web Services (JAX-WS)**, and **Java API for RESTful Web Services (JAX-RS)**, among others.

Several commercial and open source application servers exist that allow developers to run applications compliant with Java EE; JBoss AS is the leading open source solution adopted by developers and, although this is difficult to measure in exact terms, it is likely to be the most widely used application server in the market.

JBoss AS, the most used application server - myth or fact?

We just threw the stone so we cannot avoid discussing it. There is a common belief that JBoss AS is the favorite application server of developers. Actually, there is no empiric way to measure the popularity of open source software; you may be able to guess it from a number of clues such as the number of downloads and the amount of registered users in the community.

Evaluating each product's community statistics can however be misleading and maybe not even be available to all players in this market. Therefore, if we want to try an approximate comparison, let's move to a neutral field where the world's most used software—Google—rules. A one-minute search on **Google trends** that includes as search keywords the other big players (Oracle WebLogic, IBM WebSphere, and the open source GlassFish application server) reveals that JBoss AS has the highest trend for 2012 at the time of writing. For more information on this, visit `http://www.google.com/trends/?q=jboss,oracle+weblogic,+websphere,glassfish&ctab=0&geo=all&date=2012&sort=0`. We will get similar results if we query for 2011.

Another popular instrument of Google is **Adwords;** it is used to count the search keywords on a national/worldwide basis. Adwords reveals that JBoss accounts for 1.220.000 monthly searches on Google while WebSphere stops at 1.000.000, Oracle WebLogic stays at 823.000, and Glassfish is around 368.000.

So, although these numbers do not provide the last word on our question (nor do they speak about the quality of the product), they are a good indicator of the developer's sentiment. A word to the wise is enough!

As with all application servers compliant with Java EE, JBoss ships with all the required libraries to allow us to develop and deploy Java applications that comply with Java EE specifications.

Welcome to Java EE 6

Java EE 6, includes several improvements and additions to the specification. The following sections list the major improvements to the specification that are of interest to enterprise application developers.

JavaServer Faces (JSF) 2.0

Java EE 6 includes a new version of JSF. JSF 2.0 includes the following new notable features:

- JSF 2.0 adopts **Facelets** as an official part of the specification. Facelets are an alternative view technology based on pure XML templates that was introduced with Version 2 of the JSF standard. Some of the advantages of Facelets include the ability to define a view in XHTML, the ability to easily create templates, and the ability to develop JSF components using markup, without having to use any Java code.
- JSF 2.0 also includes the ability to replace XML configuration elements with annotations, thus greatly speeding up the development of the applications.

Enterprise JavaBeans (EJB) 3.1

EJB 3.1 was designed around the concept of ease of development for users. Now designing an EJB application is much easier and less error-prone than in the past. Some enhancements provided with this application are as follows:

- Local interfaces are now optional as an actual bean instance and can be injected into local clients. Singleton session beans can be used to manage application states. Session beans can now be invoked asynchronously, allowing us to use session beans for tasks that were previously reserved for JMS and message-driven beans.
- The EJB timer service of the enterprise bean container enables you to schedule timed notifications for your EJBs. You can schedule a timed notification to occur according to a calendar schedule either at a specific time or at timed intervals.

Finally, Enterprise JavaBeans can now be packaged inside a **Web ARchive** (**WAR**) file. This feature greatly simplifies EJB packaging, as in the past an **Enterprise ARchive** (**EAR**) file was needed to package web functionality and EJB functionality into a single module.

Java Persistence API (JPA) 2.0

JPA was introduced as a standard part of Java EE in Version 5 of the specification. JPA was intended to replace entity beans as the standard object-relational mapping framework for Java EE. JPA adopted ideas from third-party object-relational frameworks such as Hibernate and JDO and made them part of the standard.

JPA 2.0 improves on JPA 1.0 in a number of areas:

- It provides transparent support for bean validation (JSR-303)
- It provides enhanced collection support with the introduction of the `@ElementCollection` and `@OrderColumn` annotations
- JPA queries can now be built through the new Criteria API, reducing the reliance on JPQL
- The **JPA Query Language (JPQL)** has improved; it allows adding support for SQL-like CASE expressions, and NULLIF and COALESCE operators

Contexts and Dependency Injection for Java

Contexts and Dependency Injection (**CDI**) (JSR 299) defines a set of services for the Java EE environment that makes applications much easier to develop. CDI leverages a simpler integration between the Web (JSF) and business logic (EJB) tiers, resulting in a significantly simplified programming model for web-based applications; it also provides a programming model suitable for rapid development of simple, data-driven applications. This is a domain where Java EE has been perceived as overly complex in the past.

Java Servlet API 3.0

Java Servlets API 3.0 provides easier web application development with enhanced annotations and integrated Web 2.0 programming model support, security enhancements, asynchronous support, pluggability, simplified configuration, and other improvements.

Java API for web services (JAX-RS and JAX-WS)

Java EE 6 has adopted JAX-RS as an official part of the Java EE specification. JAX-RS is a Java API for developing RESTful web services. A RESTful web service exposes a set of resources that identify the targets of the interaction with its clients. Resources are identified by URIs; they provide a global addressing space for resource and service discovery.

Java API for XML-based web services (JAX-WS)

JAX-WS is the Java API for XML-based web services. JAX-WS is used to develop traditional SOAP-based web services. Java EE 6 includes an updated JAX-WS specification.

Java architecture for XML Binding (JAXB) 2.2

JAXB provides improved performance via new default marshalling optimizations. JAXB defines a programmer API for reading and writing Java objects to and from XML documents, thus simplifying the reading and writing of XML via Java.

New features in JBoss AS 7

The seventh release of JBoss AS is quite different from all other server releases and, as a matter of fact, has improved on several key points, especially where needed most, that is, in the management area. Some of the most notable improvements include:

- The application server can now be part of a **Managed Domain**, which provides the centralized management of multiple server instances and physical hosts, or it can just be a Standalone Server that allows for a single server instance.
- The Management **Web Console** and Management **Command Line Interface (CLI)** are brand new interfaces for managing your domain or standalone AS instance. There is no longer any need to edit XML configuration files manually. The Management CLI even offers a batch mode so that you can script and automate management tasks.
- The class-loading mechanism has been made completely modular so that modules are loaded and unloaded on demand. This provides performance and security benefits as well as very fast startup and restart times.
- JBoss AS 7 starts and stops very quickly, which is especially beneficial to developers. It uses fewer resources and is extremely efficient in its use of system resources.

Behind the scenes, the new application server is designed around a brand new kernel; this is now based on two main projects:

- **JBoss Modules**: This handles the class loading of resources in the container. You can think of JBoss Modules as a thin bootstrap wrapper for executing an application in a modular environment.
- **Modular Service Container (MSC)**: This provides a way to install, uninstall, and manage the services used by a container. MSC further enables the injection of resources into services and dependency management between services.

In the next section, we will describe all the required steps for installing and starting a new application server.

Installing the server and client components

The first step in learning about the application server will be to install all the necessary stuff on your machine in order to run it. The application server itself requires just a Java Virtual Machine environment to be installed.

As far as hardware requirements are concerned, you should be aware that the server distribution, at the time of writing, requires about 75 MB of hard-disk space and allocates a minimum of 64 MB and a maximum of 512 MB for a standalone server.

In order to get started, this is our checklist:

- Install the Java Development Kit where JBoss AS 7 will run
- Install JBoss AS 7.1.1
- Install the Eclipse development environment
- Install the Maven release management tool

At the end of this chapter, you will have all the instruments to get started with the application server.

Installing Java SE

The first mandatory requirement is to install a JDK 1.6 / JDK 1.7 environment. The Java SE download site can be found at `http://www.oracle.com/technetwork/java/javase/downloads/index.html`.

Choose to download either Java SE 6 or Java SE 7, and install it. If you don't know how to install it, please take a look at the following link:

`http://docs.oracle.com/javase/7/docs/webnotes/install/index.html`

Testing the installation

Once you have completed your installation, run the `java -version` command from a command prompt to verify that it is correctly installed. Here is the expected output from a Windows machine:

```
C:\Windows>java -version
java version "1.7.0_02"
Java(TM) SE Runtime Environment
  (build 1.7.0_02-b13)
```

```
Java HotSpot(TM) Client VM
  (build 22.0-b10, mixed mode, sharing)
```

Installing JBoss AS 7

The JBoss application server can be downloaded for free from the community site, `http://www.jboss.org/jbossas/downloads/`.

As you can see from the following screenshot, as I'm writing this book, the latest stable release is the 7.1.1 (Brontes); it features a Certified Java EE 6 Full Profile:

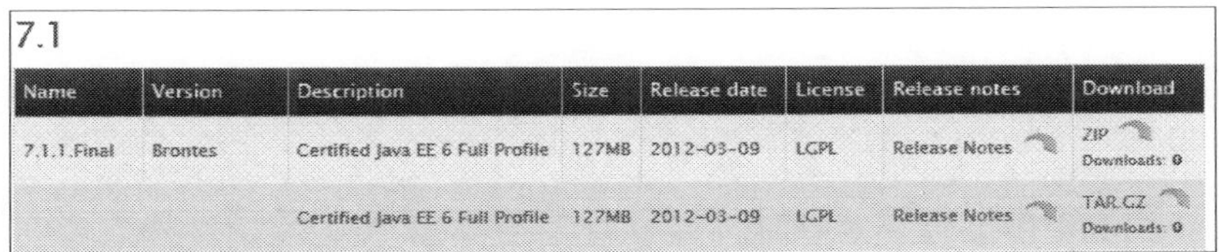

7.1

Name	Version	Description	Size	Release date	License	Release notes	Download
7.1.1.Final	Brontes	Certified Java EE 6 Full Profile	127MB	2012-03-09	LGPL	Release Notes	ZIP Downloads: 0
		Certified Java EE 6 Full Profile	127MB	2012-03-09	LGPL	Release Notes	TAR.GZ Downloads: 0

Once you have chosen the appropriate server distribution, you will then be warned that this download is part of a community release and, as such, is not supported.

> If you need Enterprise support for your applications, you can opt for the Red Hat **Enterprise Platform** (**EAP**). It is now available at the same URL location as the AS 7 release and pick up a trial of the EAP 6.0 that was built from JBoss AS 7. Compared to the community version, the EAP has gone through different quality tests and might be different in terms of features/packaging from the Community version.

Installing JBoss AS is a piece of cake: it does not require anything else besides unpacking the archive `jboss-as-7.1.1.Final.zip`.

Windows users can simply use any uncompress utility such as WinZip or WinRAR, taking care to choose a folder name that does not contain empty spaces. Unix /Linux should use the `unzip` shell command to explode the archive:

```
$ unzip jboss-as-7.1.1.Final.zip
```

> **Security warning**
>
> Unix/Linux users should be aware that JBoss AS does not require root privileges as none of the default ports used by JBoss are below the privileged port range of 1024. To reduce the risk of users gaining root privileges through JBoss AS, install and run JBoss as a non-root user

Starting up JBoss AS

After you have installed JBoss, it is wise to perform a simple startup test to validate that there are no major problems with your Java VM/operating system combination. To test your installation, move to the `bin` directory of your `JBOSS_HOME` directory and issue the following command:

```
standalone.bat      # Windows users
$ standalone.sh     # Linux/Unix users
```

Here is the screenshot of a sample JBoss AS 7 startup console:

```
C:\Windows\system32\cmd.exe
e Thread Pool -- 27) JBAS010403: Deploying JDBC-compliant driver class org.h2.Dr
iver (version 1.3)
16:24:27,640 INFO  [org.jboss.as.mail.extension] (MSC service thread 1-1) JBAS01
5400: Bound mail session [java:jboss/mail/Default]
16:24:27,721 INFO  [org.jboss.ws.common.management.AbstractServerConfig] (MSC se
rvice thread 1-7) JBoss Web Services - Stack CXF Server 4.0.2.GA
16:24:27,959 INFO  [org.jboss.as.server.deployment.scanner] (MSC service thread
1-2) JBAS015012: Started FileSystemDeploymentService for directory C:\jboss-as-7
.1.1.Final\standalone\deployments
16:24:28,216 INFO  [org.jboss.as.remoting] (MSC service thread 1-3) JBAS017100:
Listening on /127.0.0.1:9999
16:24:28,216 INFO  [org.jboss.as.remoting] (MSC service thread 1-1) JBAS017100:
Listening on /127.0.0.1:4447
16:24:28,236 INFO  [org.apache.coyote.http11.Http11Protocol] (MSC service thread
 1-7) Starting Coyote HTTP/1.1 on http--127.0.0.1-8080
16:24:28,681 INFO  [org.jboss.as.connector.subsystems.datasources] (MSC service
thread 1-2) JBAS010400: Bound data source [java:jboss/datasources/ExampleDS]
16:24:28,681 INFO  [org.jboss.as.connector.subsystems.datasources] (MSC service
thread 1-7) JBAS010400: Bound data source [java:jboss/datasources/MySqlDS]
16:24:28,787 INFO  [org.jboss.as] (Controller Boot Thread) JBAS015951: Admin con
sole listening on http://127.0.0.1:9990
16:24:28,791 INFO  [org.jboss.as] (Controller Boot Thread) JBAS015874: JBoss AS
7.1.1.Final "Brontes" started in 3096ms - Started 139 of 215 services (74 servic
es are passive or on-demand)
```

The preceding command starts up a JBoss standalone instance that's equivalent to starting the application server with the `run.bat/run.sh` script used by earlier AS releases. You will notice how amazingly fast-starting the new release of the application server is; this is due to the new modular architecture that only starts up necessary parts of the application server container needed by loaded applications.

If you need to customize the startup properties of your application server, open the `standalone.conf` file (or `standalone.conf.bat` for Windows users) where the memory requirements of JBoss have been declared. Here is the Linux core section of this file:

```
if [ "x$JAVA_OPTS" = "x" ]; then
   JAVA_OPTS="-Xms64m -Xmx512m -XX:MaxPermSize=256m -Dorg.jboss.resolver.
warning=true -Dsun.rmi.dgc.client.gcInterval=3600000 - Dsun.rmi.dgc.
server.gcInterval=3600000"
fi
```

So, by default, the application server starts with a minimum memory requirement of 64 MB of heap space and a maximum of 512 MB. This will be just enough to get started; however, if you need to run core Java EE applications on it, you will likely require at least 1 GB of heap space or up to 2 GB or more depending on your application type. Generally speaking, 32-bit machines cannot execute a process whose space exceeds 2 GB; however, on 64-bit machines, there is essentially no limit to the process size.

You can verify that the server is reachable from the network by simply pointing your browser to the application server's welcome page, which is reachable by default at the well-known address, `http://localhost:8080`.

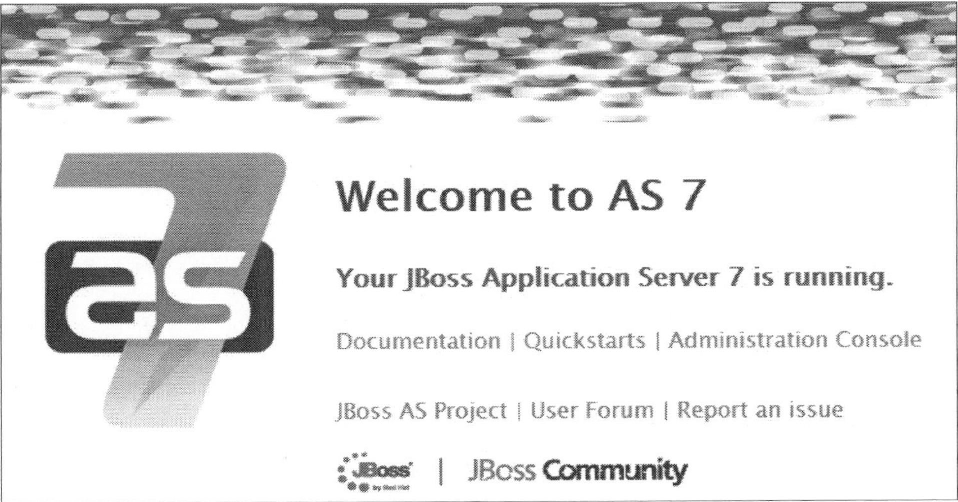

Connecting to the server with the Command Line Interface

If you have been using previous releases of the application server, you might have heard about the **twiddle** command-line utility that queried the MBeans installed on the application server. This utility has been replaced by a more sophisticated interface named the **Command Line Interface (CLI)**; it can be found in `JBOSS_HOME/bin` .

Just launch the `jboss-cli.bat` script (or `jboss-cli.sh` for Linux users), and you will be able to manage the application server via a shell interface.

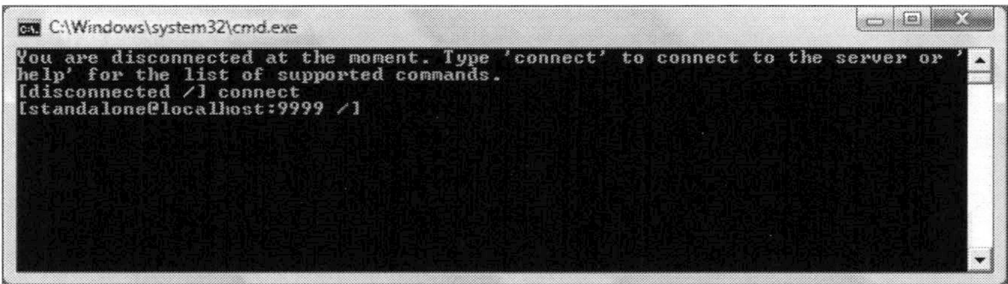

We have just started an interactive shell session that is also able to use the command-line completion (by pressing the *Tab* key) to match partly typed command names. No more searches are needed for finding the exact syntax of commands!

In the previous screenshot, we have just connected to the server using the `connect` command; it uses the loopback server address and plugs into port 9999 by default.

The command-line interface is discussed in depth in *Chapter 9, Managing the Application Server*, which is all about server-management interfaces; we will, however, get an initial taste of its basic functionalities in the next sections to get you accustomed to this powerful tool.

Stopping JBoss

Probably the easiest way to stop JBoss is by sending an interrupt signal with *Ctrl* + *C*.

However, if your JBoss process was launched in the background or, rather, is running on another machine, you can use the CLI interface to issue an immediate `shutdown` command:

```
[disconnected /] connect
Connected to localhost:9999
[localhost:9999 /] :shutdown
```

Locating the shutdown script

There is actually one more option to shut down the application server that is pretty useful if you need to shut down the server from within a script. This option consists of passing the `--connect` option to the admin shell, thereby switching off the interactive mode:

```
jboss-cli.bat --connect command=:shutdown      # Windows
jboss-cli.sh --connect command=:shutdown       # Unix / Linux
```

Stopping JBoss on a remote machine

Shutting down the application server, which is running on a remote machine, is just a matter of providing the server's remote address to the CLI, and for security reason, a username and password (See next chapter to learn more about user creation):

```
[disconnected /] connect 192.168.1.10
Authenticating against security realm: ManagementRealm
Username: admin1234
Password:
Connected to 192.168.1.10:9999
[192.168.1.10:9999 / ] :shutdown
```

Restarting JBoss

The command-line interface contains many useful commands. One of the most interesting options is the ability to reload the AS configuration or parts of it using the `reload` command.

When issued on the **root node path** of the AS server, it is able to reload the services' configuration:

```
[disconnected /] connect
Connected to localhost:9999
[localhost:9999 /] :reload
```

Installing the Eclipse environment

The development environment used in this book is Eclipse, known by Java developers worldwide, and it contains a huge set of plugins to expand its functionalities. Besides this, Eclipse is the first IDE that is compatible with the new application server.

So, let's move to the downloading page of Eclipse that is located at `http://www.eclipse.org`.

From there, download the latest Enterprise Edition (at the time of this writing, it is Version 4.2 and is also known as **Juno**). The compressed package contains all the Java EE plugins already installed and requires about 210 MB of disk space:

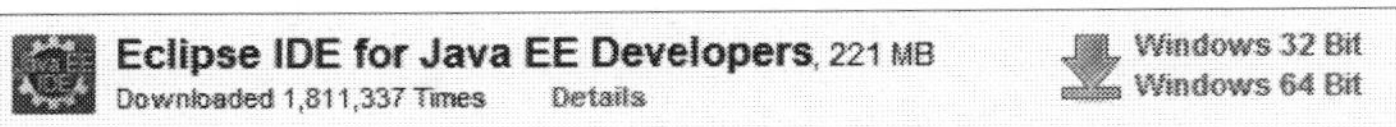

Once you have unzipped the previously downloaded file, you will see a folder named `eclipse`. In that folder, you will find the Eclipse application (a big blue dot). It is recommended that you create a shortcut on the desktop to simplify the launching of Eclipse. Note that, just as with JBoss AS, Eclipse does not have an installation process. Once you have unzipped the file, you are done!

Installing JBoss Tools

The next step will be installing the JBoss AS plugin that is a part of the suite of plugins named JBoss Tools. Installing new plugins in Eclipse is pretty simple; just follow these steps:

1. From the menu, navigate to **Help | Install New Software**.
2. Then, click on the **Add** button where you will enter JBoss Tools' download URL (along with a description) `http://download.jboss.org/jbosstools/updates/stable/juno/`:

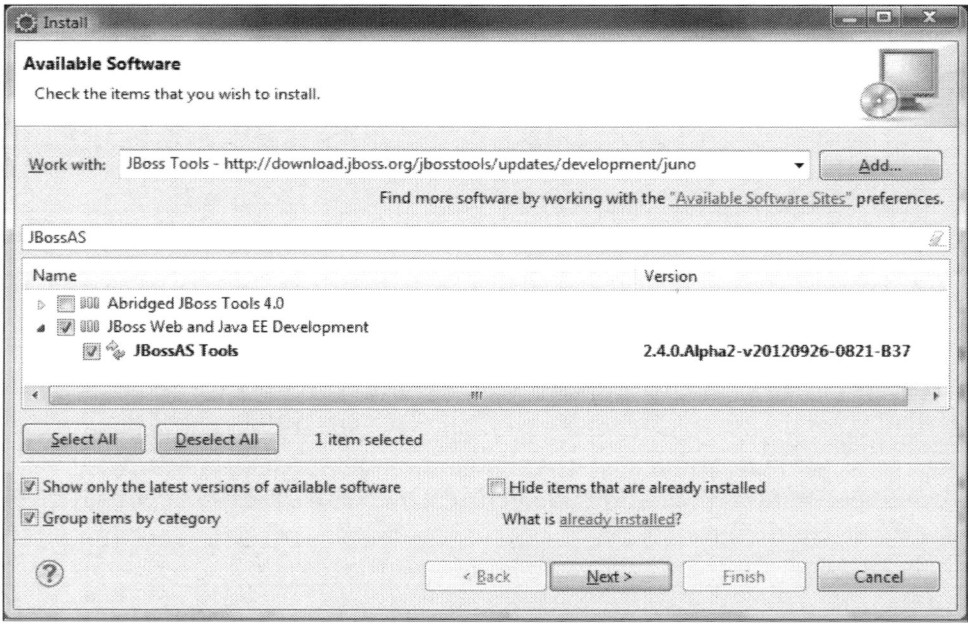

3. As you can see in the preceding screenshot, you need to check the **JBossAS Tools** plugin and move forward to the next options to complete the installation process.

Enter `JBossAS` into the filter field to quickly find out which is the JBoss AS Tools plugin among the large set of JBoss Tools.

4. Once done, restart it when prompted.

You can also download JBoss Tools as individual zips for offline installation. See **JBoss Tools Downloads** (`http://www.jboss.org/tools/download`).

5. Now, you should be able to see JBoss AS 7 enlisted as a server by navigating to **New** | **Server** from the upper menu and expanding the **JBoss Community** option:

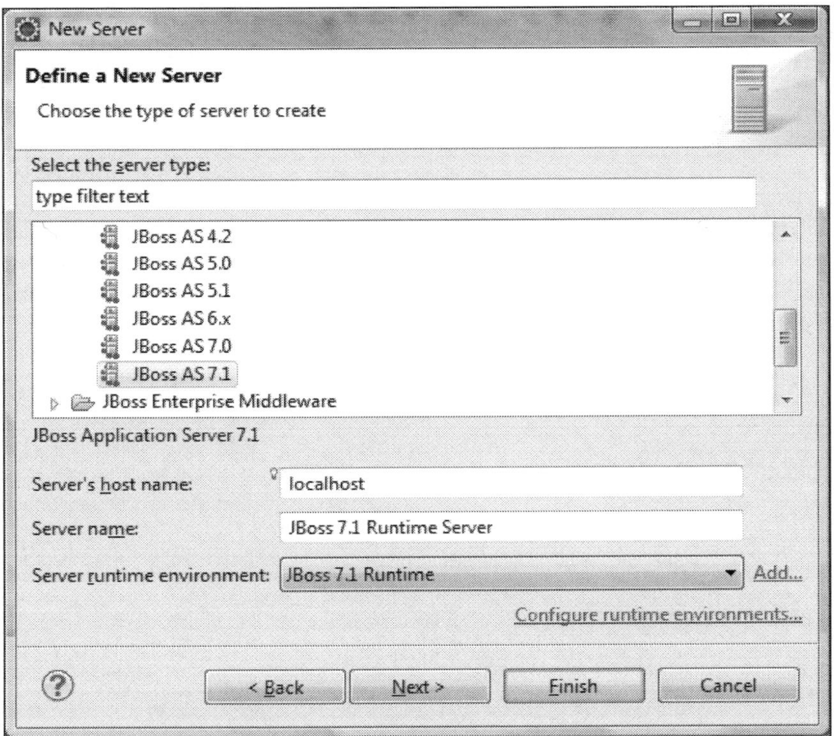

Completing the server installation in Eclipse is quite straightforward as it just requires pointing to the folder where your server distribution is; we will therefore leave this to the reader to implement as a practical exercise.

Alternative development environments

Since this book is all about development, we should also account for some other alternatives that might suit your programming styles or your company standards better. So, another valid alternative is IntelliJ IDEA that is available at `http://www.jetbrains.com/idea/index.html`.

IntelliJ IDEA is a code-centric IDE focused on developer productivity. The editor exhibits a nice understanding of your code and makes great suggestions right when you need them, and is always ready to help you shape your code.

Two versions of this product exist—**Community edition** and **Ultimate edition**—that require a license. In order to use Java EE and the JBoss AS plugin, you need to download the ultimate edition from `http://www.jetbrains.com/idea/download/index.html` and then simply install it using the installation wizard.

Once you have installed the Ultimate edition, you will be able to get started with developing applications with JBoss AS 7 by going to **File | Settings** and choosing the **IDE Settings** option from there. There you can choose to add new application server environments:

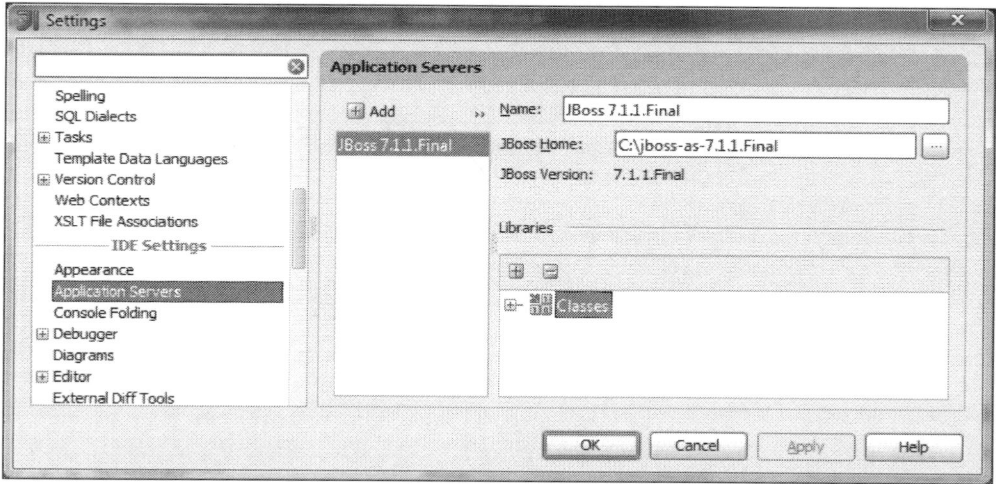

Another development option that is quite popular among developers is **NetBeans** (`http://netbeans.org`), which has recently added support for JBoss AS 7 in its development built 7.3.1

Installing Maven

Besides graphical tools, you are strongly encouraged to learn about Maven, the popular software and release management tool. By using Maven, you will enjoy:

- A standard structure for all your projects
- A centralized and automatic management of dependencies

Maven is distributed in several formats, for your convenience, and can be downloaded from `http://maven.apache.org/download.html`.

Once the download is complete, unzip the distribution archive (for example, `apache-maven-3.0.4-bin.zip`) to the directory in which you wish to install Maven 3.0.4 (or the latest available version), for example, `C:\apache-maven-3.0.4`.

Once done, add the `M2_HOME` environment variable to your system so that it will point to the folder where Maven has been unpacked.

Next, update the `PATH` environment variable by adding the Maven binaries to your system path. For example, on the Windows platform, you should include `%M2_HOME%/bin` in order to make Maven available in the command line.

Testing the installation

Once you have completed your installation, run `mvn --version` to verify that Maven has been correctly installed:

```
mvn --version

Apache Maven 3.0.4 (r1075438; 2011-02-28 18:31:09+0100)

Maven home: C:\apache-maven-3.0.4\bin\..

Java version: 1.6.0, vendor: Sun Microsystems Inc.

Java home: C:\Programmi\Java\jdk1.6.0\jre

Default locale: it_IT, platform encoding: Cp1252

OS name: "windows xp", version: "5.1",
  arch: "x86", family: "windows"
```

Downloading the example code

You can download the example code files for all Packt books you have purchased from your account at `http://www.packtpub.com`. If you purchased this book elsewhere, you can visit `http://www.packtpub.com/support` and register to have the files e-mailed directly to you.

Summary

In this chapter, we have run our first mile on the track to application server development. We have introduced the new features of the application server and we had an overview of the Java EE 6 API.

Next, we have discussed the installation of the AS and all the core components that include the **Java Development Kit** (**JDK**) and a set of development tools, such as Eclipse and Maven, that will be your companions on this journey.

In the next chapter, we will summarize all the application server features, with a special focus on the components and commands needed to deliver an application, which is the main aim of this book.

2

What's New in JBoss AS 7

This chapter will provide you with a crash course in the new application server so that we will be able to deploy our first Java EE 6 application in the next chapter. More specifically, we will cover the following topics:

- An introduction to the AS 7 core concepts
- The anatomy of the JBoss AS 7 filesystem
- An introduction to the available management instruments
- Deploying your first HelloWorld application

AS 7 core concepts

Now that we have downloaded and installed JBoss AS 7, it is worth familiarizing ourselves with some basic concepts. Initially, JBoss AS 7 can be run in two modes: the standalone mode and the domain mode.

In the **standalone** mode, each JBoss Application Server 7 instance is an independent process (similar to the previous JBoss AS versions, such as Version 4, Version 5, or Version 6). The standalone configuration files are located under the standalone/configuration of the application server.

In the **domain** mode, you can run multiple application servers and manage them from a central point. A domain can span multiple physical (or virtual) machines. On each machine we can install several instances of JBoss Application Server 7, that are under the control of a Host Controller process. The configuration files in the domain mode are located under the `domain/configuration` folder of the application server.

From the process point of view, a domain is made up of three elements:

- **Domain Controller**: The domain controller is the management control point of your domain. An AS instance running in the domain mode will have, at the most, one process instance acting as a domain controller. The domain controller holds a centralized configuration, which is shared by the node instances belonging to the domain.
- **Host Controller**: It is a process that is responsible for coordinating the lifecycle of server processes and the distribution of deployments from the domain controller to the server instances.
- **Application server nodes**: These are regular Java processes that map to instances of the application server. Each server node, in turn, belongs to a domain group. Domain groups are explained in detail when we discuss the domain configuration file.

Additionally, when starting a domain, you will see another JVM process running on your machine: this is the Process Controller. It is a very lightweight process whose primary function is to spawn server processes and Host Controller processes, and manage their input/output streams. Since it is not configurable, we will not discuss it any further.

The following diagram depicts a typical domain deployment configuration:

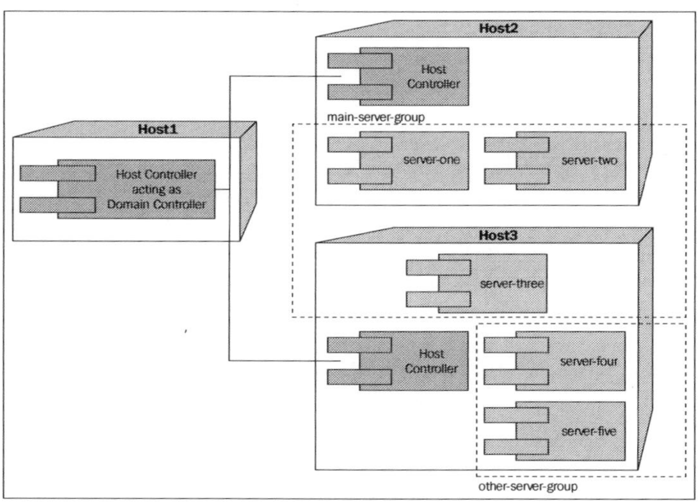

As you can see from the preceding screenshot, one host (**Host1**) acts as a dedicated domain controller. This is a common best practice adopted in domain-managed servers in order to logically and physically separate the administration unit from the servers where the applications are hosted.

The other hosts (**Host2** and **Host3**) contain the domain application servers, which are divided into two server groups: **main-server-group** and **other-server-group**. A server group is a logical set of server instances that will be managed and configured as one. Each server group can in turn be configured with different profiles and deployments; for example, in the preceding domain you can provide some services with **server-group-one** and other services with **other-server-group**.

Going into the details of the domain configuration is beyond the scope of this book; however, by the end of this chapter we will show how to deploy application units in a domain using the **Command Line Interface** available in AS 7.

The AS 7 filesystem

The difference between standalone and domain reflects in the filesystem of the application server, as shown in the following diagram:

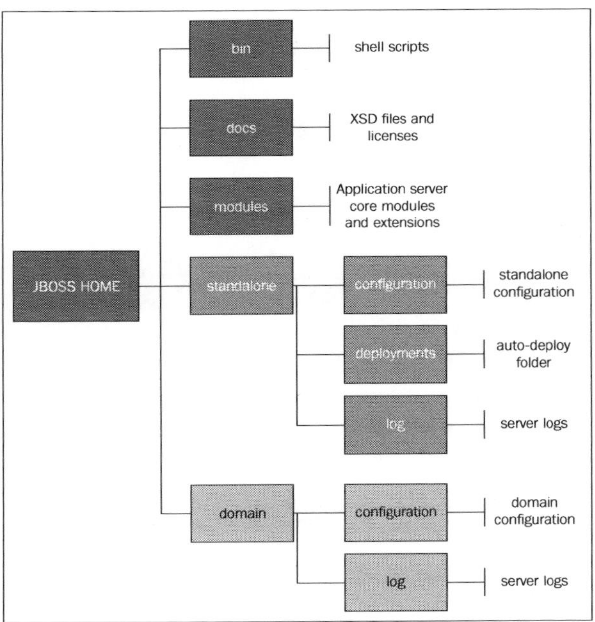

As you can see, the AS 7 filesystem is divided into two main parts: the first one is pertinent to a standalone server mode and the other is dedicated to a domain server mode. Common to both server modes is the `modules` directory, which is the heart of the application server.

JBoss AS 7 is based on the **JBoss Modules** project, which provides an implementation of a modular (non-hierarchical) class loading and execution environment for Java. In other words, rather than a single class loader that loads all JARs into a flat class path, each library becomes a module, which only links against the exact modules it depends on and nothing more. It implements a thread-safe, fast, and highly concurrent delegating class loader model, coupled with an extensible module resolution system, which combine to form a unique, simple, and powerful system for application execution and distribution.

The following table details the content of each folder contained at the root of `JBOSS_HOME`:

Folder	Description
`bin`	This folder contains startup scripts, startup configuration files, and various command-line utilities such as vault, add-user, and Java diagnostic reports available for Unix and Windows environments.
`bin/client`	This folder contains a client jar for use by non Maven-based clients.
`docs/schema`	This folder contains XML schema definition files.
`docs/example`	This folder contains some sample standalone configurations, such as a minimal standalone configuration (`standalone-minimalistic.xml`).
`domain`	This folder contains configuration files, deployment content, and writable areas used by the domain mode processes run from this installation.
`modules`	This folder contains all the modules installed on the application server.
`standalone`	This folder contains configuration files, deployment content, and writable areas used by the single standalone servers run from this installation.
`appclient`	This folder contains configuration files, deployment content, and writable areas used by the application client container run from this installation.
`welcome-content`	This folder contains the default Welcome Page content.

Digging into the `standalone` server tree, we can find folders that are pertinent to standalone independent processes. If you have experience on earlier server releases, you will find these folders quite intuitive to you:

Directory	Description
`configuration`	This directory contains configuration files for the standalone server that runs off this installation. All configuration information for the running server is located here and is the single place for configuration modifications for the standalone server.
`data`	This directory contains the persistent information written by the server to survive a restart of the server.
`deployments`	The end user deployment content can be placed in this directory for automatic detection and deployment of that content into the server's runtime.
`lib/ext`	This directory is the location for the installed library jars referenced by the applications using the `Extension-List` mechanism.
`log`	This directory contains the standalone server logfiles.
`tmp`	This directory contains the location of the temporary files written by the server.

The `domain` directory structure is quite similar to the standalone equivalent, with one important difference: as you can see from the following table, the `deployments` folder is not present here since the domain mode does not support deploying content based on scanning a filesystem. We need to use the JBoss AS 7 managed instruments (CLI and Web Admin console) in order to deploy applications to a domain.

Directory	Description
`configuration`	This directory contains configuration files for the domain, Host Controller, and any servers running off of this installation. All the configuration information for the servers managed within the domain is located here and is the single place for configuration information.
`content`	This directory is an internal working area for the Host Controller that controls this installation. This is where it internally stores the deployment content. This directory is not meant to be manipulated by the end users. It is created after the first server startup.
`lib/ext`	This directory is the location for installed library jars referenced by applications using the `Extension-List` mechanism.
`log`	This directory is the location where the Host Controller process writes its logs. The Process Controller, a small, lightweight process that actually spawns the other Host Controller processes and any application server processes, also writes a log here. It is created after the first server startup.

Directory	Description
`servers`	This directory is a writable area used by each application server instance that runs from this installation. Each application server instance will have its own subdirectory, created when the server is first started. In each server's subdirectory, the following subdirectories will be present: `data`: The information written by the server that needs to survive a restart of the server `log`: The server's logfiles `tmp`: The location of the temporary files written by the server. This folder is created after the first server startup.
`tmp`	The location for the temporary files written by the server.

Managing the application server

JBoss AS 7 provides three different approaches to configure and manage servers: a web interface, a command-line client, and a set of XML configuration files. No matter what approach you choose, the configuration is always synchronized across the different views and finally persisted to the XML files.

Managing JBoss AS 7 with the web interface

The web interface is a **Google Web Toolkit** (**GWT**) application, which can be used to manage a standalone or domain JBoss AS distribution. By default, it is deployed on a local host on the `9990` port; the property that controls the port socket binding is `jboss.management.http.port`, as contained in the server configuration (`standalone.xml`/`domain.xml`):

```
<socket-binding-group name="standard-sockets" default-
interface="public">
        <socket-binding name="management-http" interface="management"
port="${jboss.management.http.port:9990}"/>
        . . . . . . . . .
</socket-binding-group>
```

JBoss AS 7.1.x is distributed and is secured by default, and the default security mechanism is username- or password-based, making use of HTTP Digest for the authentication process.

> The reason for securing the server by default is that, if the management interfaces are accidentally exposed on a public IP address, authentication is required to connect. For this reason, there is no default user in the distribution.

The users are stored in a properties file called `mgmt-users.properties` under `standalone/configuration` or `domain/configuration` depending on the running mode of the server. This file contains the username information along with a pre-prepared hash of the username plus the name of the realm and the user's password.

To manipulate the files and add users, it has provided utilities such as `add-user.sh` and `add-user.bat` to add the users and generate the hashes. So just execute the script and follow the guided process.

```
C:\Windows\system32\cmd.exe
What type of user do you wish to add?
 a) Management User (mgmt-users.properties)
 b) Application User (application-users.properties)
(a): a

Enter the details of the new user to add.
Realm (ManagementRealm) :
Username : useradmin123
Password :
Re-enter Password :
About to add user 'useradmin123' for realm 'ManagementRealm'
Is this correct yes/no? yes
Added user 'useradmin123' to file 'C:\jboss-as-7.2.0.Alpha1-SNAPSHOT\standalone\
configuration\mgmt-users.properties'
Added user 'useradmin123' to file 'C:\jboss-as-7.2.0.Alpha1-SNAPSHOT\domain\conf
iguration\mgmt-users.properties'
Is this new user going to be used for one AS process to connect to another AS pr
ocess?
e.g. for a slave host controller connecting to the master or for a Remoting conn
ection for server to server EJB calls.
yes/no? yes
To represent the user add the following to the server-identities definition <sec
ret value="RnJhbmsxMjMh" />
Press any key to continue . . .
```

In order to create a new user you need to enter the following values:

- **Type of user**: The type will be `Management User` since it will manage the application server
- **Realm**: This must match the realm name used in the configuration; so unless you have changed the configuration to use a different realm name, leave this set to `ManagementRealm`
- **Username**: This is the username of the user you are adding
- **Password**: This is the user's password

Provided the validation is successful, you will be asked to confirm if you want to add the user; then the properties files will be updated.

The final question (`Is this new user going to be used for one AS process to connect to another AS process?`) will be displayed if you are running a release newer than 7.1.1, and can be used for adding slave Host Controllers that authenticate against a master domain controller. This in turn requires adding the secret key to your slave host's configuration in order to authenticate with the master domain controller. (For more information about domain configuration, check `https://docs.jboss.org/author/display/AS71/Admin+Guide#AdminGuide-ManagedDomain`.)

Launching the web console

Now that we have added at least one user, we can launch the web console at the default address, `http://<host>:9990/console`.

The login screen will be prompted. Enter data into the **User name** and **Password** fields that we had formerly created:

Once logged in, you will be redirected to the web administration main screen. The web console, when running in the standalone mode, will be divided into two main tab screens: the **Profile** tab and the **Runtime** tab.

The **Profile** tab contains all the single subsystems that are part of a server profile (here, **Profile** can also be understood as server configuration). So, once you select the **Profile** tab, on the left frame you can access all the subsystems and edit their configurations. (In the previous screenshot, we were watching the **Datasources** subsystem.)

The other tab named **Runtime** can be used for two main purposes: managing the deployment of applications and checking the server metrics:

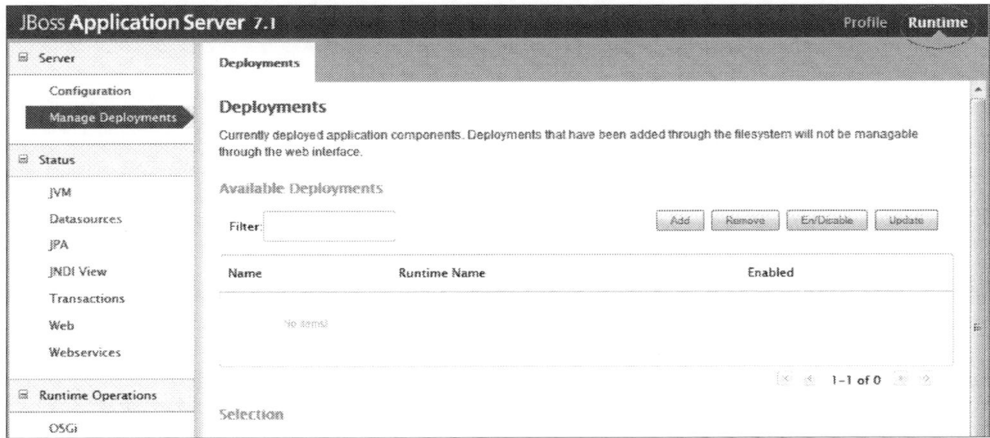

Once we have learnt how to access the web console, it is about time to try our first example application.

Deploying your first application to JBoss AS 7

In order to test-launch our first application, we will create a `HelloWorld` web application using Eclipse. So launch Eclipse and choose to create a new web project using **File** | **New** | **Dynamic Web Project**.

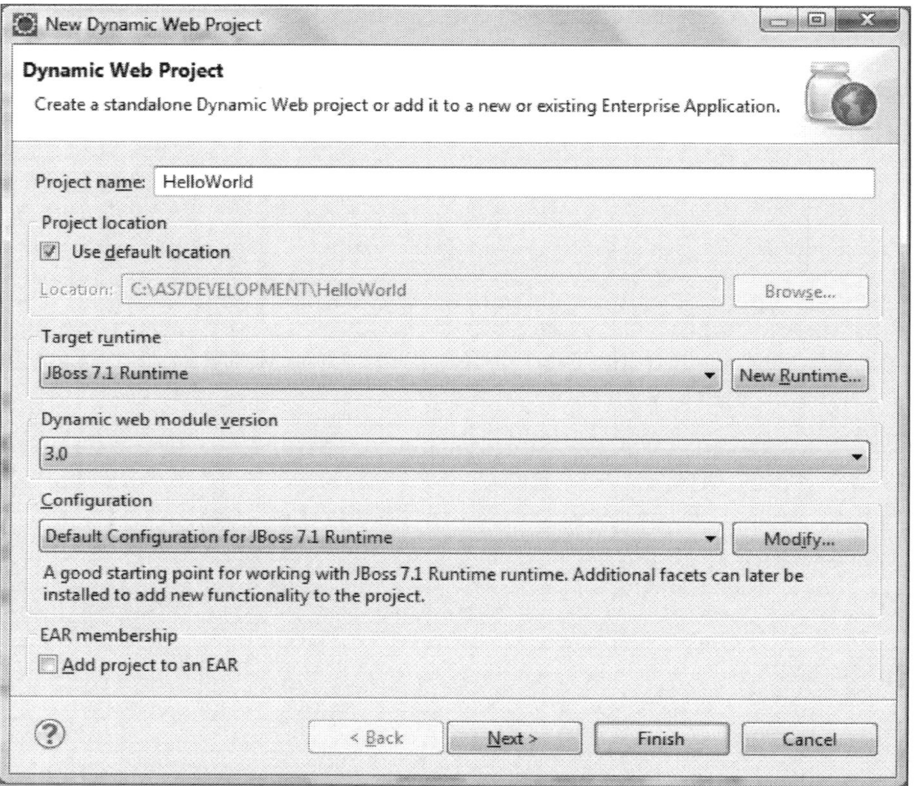

Choose a name for your application and check the **Use default location** box if you want to create your project within the same location of your Eclipse workspace. If you have correctly configured a new JBoss AS 7.1 server in Eclipse, you should see the **JBoss 7.1 Runtime** option selected by default and **Target Runtime** and **Default Configuration for JBoss 7.1 Runtime** preselected in the **Configuration** combobox.

Select **3.0** as **Dynamic web module version**, which buys us ease of development by using the Servlet 3.0 specifications, and also leave the **EAR membership** checkbox unselected.

Click on **Finish** to continue.

Now let's add a quintessential servlet to our project that merely dumps a HelloWorld message. From the **File** menu, select **New | Servlet** and enter a meaningful name and package for your servlet, such as `TestServlet` as the name and `com.packtpub.as7development.chapter2` as the package name.

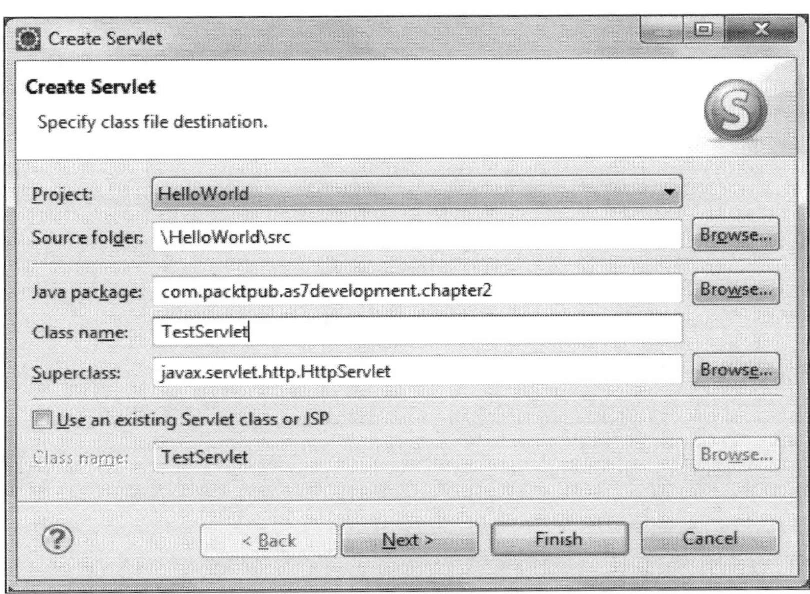

The wizard will serve a basic servlet skeleton that needs to be completed with a minimal set of code lines:

```
@WebServlet("/test")
public class TestServlet extends HttpServlet {
  protected void doGet(HttpServletRequest request,
         HttpServletResponse response) throws ServletException,
         IOException {
    PrintWriter out = response.getWriter();
    out.println("Hello World JBoss AS 7");
    out.close();
  }
  protected void doPost(HttpServletRequest request,
         HttpServletResponse response) throws ServletException,
         IOException {
  }
}
```

Notice that this small class bears the `@WebServlet` annotation, which has been introduced by the Servlet 3.0 API, and it allows registering a servlet without using the `web.xml` configuration file. In our example, we have used it to customize the servlet URL binding to use `"/test"`, which would otherwise be defaulted by Eclipse to the class name.

We will complete the application with a JBoss file descriptor named `jboss-web.xml`; although this not mandatory, it can be used to redefine the context root:

```
<jboss-web>
    <context-root>/hello</context-root>
</jboss-web>
```

The schema definition file for `jboss-web.xml` is named `jboss-as-web_1_1.xsd` and can be located in the `JBOSS_HOME/docs/schema` folder.

Now we will add the web application to the list of deployed resources by right-clicking on the Eclipse **Server** tab and selecting **Add and Remove**:

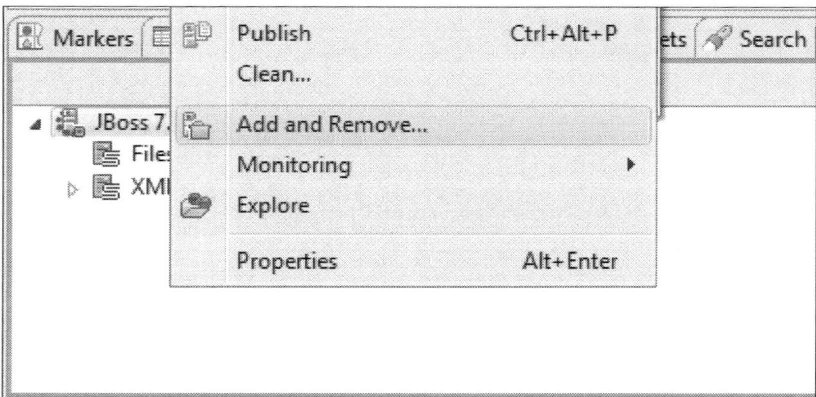

Next, click on **Add** to add the project to the list of configured resources on the server:

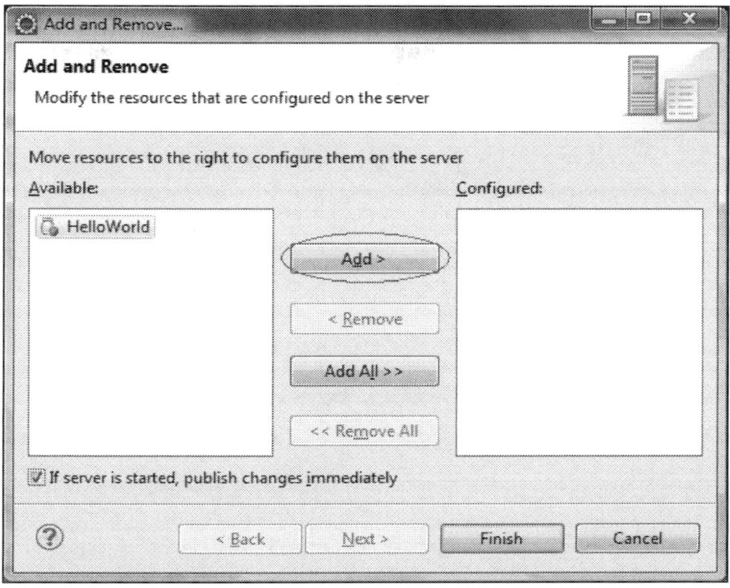

If you have started JBoss AS from inside Eclipse, the resource will be automatically deployed by checking the flag **If server is started, publish changes immediately**.

If, on the other hand, you have started the application server externally, then you can fully publish your resource by right-clicking on the application and selecting **Full Publish**:

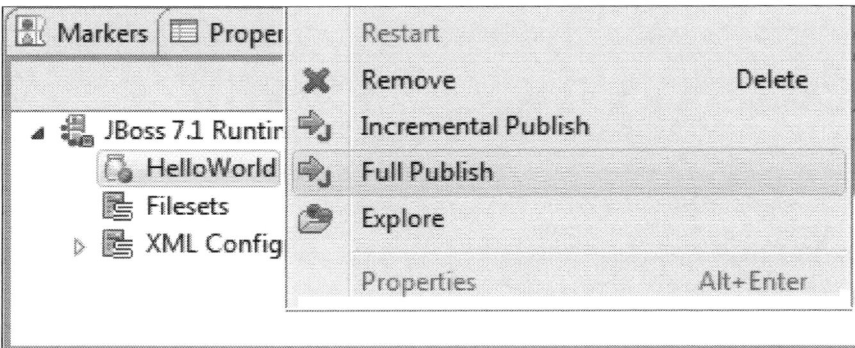

Now move to the browser and check that the application responds at the configured URL:

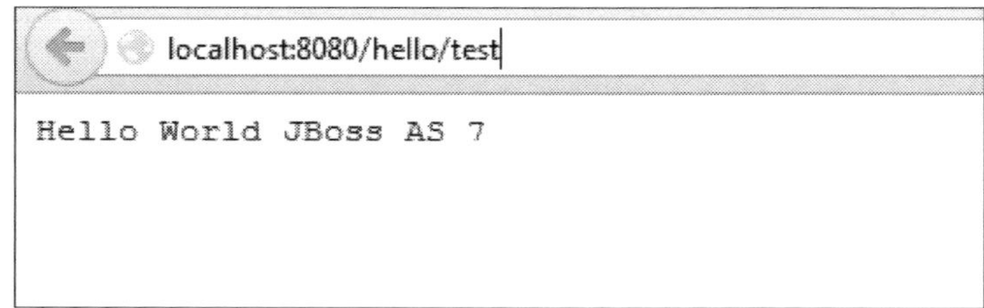

Advanced Eclipse deployment options

As it is, Eclipse has published a `HelloWorld.war` folder in `JBOSS_HOME/standalone/deployments`.

> You might have also noticed that Eclipse has also added a marker file named `HelloWorld.war.dodeploy`. This step is necessary because, by default, exploded deployments in AS 7 aren't automatically deployed but they can be triggered with a marker file named `application.[jar/war/ear].dodeploy`.
>
> Once the application is deployed, the application server replaces the `.dodeploy` marker file with a `HelloWorld.war.deployed` or with a `HelloWorld.war.failed` file, should the deployment fail.

You can change the default deployment options by double-clicking on **JBoss AS 7.1.1** (in the **Server** tab) and selecting the **Deployment** tab:

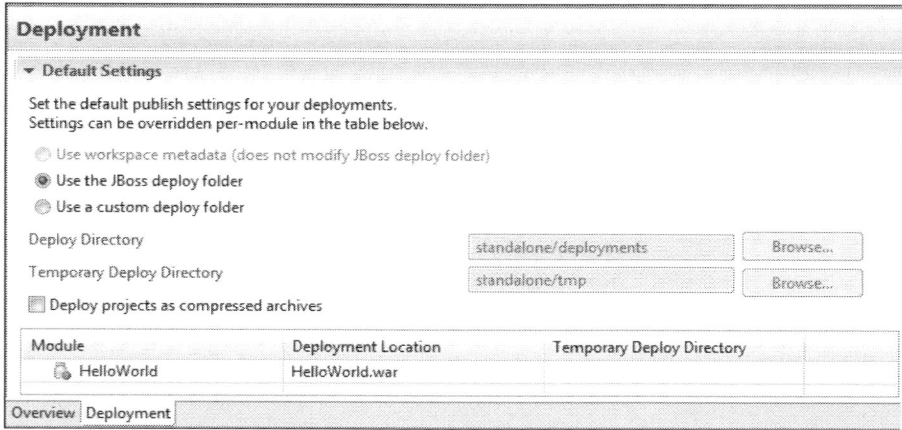

In this tab, you can choose to deploy your application on a custom deploy folder by checking the **Use a custom deploy folder** option and entering an appropriate value into the corresponding textbox.

Please note that the custom deployment folder needs to be defined as well into JBoss AS 7; check the next section for more information about it.

Also, take note of the option **Deploy projects as compressed archives**, which can be useful in some circumstances, for example if you are distributing the application via other instruments such as the CLI, which is able to deploy only compressed archives.

Managing deployments with the web console

Deploying the application using Eclipse is a straightforward task and it is likely to be your option when you are developing apps. We will show here how to use the web console to deploy the application, which can be one more arrow in your quiver.

A typical scenario for this example could be if you are running the AS in the domain mode, or simply deploying your application on a remote JBoss AS instance.

Start the web console and select the **Runtime** tab. From the options on the left panel, select **Deployments** | **Manage Deployments** as shown in the following screenshot:

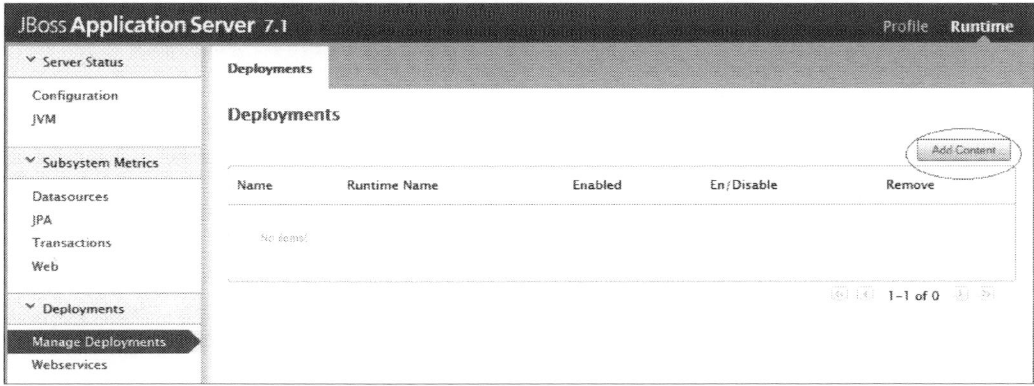

In the central panel, we can manage deployments using the **Add**, **Remove**, **En/Disable**, and **Update** buttons. Select the **Add** button to add a new deployment unit. In the next screen, pick up the file you want to deploy (for example, the `HelloWorld.war` artifact) from your local filesystem:

Complete the wizard by verifying the deployment's name and click on **Save**:

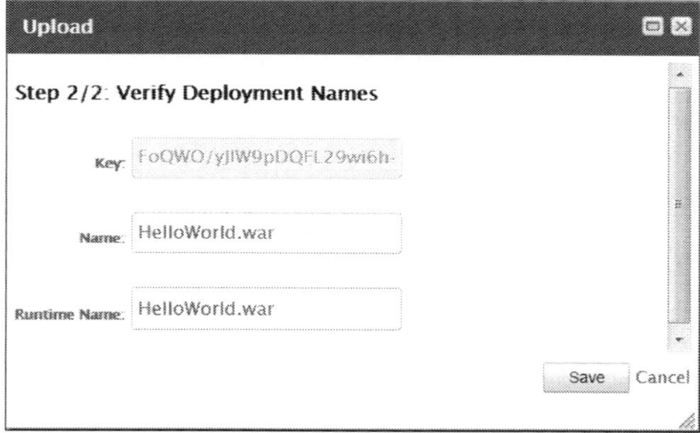

Now the deployment is enlisted into the `Deployments` table. It is however not enabled by default. Click on the **En/Disable** button to enable the deployment of the application.

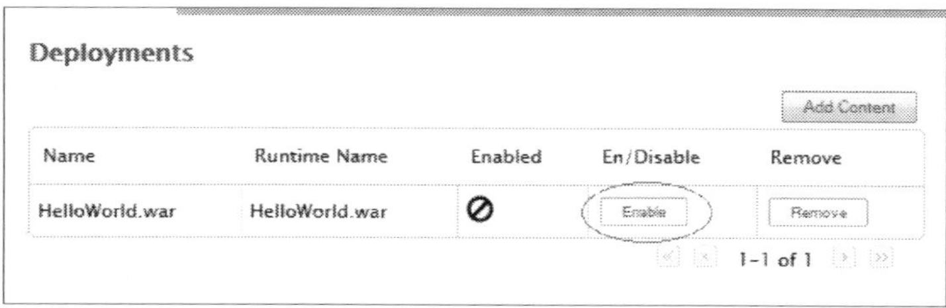

Changing the deployment scanner properties

As we have seen before, applications running in the standalone mode are scanned in the `deployments` folder by default. You can change this behavior (and also the deployment scanner's properties) by navigating to the **Profile** tab and selecting **Core | Deployment Scanners** from the left menu:

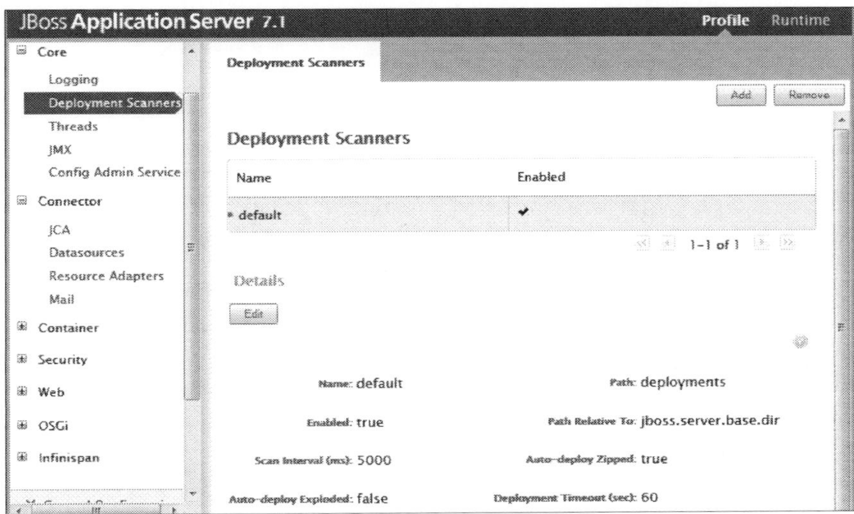

There you can set the core deployment's attributes. You can click on the **Edit** button to define new values for these properties. Most of them are self-explanatory; however, the following table summarizes them:

Attribute	Description
`name`	This is the deployment scanner's name. (By default the name `default` is provided.)
`path`	This is the absolute path where deployments are scanned. If the attribute `Path Relative to` is set, then it's appended to the relative path definition.
`Enabled`	This attribute determines if the deployment scanner is enabled or not.
`Path Relative to`	If included, this attribute must point to a system path that will be used to build the relative path expression.
`Scan Interval`	This is the time frequency (in ms) for which deployments will be scanned.
`Auto-deploy Zipped`	Setting this to `true`, it enables automatic deployments for zipped applications. It defaults to `true`.

Attribute	Description
`Auto-deploy Exploded`	Setting this to `true`, it enables automatic deployments for exploded applications. It defaults to `false`.
`Deployment timeout`	This is the timeout after which a deployment action will be marked as `failed`.

Deploying applications using the CLI

Another way to deploy an application is via the **Command Line Interface**, which can be started from `jboss-cli.bat` (or `jboss-cli.sh` for Linux users). Don't be afraid of using a textual interface to manage your application server; as a matter of fact, the console provides built-in autocomplete features and you can display the available commands at any time by simply hitting the *Tab* key as shown in the following screenshot:

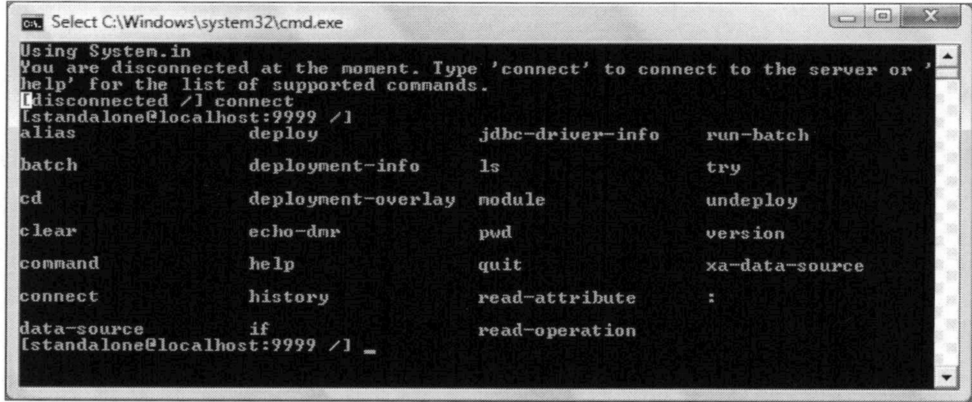

As you might guess, in order to deploy an application you need to issue the `deploy shell` command. When used without arguments, the deploy command provides a list of applications that are currently deployed:

```
[localhost:9999 /] deploy
ExampleApp.war
```

If you feed a resource archive such as `.war` to the shell, it will deploy it on the standalone server right away:

```
[standalone@localhost:9999 /] deploy ../HelloWorld.war
```

As you can see from the preceding command line, the CLI uses the folder where your deployments were actually launched as its initial location, which is `JBOSS_HOME/bin` by default You can, however, use absolute paths when specifying the location of your archives; the CLI expansion facility (using the *Tab* key) makes this option fairly simple:

```
[standalone@localhost:9999 /] deploy c:\deployments\HelloWorld.war
HelloWorld.war' deployed successfully.
```

As it is, the application is deployed and activated so that the user can access it. If you want to just perform the deployment of the application and defer the activation to a later time, you have to add the `--disabled` switch:

```
[standalone@localhost:9999 /] deploy ../HelloWorld.war --disabled
HelloWorld.war' deployed successfully.
```

In order to activate the application, simply issue another deploy command without the `--disabled` switch:

```
[standalone@localhost:9999 /] deploy --name= HelloWorld.war
HelloWorld.war' deployed successfully.
```

Redeploying the application requires an additional flag to the deploy command. Use the `-f` argument to force the application's redeployment:

```
[localhost:9999 /] deploy -f ../HelloWorld.war
HelloWorld.war' re-deployed successfully.
```

Undeploying the application can be done with the `undeploy` command, which takes as an argument the application that is deployed:

```
[localhost:9999 /] undeploy HelloWorld.war
HelloWorld.war' undeployed successfully.
```

Deploying applications to a domain

Deploying applications when running in the domain mode is slightly different from doing the same in the standalone mode. The difference boils down to the fact that an application can be deployed just to one server group or to all the server groups. As a matter of fact, one reason why you might split your domain into different server groups might be that you are planning to offer different types of services (and hence applications) on each server group.

So, in order to deploy your `HelloWorld.war` application to all server groups, issue the following command:

```
[domain@localhost:9999 /] deploy HelloWorld.war --all-server-groups
Successfully deployed HelloWorld.war
```

If, on the other hand, you want to undeploy an application from all server groups belonging to a domain, you have to issue the `undeploy` command:

```
[domain@localhost:9999 /] undeploy HelloWorld.war --all-relevant-server-groups
Successfully undeployed HelloWorld.war
```

You can also deploy your application just to one server group of your domain by specifying one or more server groups (separated by a comma) with the `--server-groups` parameter, shown as follows:

```
[domain@localhost:9999 /] deploy HelloWorld.war --server-groups=main-server-group
Successfully deployed HelloWorld.war
```

You can use the tab-completion facility in order to complete the value for the list of `--server-groups` elected for deployment.

Now, suppose we wish to undeploy the application from just one server group. There can be two possible scenarios: if the application is available just on that server group, you will just need to feed the server group to the `--server-groups` flag, shown as follows:

```
[domain@localhost:9999 /] undeploy HelloWorld.war --server-groups=main-server-group
Successfully undeployed HelloWorld.war.
```

On the other hand, if your application is available on other server groups as well, you need to provide the additional `--keep-content` flag, otherwise the CLI will complain that it cannot delete an application that is referenced by other server groups:

```
[domain@localhost:9999 /] undeploy HelloWorld.war --server-groups=main-server-group --keep-content
```

Summary

In this chapter, we went through a crash course on the application server, focusing on the available management instruments: the web interface and the Command Line Interface. We then saw how to use these tools to deploy a sample application to a standalone and domain environment.

In the next chapter, we will dive deep into Java EE 6 components, starting from Enterprise JavaBeans, which still play an important role in the evolving scenario of Java Enterprise applications.

3

Beginning Java EE 6 – EJBs

In the previous chapter, we learned some basics about how to set up and deploy a HelloWorld application on JBoss AS 7. In this chapter, we will go a little deeper and learn how to create, deploy, and assemble Enterprise JavaBeans, which are at the heart of most Enterprise applications.

In greater detail, here is what you will learn in this chapter:

- What the new EJB 3.1 features introduced by the Java EE 6 specification are
- How to develop a singleton EJB
- How to create stateless and stateful Enterprise JavaBeans
- How to add schedulers and timers to your application
- How to make use of asynchronous APIs in an EJB project

EJB 3.1 – new features

Based on the **Enterprise JavaBeans (EJB)** specification, Enterprise JavaBeans are Java components that typically implement the business logic of **Java Enterprise Edition (JEE)** applications as well as data access.

There are basically three types of Enterprise JavaBeans:

- **Stateless Session Beans (SLSB)**: SLSB are objects whose instances have no conversational state. This means that all these bean instances are equivalent when they are not servicing a client.
- **Stateful Session Beans (SFSB)**: SFSB support conversational services with tightly coupled clients. A stateful session bean accomplishes a task for a particular client. It maintains the state for the duration of a client session. After session completion, the state is not retained.

- **Message-driven beans** (**MDB**): MDB are a kind of Enterprise Bean that are able to asynchronously process messages sent by any JMS producer. (We will discuss MDB in *Chapter 7, Adding Java Message Service to Your Applications*.)

Besides standard EJB components, the application server also supports the new EJB 3.1 variants introduced by Java EE 6; they are:

- **Singleton EJB**: This is essentially similar to a stateless session bean; however, it uses a single instance to serve client requests. So, you can guarantee the use of the same instance across invocations. Singletons can use a richer life cycle for a set of events and a stricter locking policy to control concurrent access to the instance.
- **No-interface EJB**: This is just another view of the standard session bean, except that the local clients do not require a separate interface, that is, all public methods of the bean class are automatically exposed to the caller.
- **Asynchronous EJB**: These are able to process client requests asynchronously, just as with MDBs, except that they expose a typed interface and follow a more complex approach for processing client requests; it is composed of:
    - Fire-and-forget asynchronous void methods that are invoked by the client
    - Retrieve-result-later asynchronous methods having the `Future<?> Return` type

Since it's easier to grasp concepts with concrete examples, we will provide, in the next sections, a concrete application example that introduces all the features we have mentioned previously.

Developing singleton EJBs

As the name implies, `javax.ejb.Singleton` is a session bean that guarantees that there is one instance in the application, at most.

Besides this, singleton EJBs fill up a well-known gap in EJB applications, that is, the ability to have an EJB that is notified when the application starts and also when the application stops. So, you can do all sorts of things with an EJB that you previously could only do with a load-on-startup servlet. It also gives you a place to hold data that pertains to the entire application and all the users using it, without the need for static class fields.

In order to turn your EJB into a singleton, all that is needed is to apply the `@ javax.ejb.Singleton` annotation on top of it.

> A singleton bean is similar to a stateful bean in that state information is maintained across method invocations. However, there is just one singleton bean for each server JVM, and it is shared by all of the EJBs and clients of an application. This type of bean provides a convenient means of maintaining the overall state of an application.

Another annotation that is worth learning is `@javax.ejb.Startup` that causes the bean to be instantiated by the container when the application starts. This invokes the `@javax.annotation.PostConstruct` annotation if you have defined one in your EJB.

We now have enough information to understand our first EJB example. There is more than one alternative for creating a Java Enterprise project. In the earlier chapter, we have illustrated how to start from a project based on Eclipse JEE (dynamic web project), binding it later to a JBoss runtime installation. That's obviously the simplest choice, and you can easily run the examples contained in this book using this pattern; however, when it comes to enterprise solutions, it's no surprise that almost every project is now Maven-based. Some of the benefits that you will achieve when turning to Maven projects include a well-defined dependency structure, the enforcement of a project's build best practices, and project modular design, just to mention a few.

> In order to integrate Maven with Eclipse, you need to install the Maven Integration for the Eclipse plugin. This can be done in a minute by navigating to **Help** | **Eclipse Market Place** and from there search and install the **Maven Integration for Eclipse** (m2e) plugin which will need restarting Eclipse thereafter.

So let's create our first Maven project directly from Eclipse. Navigate to **File** | **New** | **Other** | **Maven Project**:

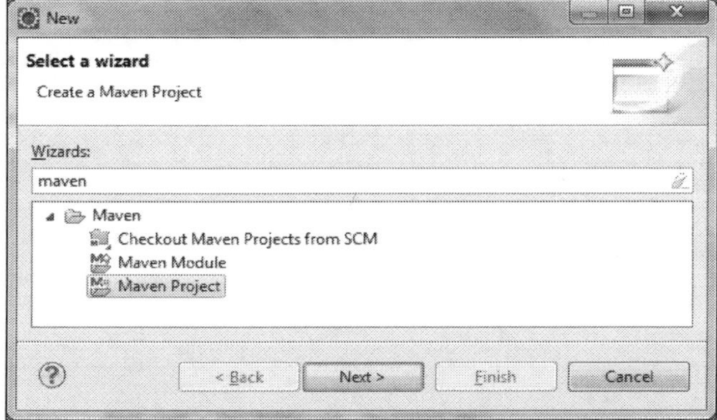

Click on **Next**; you will be taken to the following intermediary screen:

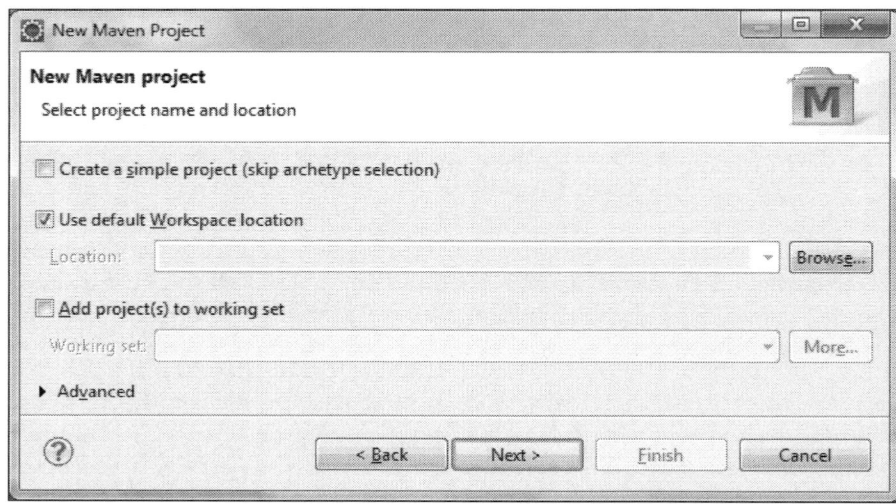

You can leave the default options selected since we would like to use a Maven EJB archetype so as to verify that the **Create a simple project** checkbox is not selected. In the next screen, we will select the archetype option that will pick up an archetype that is fit for our purpose:

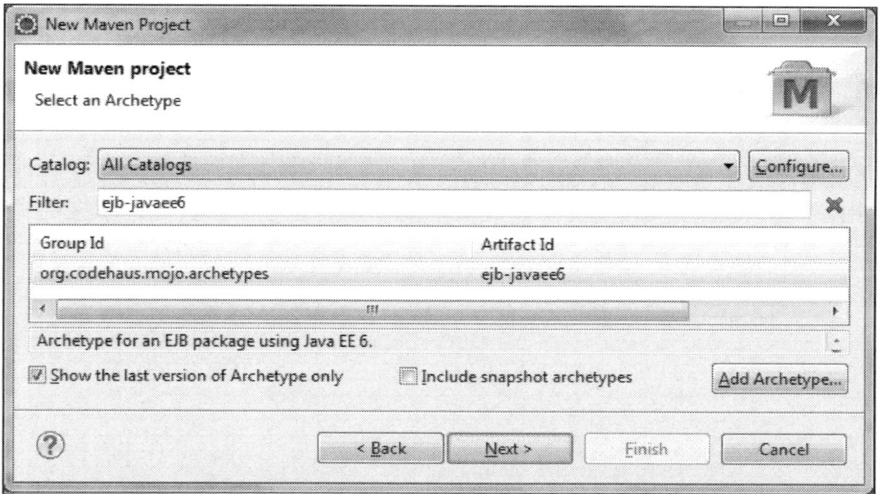

You can enter the archetype name (**ejb-javaee6**) in the filter box in order to facilitate your selection. Once selected, you can click on **Next**. You can complete the wizard by entering some package-specific information as shown in the following screenshot:

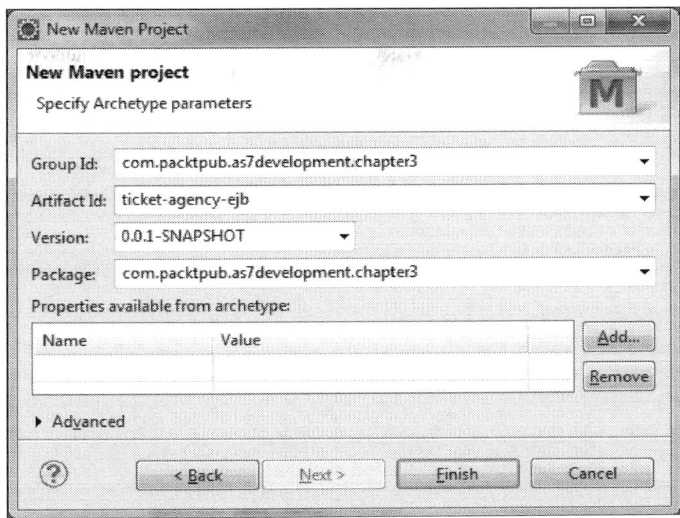

You can enter as **Group Id** the same package information, which is `com.packtpub.as7development.chapter3`. The artifact ID that corresponds to our project name will be `ticket-agency-ejb` and you can leave the default selection for the project's **Version** field. Click on **Finish** in order to complete the wizard.

The expected outcome of the Maven wizard should match the following screenshot that has been taken from the **Enterprise Explorer** view:

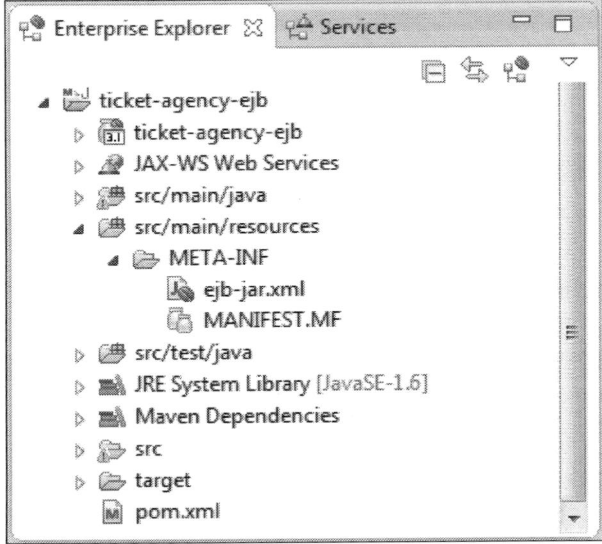

As you can see, the project has been organized as a standard Maven project under `src/main/java`, where we will add our source code, `src/main/resources`, for the configuration (containing a bare-bones `ejb-jar.xml` configuration file), and for `src/test/java`, which can be used to host the `test` classes. At the moment, we will concentrate on the main file, `pom.xml`, which needs to be aware of the JBoss enterprise dependencies.

Configuring the project object module (pom.xml)

You need to resist just a few more minutes before digging into the code examples—configuring Maven's `pom.xml` is your first priority, otherwise you will not even be able to compile a single class for your project.

The `pom.xml` file is quite verbose, so we will illustrate here just the core elements that are required to understand our example, leaving the full listing to the code example package of this book.

The first thing we are going to add, just after the `properties` section, is a reference to **JBoss' Bill of Material (BOM)**:

```
<dependencyManagement>
        <dependencies>
            <dependency>
                <groupId>org.jboss.spec</groupId>
                <artifactId>jboss-javaee-6.0</artifactId>
                <version>3.0.2.Final</version>
                <type>pom</type>
                <scope>import</scope>
            </dependency>
        </dependencies>
 </dependencyManagement>
```

This dependency will import a project object module that contains a reference to all the libraries that are part of the JBoss Enterprise stack—its most evident advantage is that you will not need to specify the single dependency version but just state which JBoss Enterprise stack version you are going to use (in our example, it is `3.0.2.Final`).

Now for the project dependencies. Since we are going to use the EJB 3.1 API with annotations, we would need the **Common Annotations API** (JSR-250) and the **EJB 3.1 API dependencies**; so, add the following block just after the BOM section:

```
<dependencies>

    <dependency>
      <groupId>org.jboss.spec.javax.annotation</groupId>
      <artifactId>jboss-annotations-api_1.1_spec</artifactId>
      <scope>provided</scope>
    </dependency>

    <dependency>
      <groupId>org.jboss.spec.javax.ejb</groupId>
      <artifactId>jboss-ejb-api_3.1_spec</artifactId>
      <scope>provided</scope>
    </dependency>

    <dependency>
      <groupId>org.jboss.logging</groupId>
      <artifactId>jboss-logging</artifactId>
      <version>3.1.3.GA</version>
    </dependency>

</dependencies>
```

We have also added the JBoss logging API, which is not part of the enterprise bill of material; therefore, a version needs to be specified.

The scope `provided`, included in the enterprise dependencies, corresponds to adding a library to the compilation path. Therefore, it expects the JDK or a container to provide the dependency at runtime.

At this point, you will be able to compile your project; so we will start adding classes, but we will return to the `pom.xml` file when it's time to deploy your artifact.

Coding our EJB application

Creating EJB classes does not require getting mixed up with fancy wizards; all you need to do is add bare Java classes. Therefore, from the **File** menu go to **New | Java Class**, and enter `TheatreBox` as the classname and `com.packtpub.as7development.chapter3.ejb` as the package name.

We will add the following implementation to the class:

```
@Singleton
@Startup
```

```
public class TheatreBox {
  private ArrayList<Seat> seatList;
  private static final Logger logger =
      Logger.getLogger(TheatreBox.class);

  @PostConstruct
  public void setupTheatre(){
    seatList = new ArrayList<Seat>();
    int id = 0;
    for (int i=0;i<5;i++) {
      Seat seat = new Seat(++id, "Stalls",40);
      seatList.add(seat);
    }
    for (int i=0;i<5;i++) {
      Seat seat = new Seat(++id,"Circle",20);
      seatList.add(seat);
    }
    for (int i=0;i<5;i++) {
      Seat seat = new Seat(++id, "Balcony",10);
      seatList.add(seat);
    }
    logger.info("Seat Map constructed.");
  }

  @Lock(READ)
  public ArrayList<Seat> getSeatList() {
    return seatList;
  }
  @Lock(READ)
  public int getSeatPrice(int id) {

    return getSeatList().get(id).getPrice();
  }

  @Lock(WRITE)
  public void buyTicket(Seat seat)    {
    seat.setBooked(true);
  }
}
```

Let's see our application code in detail; the void method `setupTheatre` is invoked as soon as the application is deployed and takes care of assembling the theatre seats, creating a simple list of `Seat` objects. Each `Seat` object is constructed using a set of three field constructors that includes the seat ID, its description, and the price:

```
public class Seat {

  public Seat(int id, String seat, int price) {
    this.id = id;
    this.seatName = seat;
    this.price = price;
  }
// Fields and Getters/Setters omitted for brevity
}
```

Next, the singleton bean exposes three public methods; the `getSeatList` method returns a list of `Seat` objects that will return to the user the information regarding whether they have been reserved or not.

The `getSeatPrice` method is a utility method that will pick up the seat price and return it as `int` so it can be used to verify the user is able to afford buying the ticket.

Finally, the `buyTicket` method is the one that actually buys the ticket and therefore sets up the ticket as booked.

Controlling bean concurrency

As you might have noticed, the bean includes an `@Lock` annotation on top of the methods managing our collection of `Seat` objects. This kind of annotation is used to control the concurrency of the singleton.

Concurrent access to a singleton EJB is, by default, controlled by the container. Read and write access to a singleton is limited to one client at a time. However, it is possible to provide a finer level of concurrency control through the use of annotations. This can be achieved using the `@Lock` annotation whose arguments determine the type of concurrency access permitted.

By using an `@Lock` annotation of type `javax.ejb.LockType.READ`, multithreaded access will be allowed to the bean.

```
@Lock(READ)
public ArrayList<Seat> getSeatList() {
  return seatList;
}
```

On the other hand, if we apply `javax.ejb.LockType.WRITE`, the single-threaded access policy is enforced.

```
@Lock(WRITE)
public void buyTicket(Seat seat)    {
   seat.setBooked(true);
}
```

The general idea is to use `READ` type locks on methods that just read values from the cache and `WRITE` type locks for methods that change the values of elements contained in the cache.

Using bean-managed concurrency

The other possible option is using a bean-managed concurrency that can be pursued by applying the `@javax.ejb.ConcurrencyManagement` annotation with an argument of `ConcurrencyManagementType.BEAN`. This annotation will disable the effect of the `@Lock` annotation we have used so far, putting the responsibility of ensuring that the singleton cache does not get corrupted on the developer.

So, in order to ensure that our bookings are preserved, we will need to use a well-known **synchronized** keyword on top of the `buyTicket` method:

```
@Singleton
@Startup
@ConcurrencyManagement(ConcurrencyManagementType.BEAN)
public class TheatreBox {
. . . .
  public void buyTicket(Seat seat)    {
      synchronized (this){
         seat.setBooked(true);
      }
}
```

Since concurrent access is restricted when a thread enters the synchronized block, no other methods are then allowed to access the object while the current thread is in the block.

Cooking session beans

Our singleton EJB is equipped with the methods for handling our cache of theatre seats. We will now add a couple of session beans to our project for managing the business logic: a stateless session bean that will provide a view of the theatre seats and a stateful bean that will behave as a payment gateway to our system.

The choice of splitting our information system into two different beans is not part of a design pattern in particular, but serves a different purpose. That is, we would like to show how to look up both types of beans from a remote client.

Adding a stateless bean

So, the first bean we will create is `com.packtpub.as7development.chapter3.ejb TheatreInfoBean` that barely contains the logic for looking up the list of theatre seats. In practice, this acts as a façade for our singleton bean.

```
@Stateless
@Remote(TheatreInfo.class)
public class  TheatreInfoBean implements TheatreInfo  {
  @EJB TheatreBox box;

  @Override
  public String printSeatList() {
    ArrayList<Seat> seats= box.getSeatList();
    StringBuffer sb = new StringBuffer();
    for (Seat seat: seats) {
      sb.append(seat );
      sb.append("\n");
    }
    return sb;
  }
}
```

Since we are planning to invoke this EJB from a remote client, we have provided a remote interface for it with the `@Remote(TheatreInfo.class)` annotation.

Next, have a look at the `@EJB TheatreBox` box that can be used to safely inject an EJB into your class without the need of your manually performing a JNDI lookup. This practice can be used to increase the portability of your application between different application servers where different JNDI rules might exist.

The remote interface of your bean will be as simple as this:

```
public interface TheatreInfo {
   public String printSeatList();

}
```

> If you are planning to expose your EJB to local clients only (for example, to a servlet), you can leave out the remote interface definition and simply annotate your bean with `@Stateless`. The application server will create a `no-interface` view of your session bean, which can safely be injected into your local clients such as servlets or other EJBs.

Adding a stateful bean

In order to control how much money our customer has got in his pocket, we would need a session-aware component. Turning a Java class into a stateful session bean is just a matter of adding an `@Stateful` annotation on top of it, as in our example class `com.packtpub.as7development.chapter3.ejb.TheatreBooker`.

```
@Stateful
@Remote(TheatreBooker.class)
public class TheatreBookerBean implements TheatreBooker {
   private static final Logger logger =
          Logger.getLogger(TheatreBookerBean.class);

  int money;
  @EJB TheatreBox theatreBox;

  @PostConstruct
  public void createCustomer() {
    this.money=100;
  }
   @Override
  public String bookSeat(int seatId) throws SeatBookedException,
NotEnoughMoneyException {

    Seat seat = theatreBox.getSeatList().get(seatId);
                      // Business checks
    if (seat.isBooked()) {
      throw new SeatBookedException("Seat Already booked!");
    }
    if (seat.getPrice() > money) {
      throw new NotEnoughMoneyException("You don't have enough money
to buy this ticket!");
    }
```

```
        theatreBox.buyTicket(seat);
        money = money - seat.getPrice();
        logger.info("Seat "+seatId+ " booked.");
        return "Seat "+seatId+ " booked.";
    }

}
```

As you can see, this bean bears an `@PostConstruct` annotation for initializing a session variable (money) that will be used to check that the customer has enough money to buy the ticket.

Besides this, the ultimate purpose of our SFSB is to contact the `buyTicket` method of our singleton after having performed some business checks.

If the business checks do not pass, the application will issue some exceptions. This is the case, for example, if the seat has already been booked or if the customer hasn't got enough money to buy the ticket. In order to keep our conversation going, it's important that our exceptions be an extension of the generic `Exception` class.

```
public class SeatBookedException extends Exception {
  . . . .
}
```

If we'd rather use a runtime exception (for example, `EJBException`), the bean instance will be discarded, resulting in our communication being dropped between the remote client and the server. So, always take care to choose the appropriate type of exception when dealing with EJBs—choose to throw a runtime exception if you are dealing with an unrecoverable scenario (the connection with the enterprise information system is dropped). On the other hand, consider throwing a checked exception (or simply not throwing exceptions at all) if you are dealing with a business kind of exception; for example, if the booked seat is already engaged.

Deploying the EJB application

As it is, you should be able to package your EJB project by issuing the following Maven goal, by starting a command-line prompt from your project root:

```
mvn install
```

The preceding command will compile and package the application that needs to be copied into the `deployments` folder of your application server. That's fine; however, we can expect lots more from Maven by installing just a couple of plugins. In our case, we will configure our project to use Maven's JBoss plugin by adding the following section:

```
<build>
   <finalName>${project.artifactId}</finalName>
   <plugins>
      <plugin>
         <groupId>org.jboss.as.plugins</groupId>
         <artifactId>jboss-as-maven-plugin</artifactId>
         <version>${version.jboss.maven.plugin}</version>
         <configuration>
            <filename>${project.build.finalName}.jar</filename>
         </configuration>
      </plugin>
      <plugin>
         <artifactId>maven-compiler-plugin</artifactId>
         <version>2.3.1</version>
         <configuration>
            <source>1.6</source>
            <target>1.6</target>
         </configuration>
      </plugin>
      <plugin>
         <groupId>org.apache.maven.plugins</groupId>
         <artifactId>maven-ejb-plugin</artifactId>
         <version>2.3</version>
         <configuration>
            <ejbVersion>3.1</ejbVersion>
            <generateClient>true</generateClient>
         </configuration>
      </plugin>
   </plugins>
</build>
```

In the first part of the XML fragment, we have specified the project's `finalName` attribute that will dictate the name of the packaged artifact (in our example, the project's name corresponds to our project's artifact ID, so it will be named `ticket-agency-ejb.jar`).

The artifact ID named `jboss-as-maven-plugin` will actually trigger the JBoss Maven plugin that will be used to deploy our project.

You should also include the `maven-compiler-plugin` artifact that can be used to enforce the Java 1.6 compatibility and activate the annotation processors as well. Finally, `maven-ejb-plugin` should already be part of your `pom.xml` file since we have chosen an EJB archetype. You should set the `generateClient` option to `true` (the default is `false`) in order to create the EJB client classes.

> All information about plugin versions has been hardcoded into the plugin configuration for the sake of readability. As you can see from the source code that is part of this book, you should use properties to set up the core project's attributes.

So, once you have configured the JBoss plugin, your application can be deployed automatically by entering from your project root:

```
mvn jboss-as:deploy
```

Since deployment is a repetitive task for a developer, it could be convenient to execute this operation from within the Eclipse environment. All you need is to create a new **Run Configuration** setting from the upper menu by navigating to **Run | Run Configurations**.

Enter the project's base directory (hint—the **Browse workspace** utility will help you to pick up the project from your project list) and type your Maven goal into the **Goals** textbox:

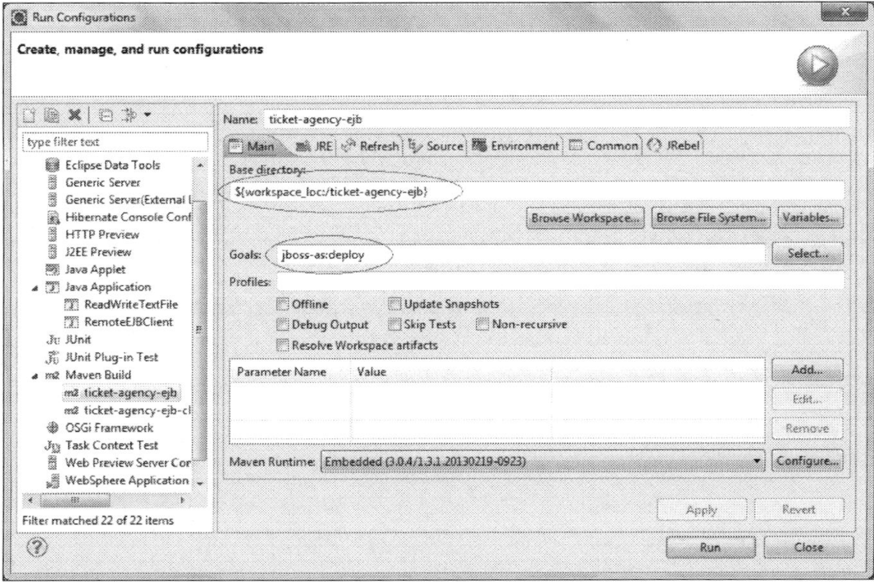

Once done, click on **Apply** to save your configuration and then click on **Run** to execute the deployment of the application. The Maven plugins will activate and, once verified that all classes are up-to-date, start deploying the applications to JBoss AS using the remote API. You should expect a success message on the Maven console:

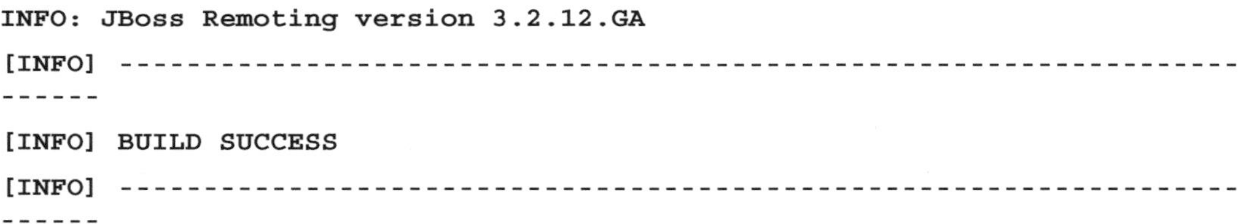

```
INFO: JBoss Remoting version 3.2.12.GA
[INFO] ----------------------------------------------------------------
------
[INFO] BUILD SUCCESS
[INFO] ----------------------------------------------------------------
------
```

On the other hand, on the JBoss AS 7 console, you have quite a verbose output that points out some important EJB JNDI bindings (we will return to it in a minute) and informs us that the application has been deployed correctly:

```
09:09:32,782 INFO  [org.jboss.as.server] (management-handler-thread - 1)
JBAS018562: Deployed "ticket-agency-ejb.jar"
```

Creating a remote EJB client

Creating a remote EJB client for the AS 7 application server is a bit different compared to other releases of the application server.

As a matter of fact, previous versions of JBoss AS (versions < 7.*x*) used the JNP project as the JNDI naming implementation so developers are familiar with `jnp://PROVIDER_URL` to communicate with the application server.

Starting with AS7, the JNP project is no longer used, neither on the server side or on the client side. The client side of the JNP project has now been replaced by the **jboss-remote-naming** project (`https://github.com/jbossas/jboss-remote-naming`). There were various reasons why the JNP client was replaced by the jboss-remote-naming project. One of them was that the JNP project did not allow fine-grained security configurations while communicating with the JNDI server. The jboss-remote-naming project is backed by the **jboss-remoting** project (`https://github.com/jboss-remoting/jboss-remoting`); it allows much more and better control over security.

Besides the new naming implementation, in AS7 there is no longer support for binding custom JNDI names to EJBs. So the beans are always bound to the spec's mandated `java:global`, `java:app` and `java:module` namespaces. Therefore, setting the JNDI name for the session bean element via an annotation or configuration file is no longer supported.

So what will be the JNDI name used to invoke a stateless session bean? Here is it:

```
ejb:<app-name>/<module-name>/<distinct-name>/<bean-name>!<fully-
qualified-classname-of-the-remote-interface>
```

A bit verbose, isn't it? However, the following table will help you to get through it:

Element	Description
`app-name`	This is the enterprise application name (`without.ear`) if your EJB has been packed in an EAR
`module-name`	This is the module name (`without.jar` or `without.war`) where your EJB has been packed
`distinct-name`	You can optionally set a distinct name for each deployment unit
`bean-name`	This is the bean's classname
`fully-qualified-classname-of-the-remote-interface`	This is the fully qualified classname of the remote interface

So the corresponding JNDI binding for your `TheatreInfo` EJB, packaged into a file named `ticket-agency-ejb.jar`, will be:

```
ejb:/ticket-agency-ejb//TheatreInfoBean!com.packtpub.as7development.
chapter3.ejb.TheatreInfo
```

On the other hand, stateful EJBs will contain one more attribute—`?stateful`—at the bottom of the JNDI string; this will result in the following JNDI naming structure:

```
ejb:<app-name>/<module-name>/<distinct-name>/<bean-name>!<fully-
qualified-classname-of-the-remote-interface>?stateful
```

And here's the corresponding binding for the `TheatreBookerBean` class:

```
ejb:/ticket-agency-ejb//TheatreBookerBean!com.packtpub.as7development.
chapter3.ejb.TheatreBooker?stateful
```

If you pay attention to the server logs, you will see that once your application is deployed, a set of JNDI bindings will be displayed on the server console. For example:

```
java:global/ticket-agency-ejb/TheatreInfoBean!com.
packtpub.as7development.chapter3.ejb.TheatreInfo
java:app/ticket-agency-ejb/TheatreInfoBean!com.packtpub.
as7development.chapter3.ejb.TheatreInfo
java:jboss/exported/ticket-agency-ejb/
TheatreInfoBean!com.packtpub.as7development.chapter3.ejb.
TheatreInfo
```

Some of these bindings reflect the standard bindings as per Java EE specifications plus JBoss custom bindings (`java:/jboss`). This information, as it is, is not relevant for us but can be used to build our EJB client lookup string by replacing the Java EE (or JBoss-specific prefix) with `ejb:/`. For example, replace `java:/global` with `ejb:`, and you will save yourself the headache of referring to the EJB lookup string.

Once we have done with coding the JNDI binding string, we will code our EJB client. The best strategy to achieve this is by creating a separate Maven project for our EJB client so we don't need to pollute the server project with specific client dependencies.

As shown for `ticket-agency-ejb`, create a new Maven project from the menu (**File** | **New** | **Maven Project**) and, in the next screen, enable the archetype selection. When you reach the specific archetype parameter's screen, enter the following suggested values for your **Group Id**, **Artifact Id**, and **Package** fields:

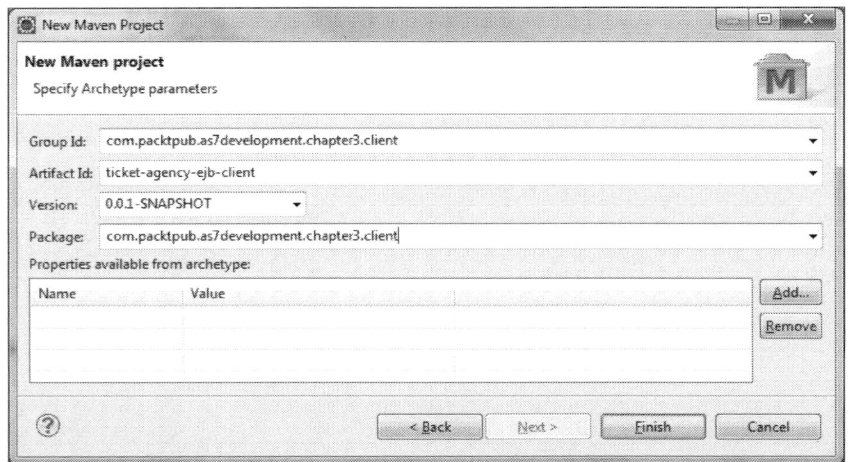

In the next screen, select a very basic archetype, `maven-archetype-quickstart`, that will generate a generic Maven-compliant project structure:

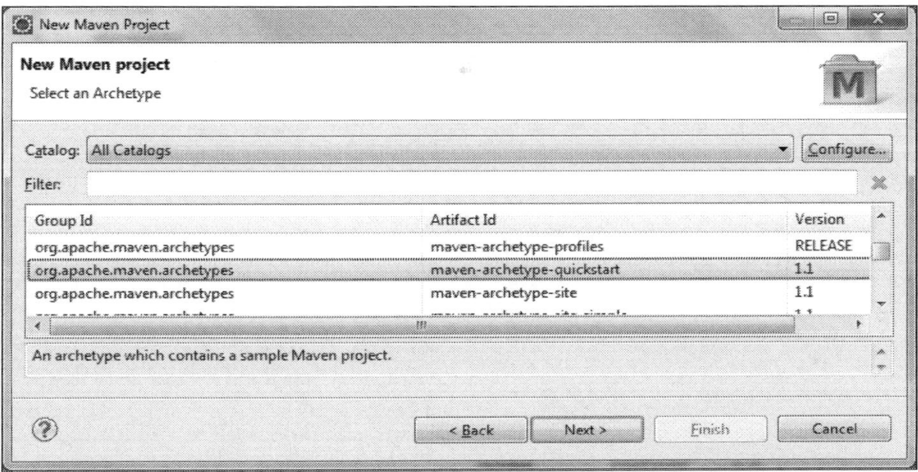

The next step will be configuring the client's `pom.xml` file.

Configuring the client's project object module

Configuring the client dependencies will require basically all the libraries that connect and transport data to the server, along with the required EJB client dependencies. The first thing we will add, just as we did for the server project, is the BOM for the EJB client dependencies:

```
<dependencyManagement>
   <dependencies>
      <dependency>
         <groupId>org.jboss.as</groupId>
         <artifactId>jboss-as-ejb-client-bom</artifactId>
         <version>7.2.0.Final</version>
         <type>pom</type>
         <scope>import</scope>
      </dependency>
   </dependencies>
</dependencyManagement>
```

Next, we will add a set of dependencies that are needed to resolve the EJB interfaces (the `ticket-agency-ejb` artifact), the JBoss' transaction API (needed as EJB are transactional-aware components), the `jboss-ejb-api` and `ejb-client` APIs, the `org.jboss.xnio` and `org.jboss.xnio` APIs (that provide a low-level input/output implementation), the `org.jboss.remoting3` API (the core transport protocol), which in turn requires `org.jboss.sasl` (for securing the transport), and finally the `org.jboss.marshalling` API (for serializing the objects that are sent to and received from the server):

```
<dependencies>
   <dependency>
      <groupId>com.packtpub.as7development.chapter3</groupId>
      <artifactId>ticket-agency-ejb</artifactId>
      <type>ejb-client</type>
      <version>${project.version}</version>
   </dependency>

   <dependency>
      <groupId>org.jboss.spec.javax.transaction</groupId>
      <artifactId>jboss-transaction-api_1.1_spec</artifactId>
      <scope>runtime</scope>
   </dependency>

   <dependency>
      <groupId>org.jboss.spec.javax.ejb</groupId>
      <artifactId>jboss-ejb-api_3.1_spec</artifactId>
      <scope>runtime</scope>
   </dependency>

   <dependency>
      <groupId>org.jboss</groupId>
      <artifactId>jboss-ejb-client</artifactId>
      <scope>runtime</scope>
   </dependency>

   <dependency>
      <groupId>org.jboss.xnio</groupId>
      <artifactId>xnio-api</artifactId>
      <scope>runtime</scope>
   </dependency>
   <dependency>
      <groupId>org.jboss.xnio</groupId>
      <artifactId>xnio-nio</artifactId>
      <scope>runtime</scope>
```

```
    </dependency>

    <dependency>
       <groupId>org.jboss.remoting3</groupId>
       <artifactId>jboss-remoting</artifactId>
       <scope>runtime</scope>
    </dependency>

    <dependency>
       <groupId>org.jboss.sasl</groupId>
       <artifactId>jboss-sasl</artifactId>
       <scope>runtime</scope>
    </dependency>

    <dependency>
       <groupId>org.jboss.marshalling</groupId>
       <artifactId>jboss-marshalling-river</artifactId>
       <scope>runtime</scope>
    </dependency>
</dependencies>
```

Coding the EJB client

We are done with the configuration. We will finally proceed with adding a new Java class `com.packtpub.as7development.chapter3.client.RemoteEJBClient` that will communicate with the Ticket Booking machine's EJB application:

```
public class RemoteEJBClient {
  private final static java.util.logging.Logger logger = Logger.
getLogger(RemoteEJBClient.class .getName());
private final static Hashtable jndiProperties = new Hashtable();

  public static void main(String[] args) throws Exception {
    Logger.getLogger("org.jboss").setLevel(Level.SEVERE); [1]
    Logger.getLogger("org.xnio").setLevel(Level.SEVERE);

    testRemoteEJB();

  }

  private static void testRemoteEJB() throws NamingException {
      jndiProperties.put(Context.URL_PKG_PREFIXES, "org.jboss.ejb.
client.naming");
    final TheatreInfo info = lookupTheatreInfoEJB(); [2]
```

```
    final TheatreBooker book = lookupTheatreBookerEJB(); [3]
    String command = "";

      /* not included for brevity. Prints out a Welcome message with
the available commands */
      dumpWelcomeMessage();

    while (true){

      command = IOUtils.readLine("> "); [4]
      if (command.equals("book")) { [5]

        int seatId = 0;

        try {
          seatId = IOUtils.readInt("Enter SeatId");
        } catch (NumberFormatException e1) {
          logger.info("Wrong seatid format!");
          continue;
        }

        try {
          String retVal = book.bookSeat(seatId-1);
        }

        catch (SeatBookedException e) {
          logger.info(e.getMessage());
          continue;
        }
        catch (NotEnoughMoneyException e) {
          logger.info(e.getMessage());
          continue;
        }
      }
      else if (command.equals("list")) { [6]
        logger.info(info.printSeatList().toString());
        continue;
      }
      else if (command.equals("quit")) { [7]
        logger.info("Bye");
        break;
      }
      else {
        logger.info("Unknown command "+command);
```

```
        }
      }

    }

     private static TheatreInfo lookupTheatreInfoEJB() throws
  NamingException {

    final Context context = new InitialContext(jndiProperties);
    return (TheatreInfo) context.lookup("ejb:/ticket-agency-
  ejb//TheatreInfoBean!com.packtpub.as7development.chapter3.ejb.
  TheatreInfo");

     }
     private static TheatreBooker lookupTheatreBookerEJB() throws
  NamingException {

    final Context context = new InitialContext(jndiProperties);
    return (TheatreBooker) context.lookup("ejb:/ticket-agency-ejb/
  TheatreBookerBean!com.packtpub.as7development.chapter3.ejb.TheatreBook
  er?stateful");

     }

  }
```

Let's see the most interesting points. At first, we set some logging rules `[1]` in order to avoid mixing the JBoss remoting log messages with the console application information.

Next, we look up the `TheatreInfo` SLSB `[2]` and the `TheatreBooker` SFSB `[3]` using the JNDI definition rules that we just discussed.

The main application loop reads from the console from input `[4]` and performs the corresponding actions: it books a ticket `[5]`, lists the theatre tickets `[6]`, and then quits the application `[7]`.

Adding EJB client configuration

As you can see from the preceding code, there is no indication about the location of the server where the EJBs are running. If you don't want to specify this by code, the simplest thing you can do is add the `jboss-ejb-client.properties` file in the client's classpath.

By default, Maven's quickstart archetype does not include a `resources` folder for your project's configuration files. You can just add one by right-clicking on your project and choosing **Add new Java Source folder** under `src/main/resources`. Once done, you need to add the `jboss-ejb-client.properties` file.

The contents of the `jboss-ejb-client.properties` file are as follows:

```
endpoint.name=client-endpoint
remote.connectionprovider.create.options.org.xnio.Options.SSL_
ENABLED=false
remote.connections=default
remote.connection.default.host=localhost
remote.connection.default.port = 4447
```

And here's some explanation to this file—the optional `endpoint.name` property represents the name that will be used to create the client side of the endpoint. If it is not specified, it will default to `config-based-ejb-client-endpoint`.

The `remote.connectionprovider.create.options.org.xnio.Options.SSL_ENABLED` property enables the encryption of the XNIO connection, otherwise plain text will be used. (In *Chapter 11, Securing JBoss AS 7 Application*, we will discuss using SSL to secure the connection between the client and the server.)

The `remote.connections` property can be used to define a list of logical names that will be used for connection purposes by the `remote.connection.[name].host` and `remote.connection.[name].port` attributes. If you'll define more than one connection, as in the following example, the connections will be split across the various destinations:

```
remote.connections=host1,host2
remote.connection.host1.host=192.168.0.1
remote.connection.host2.host=192.168.0.2
remote.connection.host1.port = 4447
remote.connection.host2.port = 4547
```

The default port used by the remoting framework is `4447`. You can, however, set a custom port using the CLI interface. For example, in order to set it to `4457`, you can issue the following command:

```
/socket-binding-group=standard-sockets/socket-binding=remoting/:write-
attribute(name=port,value=4457)
```

Running the client application

In order to run your client application, the last requirement will be to add the required Maven plugins that are needed to run the remote EJB client:

```
<build>
   <finalName>${project.artifactId}</finalName>
   <plugins>

      <!-- maven-compiler-plugin here -->

      <plugin>
         <groupId>org.codehaus.mojo</groupId>
         <artifactId>exec-maven-plugin</artifactId>
         <version>${version.exec.plugin}</version>
         <executions>
            <execution>
               <goals>
                  <goal>exec</goal>
               </goals>
            </execution>
         </executions>
         <configuration>
            <executable>java</executable>
            <workingDirectory>${project.build.directory}/exec-working-
directory</workingDirectory>
            <arguments>
               <argument>-classpath</argument>
               <classpath />                <argument>com.packtpub.
as7development.chapter3.client.RemoteEJBClient</argument>
            </arguments>
         </configuration>
      </plugin>

   </plugins>
</build>
```

As you can see in the preceding code, besides the `maven-compiler-plugin` archetype that we have omitted for the sake of brevity (we have discussed it in the server project), we have included `exec-maven-plugin` that adds the ability to execute Java programs using the `exec` goal.

Once all the plugins are in place, you can compile and execute your project by issuing the following Maven goal:

```
mvn install exec:exec
```

The preceding command can be executed either from a shell (positioned in the project's `root` folder) or from your Eclipse runtime configuration as shown in the following screenshot:

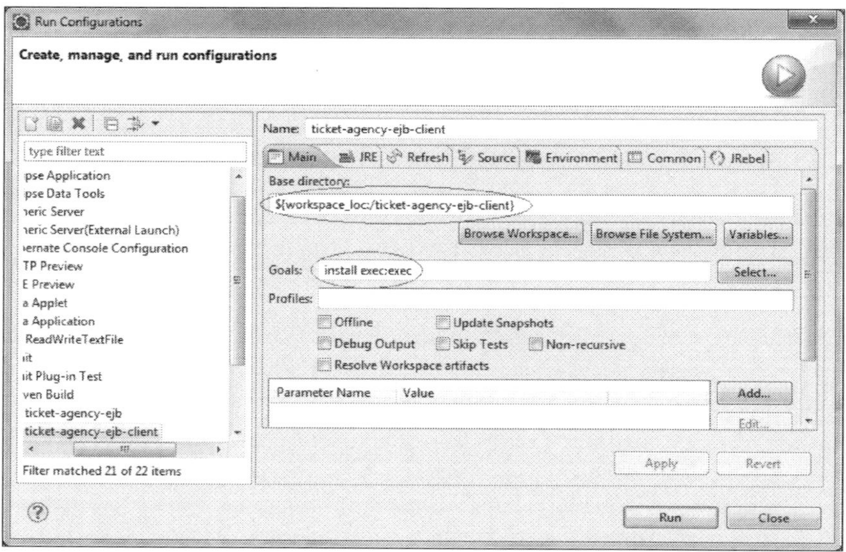

If executed from the Eclipse environment, you should be able to see the following GUI:

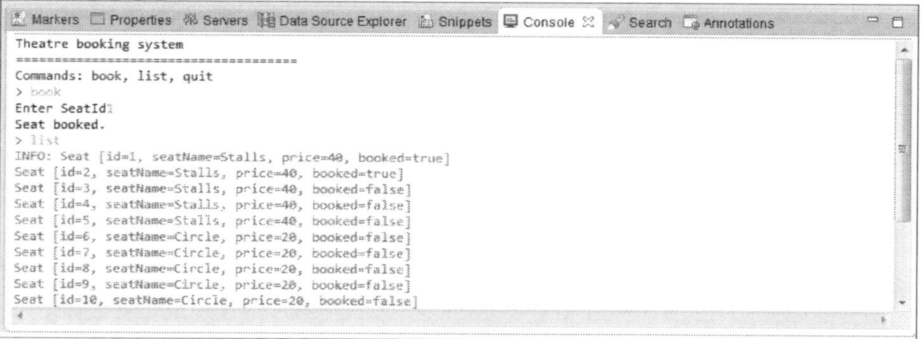

At the moment, our application provides just two functions: `book` for booking a seat and `list` for listing all the theatre seats. In the next sections, we will enrich our application by adding some more commands.

Adding user authentication

If you are running this example from a client that is located on the same machine as the application server, the remoting framework will silently allow communication between the client and your EJBs classes. On the other hand, for a client located on a remote system, you would require to provide authentication for your requests. In order to add an application user, launch the `add-user.sh` (or `add-user.bat`) script that is located under `JBOSS_HOME/bin`:

Here's a transcript of a user creation example:

```
What type of user do you wish to add?
 a) Management User (mgmt-users.properties)
 b) Application User (application-users.properties)
(a): b

Enter the details of the new user to add.
Realm (ApplicationRealm) :
Username : ejbuser
Password :
Re-enter Password :
What roles do you want this user to belong to? (Please enter a comma
separated l
ist, or leave blank for none) :
About to add user 'ejbuser' for realm 'ApplicationRealm'
Is this correct yes/no? yes
Added user 'ejbuser' to file 'C:\jboss-as-7.1.1.Final\standalone\
configuration\application-users.properties'
```

The previous user will be added for you in the `application-user.properties` file located in your `configuration` folder.

This file contains the default security realm named `ApplicationRealm`. This security realm uses the following format to store passwords:

```
username=HEX( MD5( username ':' realm ':' password))
```

With the password I've just entered, the fill will contain the following entry:

```
ejbuser=dc86450aab573bd2a8308ea69bcb8ba9
```

Now insert the username and password information into `jboss-ejb-client.properties`:

```
remote.connection.default.username=ejbuser
remote.connection.default.password=ejbuser123
```

Now, with all the previous information in the right place, you will be able to connect to your EJB application from a client that is not residing on the same machine as the server.

Using the EJB timer service

Applications that model business workflows often rely on timed notifications. The timer service of the enterprise bean container enables you to schedule timed notifications for all types of enterprise beans, except for stateful session beans. You can schedule a timed notification to occur according to a calendar schedule either at a specific time, after a duration of time, or at timed intervals.

There can be two main types of EJB timers: **programmatic timers** and **automatic timers**. Programmatic timers are set by explicitly calling one of the timer creation methods of the `TimerService` interface. Automatic timers are created upon the successful deployment of an enterprise bean that contains a method annotated with the `java.ejb.Schedule` or `java.ejb.Schedules` annotations. Let's see both approaches in the following sections.

Programmatic timer creation

To create a timer, the bean invokes one of the create methods of the `TimerService` interface. These methods allow for either single-action, interval, or calendar-based timers to be created.

The simplest way of getting a `TimerService` instance is to use resource injection. For example, in the `TheatreBox` singleton EJB, we will use the `@Resource` annotation to inject a `TimerService` object:

```
@Resource
TimerService timerService;
long duration= 6000;
```

The duration specifies the time (in ms) when the single timer is fired. The method that will fire the timer will use the `TimerService` instance to invoke the `createSingleActionTimer`, passing the duration and an instance of the `TimerConfig` class as an argument, which may optionally contain some basic information (such as a description of the timer).

```
public void createTimer(){
    timerService.createSingleActionTimer(duration, new TimerConfig());
}
```

Next, we will create a callback method named `timeout` and use the `@Timeout` annotation on top of the method. In the `timeout` method, we could, for example, reinitialize our singleton by invoking the `setupTheatre` method. Nothing fancy; however, this should give you an idea of how to get working with a single action timer.

```
@Timeout
public void timeout(Timer timer){
  logger.info("Re-building Theatre Map.");
  setupTheatre();
}
```

Scheduling timer events

If you want to schedule timed notifications at fixed intervals, the simplest way is to use the `@Schedule` annotation. The `@Schedule` annotation takes a series of comma-delimited settings to express a time or set of times, much as the Unix cron utility does. Each setting corresponds to a unit of time such as an hour or minute. A simple repeating event occurring every minute can be expressed using the `@Schedule` annotation as follows:

```
@Schedule(second="0", minute= "*", hour= "*")
```

You can find some more details about building the time string at `http://docs.oracle.com/javaee/6/tutorial/doc/bnboy.html`.

For the purpose of our example, we will create a stateless session bean that will act as an automatic buying system and therefore buy tickets at our ticketing store. So we will add one competitor in our quest for the best seat at the theatre!

```
@Stateless
public class AutomaticSellerBean
{
  private final static Logger logger = Logger.
getLogger(AutomaticSellerBean.class.getName());

  @EJB private TheatreBox   theatreBox;

  @Resource
  private TimerService timerService; [1]

  @Schedule(dayOfWeek = "*", hour = "*", minute = "*", second =
"*/60",year="*", persistent = false) [2]
```

```
    public void automatiCustomer()
    {
       int seatId = findSeat();

         if (seatId == -1) {
           cancelTimers();
           logger.info("Scheduler gone!");
           return ; // No more seats
         }

           theatreBox.buyTicket(seatId); [3]

             logger.info("Somebody just booked seat number "+seatId +1);
    }

    private int findSeat() {
      ArrayList<Seat> list = theatreBox.getSeatList();
      for (Seat s: list) {
        if (!s.isBooked()) {
          return s.getId() -1;
        }
      }
      return -1;
    }
    private void cancelTimers() {     [4]
      for (Timer timer : timerService.getTimers()) {
        timer.cancel();
      }
    }
  }
```

The first thing we should account for is the resource injection of the `Timer` object `[1]` that will be used in the `cancelTimers` method `[4]` to cancel all the scheduling when the theatre is fully booked.

Next, pay attention to the `Schedule` annotation `[2]` we are using that will fire a nonpersistent timer each minute.

Persistent timers (the default option) are able to survive application and server crashes. When the system recovers, any persistent timers will be recreated and missed callback events will be executed.

When a replay of missed timer events is not desired, a nonpersistent timer should be used, as in the preceding example.

When the action is fired, the `automaticCustomer` method starts scanning the theatre seats for an available seat. (Nothing too complex; `findSeat` starts looking from the first available seat.)

Finally, if there are seats still available, the `buyTicket` method `[3]` of the `TheatreBox` singleton will be used to short circuit the purchase of the seat (obviously, we won't need to check the money for our automatic customer).

Adding asynchronous methods to our EJBs

Before the EJB 3.1 specification, the only way to provide asynchronous capabilities to enterprise applications was using message-driven bean recipes. This remains substantially a best practice, and we are going to discuss this in depth in *Chapter 7, Developing Applications with JBoss JMS Provider*; however, in some cases it might be desirable (and easier) to use these asynchronous features from a component that follows the classical request-reply pattern.

You can make an EJB's method asynchronous by simply tagging it with the `@Asynchronous` annotation. Each time this method is invoked, it will immediately return, regardless of how long the method actually takes.

This can be used in one of two ways:

- The first technique is a fire-and-forget manner where the request is made up of the EJB and the client is not concerned about the success or failure of the request.
- The second modus operandi invokes the method but does not wait for the method to complete. The method returns a `Future` object. This object is used later to determine the result of the request.

Using fire-and-forget asynchronous calls

If you don't care about the async result, you can just have your async method return void. For this purpose, we will add a new method named `bookSeatAsync` to `TheatreBookerBean` and simply tag it as `@Asynchronous`.

```
@Asynchronous
public void bookSeatAsync(int seatId) {

  Seat seat = theatreBox.getSeatList().get(seatId);

  if (seat.isBooked()) {
    throw new SeatBookedException("Seat Already booked!");     }
```

```
    if (seat.getPrice() > money) {
      throw new NotEnoughMoneyException("You don't have enough money to
buy this ticket!");  }

    logger.info("Booking issued");
    theatreBox.buyTicket(seat);

    money = money -seat.getPrice();

     logger.info("Booking successful");

}
```

As you can see, this method does not return anything; we will need to use some other instruments to check if the transaction was completed successfully. For example, we can check from the theatre list if the seat has been booked successfully.

Returning a Future object to the client

The other available option consists of returning a `java.util.concurrent.Future` object that can later be inspected by our clients so that they know the outcome of our transaction:

```
@Asynchronous
public Future<String> bookSeatAsync(int seatId) {

  Seat seat = theatreBox.getSeatList().get(seatId);
  if (seat.isBooked()) {
    return new AsyncResult<String>("Seat "+seatId+" Already booked!");
  }
  if (seat.getPrice() > money) {
    return new AsyncResult<String>("You don't have enough money to buy
this ticket!");
  }

  logger.info("Booking issued");
  theatreBox.buyTicket(seat);
  money = money -seat.getPrice();

  return new AsyncResult<String>("Booked seat: "+seat+" - Money left:
"+money);
}
```

In this case, calls to the asynchronous `bookSeatAsync` method simply result, behind the scenes, in a `Runnable` Java object being created that wraps the method and parameters you provide. This `Runnable` object is given to an `Executor` object that is simply a work queue attached to a thread pool.

After adding the work to the queue, the proxy version of the method returns a `Future` implementation that is linked to `Runnable` that is now waiting on the queue.

When `Runnable` finally executes the `bookSeatAsync` method, it takes the return value and sets it to `Future`, making it available to the caller.

When dealing with `Future` objects, the client code needs to be adapted. As a matter of fact, in standard synchronous calls we used exceptions to intercept some events, such as when the customer does not have enough money to complete the transaction. When using `Future` calls, there's a change in this paradigm. The call to the asynchronous method is detached from the client; however, we have the option to check if the `Future` work has been completed with the `isDone` method issued on the `Future` return value.

For this purpose, let's add a `bookasync` command that will issue asynchronous booking and a `mail` command that will simulate the reading of the outcome by e-mail:

```
Future<String> futureResult = null; [1]
. . . . .
else if (command.equals("bookasync")) {

  String text = IOUtils.readLine("Enter SeatId ");
  int seatId = 0;

    try {
      seatId = Integer.parseInt(text);
    } catch (NumberFormatException e1) {

      logger.info("Wrong seatid format!");
      continue;
    }
    try {
      Thread.sleep(10000); // Simulate time consuming task
    } catch (InterruptedException e) {

      e.printStackTrace();
    }

    futureResult = book.bookSeatAsync(seatId-1); [2]
```

```
        logger.info("Booking issued. Verify your mail!");
      }
      else if (command.equals("mail")) {

          if (futureResult == null || (!futureResult.isDone())) { [3]
          logger.info("No mail received!");
          continue;
        }
        else {
          try {
            String result = futureResult.get();
            logger.info("Last mail received: "+result);

          } catch (InterruptedException e) {
              e.printStackTrace();
          } catch (ExecutionException e) {
              e.printStackTrace();
          }
          continue;
        }
    }
```

As you can see from the previous code snippet, we issue an asynchronous booking `[2]` and bind it with the `futureResult` instance `[1]`. We have introduced a pause of 10 seconds to complete the booking so that later on we can check if the work has been completed by checking the `isDone` method `[3]` of the `futureResult` object.

Here is a snapshot of our richer client application:

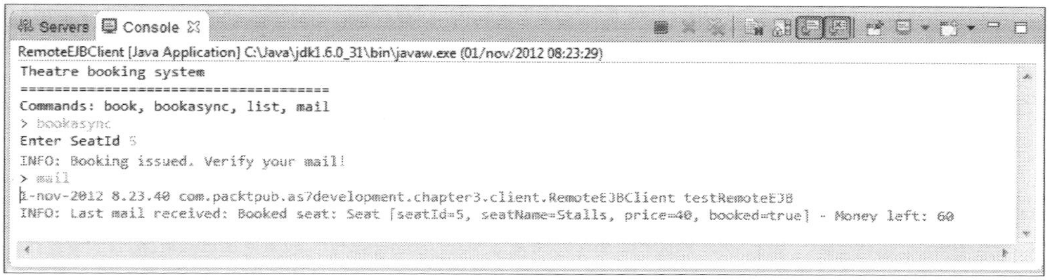

```
Servers  Console
RemoteEJBClient [Java Application] C:\Java\jdk1.6.0_31\bin\javaw.exe (01/nov/2012 08:23:29)
Theatre booking system
=====================================
Commands: book, bookasync, list, mail
> bookasync
Enter SeatId 5
INFO: Booking issued. Verify your mail!
> mail
1-nov-2012 8.23.40 com.packtpub.as7development.chapter3.client.RemoteEJBClient testRemoteEJB
INFO: Last mail received: Booked seat: Seat [seatId=5, seatName=Stalls, price=40, booked=true] - Money left: 60
```

Summary

In this chapter, we went through the new EJB 3.1 features by following a simple lab example that we enriched progressively. The example showed how the Maven framework can be used from within the Eclipse environment to assist you in assembling the project with all the necessary dependencies.

Until now, we have just coded a remote standalone client for our application. In the next chapter, we will see how to add a web frontend to our example using the context and dependency injections, to bridge the gap between the web tier and the enterprise tier.

4

Learning Context Dependency Injection

Chapter 3, Beginning Java EE 6 – EJBs, was a challenging chapter, since we had to cover lots of ground, including Java Enterprise enhancements and Maven-specific configuration. If you are still a Maven non-believer, in this chapter, we will give you one more chance to embrace this amazing framework.

This chapter discusses **Contexts and Dependency Injection** (**CDI**), which is a new addition to the Java EE specification as of Java EE 6. It provides several benefits that were missing to Java EE developers, such as allowing any JavaBean to be used as a JSF managed bean, including stateless and stateful session beans.

Some of the topics covered in this chapter include:

- What is Context Dependency Injection and how it relates to EJB
- How to rewrite our Ticket Booking example to use CDI and Java Server Faces technology
- How to run the project using Maven

This chapter assumes familiarity with **Java Server Faces** (**JSF**), which will be used to provide a graphical interface to our applications. If you are looking for a startup guide for JSF, there are several excellent resources online about JSF, including the relevant sections in the official Java EE 6 tutorial at `http://docs.oracle.com/javaee/6/tutorial/doc/bnatx.html`.

Introducing Context and Dependency Injection

Contexts and Dependency Injection for the Java EE platform introduces a standard set of component management services to the Java EE platform.

As a component of Java EE 6, CDI is in many ways a standardization of concepts that have been brewing in Spring for a long time, such as dependency injection and interceptors. In fact, CDI and Spring 3 share many similar features.

CDI lets you decouple concerns by what it refers to as loose coupling and strong typing. In doing so, it provides an almost liberating escape from the banalities of everyday Java programming, allowing injections of its objects and controlling their lifetimes.

Why CDI is for Java EE?

If you have been programming with Java EE 5, you might argue that it already features resources injection of resources. However, this kind of injection can be used only for resources known to the container (for example, `@EJB`, `@PersistenceContext`, `@PersistenceUnit`, and `@Resource`). CDI, on the other hand, provides a general-purpose dependency injection scheme, which can be used for any component.

The CDI elementary unit is still the bean. Compared with EJBs, CDI features a different, more flexible kind of bean. One of the most important differences between the two approaches is that CDI Beans are **contextual** that is, they live in a well-defined scope.

Consider the following code snippet:

```
public class HelloServlet extends HttpServlet {

@EJB EJBSample ejb;
  public void doGet (HttpServletRequestreq,
HttpServletResponse res)
    throws ServletException, IOException
  {
      PrintWriter out = res.getWriter();

      out.println(ejb.greet());
```

```
        out.close();
    }
}
```

Here, the injected EJB proxy just points to a pool of stateless instances (or a single bean instance for stateful beans). There is no automatic association between the HTTP request or HTTP session and a given EJB instance.

The opposite is true for CDI Beans, which live in well-defined scopes. For example, the following CDI Bean lives in a `RequestScoped`, that is, it will be destroyed at the end of the request:

```
@RequestScoped
@Named
public class Customer {

    private String name;
    private String surname;

    public String getName(){
        return name;
    }
    public String getSurname(){
        return surname;
    }

}
```

The above CDI Bean can be safely injected into our former servlet and, at the end of an HTTP session or HTTP request, all instances associated with this scope are automatically destroyed and, thus, garbage collected.

```
public class HelloServlet extends HttpServlet {

@InjectCustomerServiceservice;

  public void doGet (HttpServletRequest req,
  HttpServletResponse res)
    throws ServletException, IOException
  {
. . . .
  }
}
```

Named beans

In the earlier section, we have come across the `@Named` annotation. Named beans allow us to easily inject our beans into other classes that depend on them, and to easily refer to them from JSF pages via the **Unified Expression Language**(EL). Recall the earlier example:

```
@RequestScoped
@Named
public class Customer {

    private String name;
    private String surname;

    public String getName(){
        return name;
    }
    public String getSurname(){
        return surname;
    }

}
```

This class, decorated with the `@Named` annotation, can be then referenced from a JSF page.

By default, the name of the bean will be the classname with its first letter switched to lowercase; thus the `Customer` bean can be referred to as `customer`.

```
<?xml version="1.0" encoding="UTF-8"?>
<html xmlns="http://www.w3.org/1999/xhtml" xmlns:h="http://java.sun.com/jsf/html">
   <h:body>
      <h:form>
         <h:panelGrid columns="2">
            <h:outputLabel for="name" value="Name" />
            <h:inputText id="name" value="#{customer.name}" />
            <h:outputLabel for="lastName" value="Surname" />
            <h:inputText id="surname" value="#{customer.surname}" />
            <h:panelGroup />
         </h:panelGrid>
      </h:form>
   </h:body>
</html>
```

If you want to use a different naming policy for your bean, you could use the `@Named` annotation as follows:

```
@Named(value="customNamedBean")
```

This way, we will be able to reference our CDI Beans using the identified `customNamedBean` value.

CDI scopes

CDI Beans come with a set of predefined scopes and annotations and each CDI Bean has a distinct lifecycle determined by the scope they belong to. The following table describes the built-in CDI scopes and the annotations required to set them:

Scope	Description
`@RequestScoped`	The `@RequestScoped` beans are shared for the length of a single request. This could be an HTTP request, a remote EJB invocation, a web services invocation, or message-delivery to an MDB. These beans are destroyed at the end of the request.
`@ConversationScoped`	The `@ConversationScoped` beans are shared across multiple requests in the same HTTP session but only if there is an active conversation maintained. Conversations are supported for JSF requests through the `javax.enterprise.context.Conversation` bean.
`@SessionScoped`	The `@SessionScoped` beans are shared between all requests that occur in the same HTTP session and are destroyed when the session is destroyed.
`@ApplicationScoped`	An `@ApplicationScoped` bean will live for as long as the application is running and is destroyed when the application is shut down.
`@Dependent`	The `@Dependent` beans are never shared between injection points. Any injection of a dependent bean is a new instance whose lifecycle is bound to the lifecycle of the object it is being injected into.

In this chapter example, we will use the `RequestScoped` and `SessionScoped` beans to drive our simple Ticket Booking system. In the next chapter we will further enhance our example using `ConversationScoped` beans, which are a peculiar scope of CDI Beans. Providing a detailed explanation example of all named beans' scopes is beyond the scope of this book. However, you can quench your thirst for knowledge by having a look at JBoss CDI implementation docs at `http://docs.jboss.org/weld/reference/latest/en-US/html/scopescontexts.html`.

JBoss AS CDI implementation

Weld is the JBoss CDI implementation and is actually being developed as part of the Seam project (`http://www.seamframework.org/`). Weld provides a complete CDI implementation, which can be safely run on a Java EE 6 container such as JBoss AS or Oracle WebLogic.

Therefore, in order to run CDI-based applications on JBoss AS 7, you don't need to download any extra libraries as Weld is part of the JBoss AS 7 modules and it is included in all server configurations, as stated by the following extension:

```
<extension module="org.jboss.as.weld"/>
```

Having your module installed, however, does not mean that you can blindly use it in your applications. The general rule is that on JBoss AS 7, every application module is isolated from other modules; this means, by default, it does not have visibility on the AS modules, nor do the AS modules have visibility on the application.

To be accurate we should state that all JBoss AS 7 modules fall into the following three categories:

- **Modules which are implicitly added to your applications**: This category includes the most common API such as `javax.activation`, `javax.annotation`, `javax.jms`, `javax.security`, `javax.transaction`, `javax.jms`, and `javax.xml`. Using these modules does not require any extra effort as JBoss AS 7 will add them for you if you are referencing them in your application.
- **Modules which are added on condition**: This category includes `javax.ejb`, `org.jboss.resteasy`, `javax.persistence` and `org.hibernate`, `org.jboss.as.web`, and finally `org.jboss.as.weld`. All these modules will be added on the condition that you supply its core annotations (such as `@Stateless` for EJB) or its core configuration files; for example, `web.xml` for a web application.
- **Modules which need to be explicitly enabled by the application deployer**: This includes all other modules, such as your custom modules that you can add to the application server. The simplest way to allow visibility to these modules is adding an explicit dependency in your `META-INF/MANIFEST.MF` file. For example, if you want to trigger the **log4j** dependency, you have to code your manifest file as follows:

  ```
  Dependencies: org.apache.log4j
  ```

So if you followed our checklist carefully, you should be aware that in order to let Weld libraries kick in, you should add its core configuration file, which is named `beans.xml`. This file can be placed in your application at the following locations:

- In your `WEB-INF` folder if you are developing a web application
- In your `META-INF` folder if you are deploying a JAR archive

The `beans.xml` file is based on the following schema reference:

```
<beans xmlns="http://java.sun.com/xml/ns/javaee"
xmlns:xsi="http://www.w3.org/2001/XMLSchema-instance"
xsi:schemaLocation="
      http://java.sun.com/xml/ns/javaee
      http://java.sun.com/xml/ns/javaee/beans_1_0.xsd">
</beans>
```

However, it is perfectly legal to place an empty `beans.xml` file in the correct location, in order to enable CDI in your applications.

Rethinking your ticketing system

Once you have learned the basics of CDI, we will start re-engineering the Ticket Booking system using CDI Beans wherever necessary. We will turn it into a leaner application by dropping a few items such as remote interfaces or asynchronous methods, which are not needed in this example. Therefore, you will be able to focus just on the components that are actually used in the web application.

Let's create, for this purpose, a web application using a new Maven archetype that fits our purpose:

1. From the **File** menu go to **New | Maven Project**; follow the wizard to the second screen where you will select the `webapp-javaee6 archetype`, which will create the structure for a web-based Java EE 6 project:

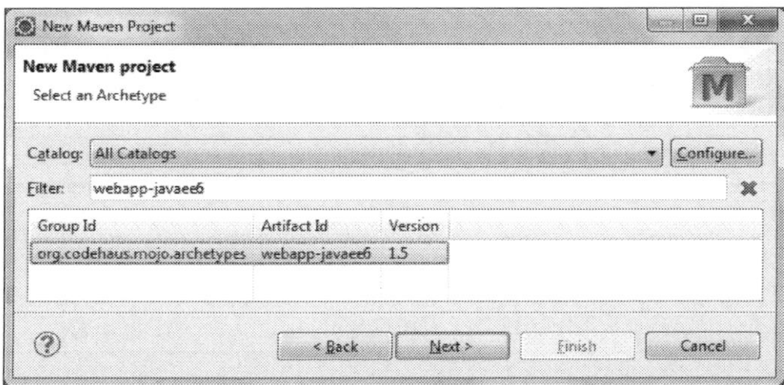

2. On the next screen, enter `com.packtpub.as7development.chapter4` as **Group Id** and **Package** and `ticket-agency-cdi` as **Artifact Id**:

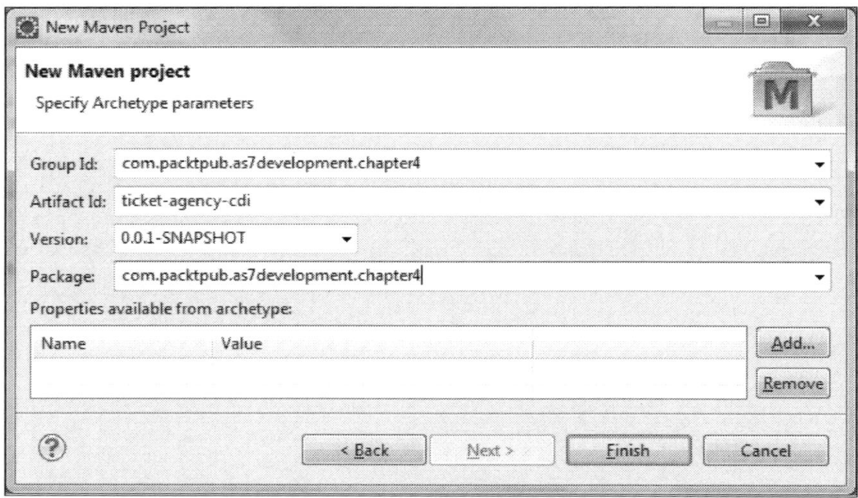

3. Click on **Finish**. The Maven plugin for Eclipse will generate for you the following project structure:

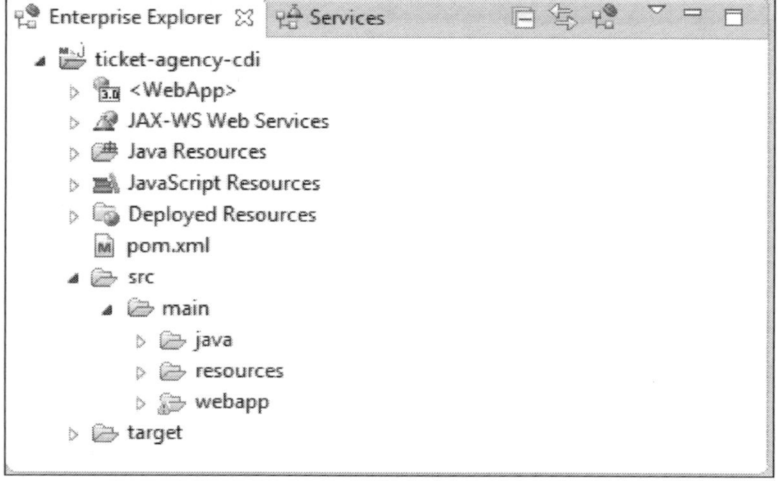

As you can see from the preceding screenshot, we have now, besides the standard `java` (for Java classes) and `resources` (for configuration files) folders, a new directory named `webapp` that will host the web application views.

Adding the required dependencies

In order to compile and run the project, our Maven's `pom.xml` now requires a more complex set of libraries, starting from Java Enterprise CDI API:

```
<dependency>
   <groupId>javax.enterprise</groupId>
   <artifactId>cdi-api</artifactId>
   <scope>provided</scope>
</dependency>
```

Next, we need the Common Annotations API (JSR-250) that we have used to annotate our beans:

```
<dependency>
   <groupId>
      org.jboss.spec.javax.annotation
   </groupId>
   <artifactId>jboss-annotations-api_1.1_spec</artifactId>
   <scope>provided</scope>
</dependency>
```

Since our project uses JBoss logging API as well to output information, you also need to include:

```
<dependency>
   <groupId>org.jboss.logging</groupId>
   <artifactId>jboss-logging</artifactId>
   <version>RELEASE</version>
</dependency>
```

Next in the list is the EJB API, which we are still using in this example:

```
<dependency>
   <groupId>org.jboss.spec.javax.ejb</groupId>
   <artifactId>jboss-ejb-api_3.1_spec</artifactId>
   <scope>provided</scope>
</dependency>
```

Remember that in order to use the JBoss Java EE 6 stack, you have to specify the `jboss-javaee-6.0` **Bill of Materials** (**BOM**) as shown in the earlier chapter, otherwise Maven will complain that dependencies are missing the appropriate library version.

In order to let Maven publish the application for us, we will include `jboss-as-maven-plugin` as well, as we did in the last chapter, taking care to specify the correct filename extension (`.war`):

```
<build>
    <finalName>${project.artifactId}</finalName>
    <plugins>
      <plugin>
        <groupId>org.jboss.as.plugins</groupId>
        <artifactId>jboss-as-maven-plugin</artifactId>
        <version>${version.jboss.maven.plugin}</version>
        <configuration>
          <filename>${project.build.finalName}.war</filename>
        </configuration>
      </plugin>
  </plugins>
  </build>
```

Coding the beans

Once your project is properly configured, we can start modeling our beans. The first bean we will upgrade is `TheatreBookerBean` which will drive the user session, accessing the `Ticket` list from our `TheatreBox` bean:

```
package com.packtpub.as7development.chapter4.service;

import java.io.Serializable;

import javax.annotation.PostConstruct;
import javax.enterprise.context.SessionScoped;
import javax.enterprise.event.Event;

import javax.faces.application.FacesMessage;
import javax.faces.context.FacesContext;
import javax.inject.Inject;
import javax.inject.Named;

import org.jboss.logging.Logger;

import com.packtpub.as7development.chapter4.ejb.TheatreBox;
import com.packtpub.as7development.chapter4.model.Seat;

@Named  [1]
@SessionScoped  [2]
```

```
public class TheatreBookerBean implements Serializable {
 private static final Logger logger =
   Logger.getLogger(TheatreBookerBean.class);

 int money;
 @Inject TheatreBox theatreBox; [3]

 @PostConstruct
 public void createCustomer() {
  this.money=100;
 }

 public void bookSeat(int seatId)    {
  FacesContext fc = FacesContext.getCurrentInstance();


  logger.info("Booking seat "+seatId);
  Seat seat = theatreBox.getSeatList().get(seatId-1);

  if (seat.getPrice() > money) {    [4]

   FacesMessage m = new FacesMessage(FacesMessage.SEVERITY_ERROR, "Not
enough Money!", "Registration successful");
   fc.addMessage(null, m);
   return;
  }

  theatreBox.buyTicket(seatId-1);

  FacesMessage m = new FacesMessage(FacesMessage.SEVERITY_INFO,
"Booked!", "Booking successful");
  fc.addMessage(null, m);
  logger.info("Seat booked.");

  money = money - seat.getPrice();


 }
 public int getMoney() {
  return money;
 }
}
```

As you can see, the bean has been tagged as `Named [1]`, which means that it can be directly referenced in our JSF pages. The bean is `SessionScoped [2]` since it stores the amount of money available to the customer during its session.

Finally, notice that we can safely inject EJBs into our CDI Beans using the `Inject [3]` annotation. Also the reverse is perfectly legal, that is, injecting CDI Beans into EJBs.

Compared with our earlier project, here we don't raise Java Exceptions when the customer is not able to afford a ticket. Since the application is web based, we simply display a warning message to the client, using `JSF Faces Messages [4]`.

The other bean that we still use in our application is `TheatreInfoBean`, which has been moved to the `producer` package, as it will actually provide the application with the list of available seats:

```
package com.packtpub.as7development.chapter4.producer;

import java.util.List;

import javax.annotation.PostConstruct;
import javax.enterprise.event.*;
import javax.enterprise.inject.*;
import javax.inject.*;

import com.packtpub.as7development.chapter4.ejb.TheatreBox;
import com.packtpub.as7development.chapter4.model.Seat;

@Model [1]
public class  TheatreInfoBean   {

@Inject TheatreBox box;

private List<Seat> seats;

@Produces [2]
@Named
public List<Seat>getSeats() {
   return seats;
}

public void onMemberListChanged(@Observes(notifyObserver = Reception.
IF_EXISTS) final Seat member) {
   retrieveAllSeatsOrderedByName(); [3]
}
```

```
@PostConstruct
public void retrieveAllSeatsOrderedByName() {

   seats = box.getSeatList();

}

}
```

At first, have a look at the `@Model` annotation `[1]`, which is an alias for two commonly used annotations: `@Named` and `@RequestScoped`. Therefore, this bean will be "named" into our JSF page and will carry a request scope.

Next, pay attention to the method `getSeats`. This method returns a list of seats, exposing it as a producer method `[2]`.

Producer methods allow control over the production of the dependency objects. As a Java Factory pattern, they can be used as a source of objects whose implementation may vary at runtime, or if the object requires some custom initialization that is not to be performed in the constructor.

It can be used to provide any kind of concrete class implementation; however, it is especially useful to inject Java EE resources into your application.

One advantage of using a `@Producer` annotation for the `getSeats` method is that its objects can be exposed directly via JSF **Expression Language(EL)**, as we will see in a minute.

Finally, another feature of CDI that was unleashed in this example is the **observer**. Observers, just like the name suggests, can be used to observe objects. An observer method is notified whenever an object is created, removed, or updated. In our example, it allows the list of seats to be refreshed whenever they are needed.

To be precise, in our example, we are using a conditional Observer which is denoted by the expression `notifyObserver = Reception.IF_EXISTS`. This means that in practice the observer method is only called if an instance of the component already exists. If not specified, the default option (`ALWAYS`) will be that the observer method is always called (If an instance doesn't exist, it will be created).

Whenever a change in our list of seats occurs, we will use the `javax.enterprise.event.Event` object to notify the observer of changes. This will be done in our Singleton Bean, which gets injected with the seat's event `[1]` and notifies the observer by firing the event when a seat is booked `[2]`.

```
package com.packtpub.as7development.chapter4.ejb;

import static javax.ejb.LockType.*;
import javax.ejb.*;import org.jboss.logging.Logger;
import com.packtpub.as7development.chapter4.model.Seat;
import java.util.*;

@Singleton
@Startup

public class TheatreBox {

@Inject Event<Seat>seatEvent;

@Lock(WRITE)
public void buyTicket(intseatId )      {
   Seat seat = getSeatList().get(seatId);

   seat.setBooked(true);
   seatEvent.fire(seat);

}

   // Code stays the same as chapter3
}
```

The last class we will include in our project is the `Seat` bean, which will be used as our model without any change in it:

```
package com.packtpub.as7development.chapter4.model;

import java.io.Serializable;

public class Seat implements Serializable {
   // Code stays the same as chapter3

}
```

Building the view

Once we have coded the server side of our example, creating the frontend will be quite easy, as we made all our resources available through CDI Beans.

One notable difference between the earlier edition of this book is that **Facelets** are now the preferred view technology for JSF. Earlier versions of JSF used JSP as their default view technology. As JSP technology predates JSF, sometimes using JSP with JSF felt unnatural or created problems. For example, the lifecycle of JSPs is different from the lifecycle of JSF.

> Compared to the simpler request-response paradigm on which the JSP lifecycle is based, the JSF lifecycle is much more complex, since the core of JSF is the MVC pattern, which has several implications. User actions in JSF-generated views take place in a client that does not have a permanent connection to the server. The delivery of user actions or page events is delayed until a new connection is established. The JSF lifecycle must handle this delay between event and event processing. Also, the JSF lifecycle must ensure that the view is correct before rendering it and also that, the JSF system includes a phase for validating inputs and another for updating the model only after all inputs pass validation.

Most of the time Facelets are used to build Java Server Faces views using HTML-style templates and component trees. Templating is a useful feature available with Facelets that allows you to create a page that will act as the template for the other pages in an application (something like Struts tiles). The idea is to obtain portions of reusable code without repeating the same code on different pages.

So here's the main application structure, which contains a template page named `default.xhtml` that is referenced by views in the template attribute of the page's `composition` element:

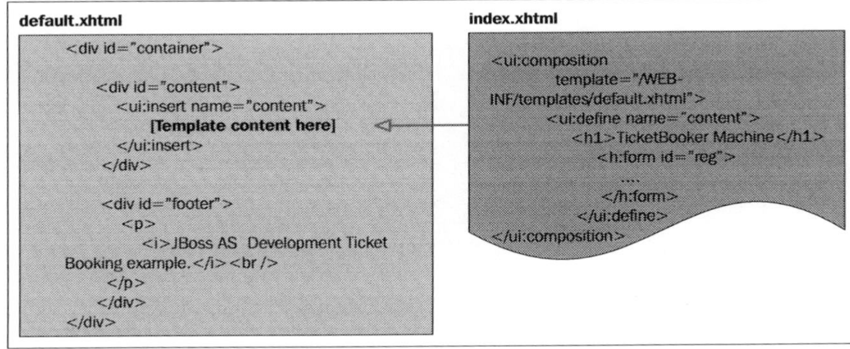

As you can see, the template contains two main HTML `div` elements that will be used to contain the main application panel (`content`) and a footer div (`footer`), which will barely output the application title.

So in order to add the template at first, add a new JSP page in the `WEB-INF/templates` folder of your application, and name it `default.xhtml`:

```
<!DOCTYPE html PUBLIC "-//W3C//DTD XHTML 1.0 Strict//EN"
    "http://www.w3.org/TR/xhtml1/DTD/xhtml1-strict.dtd">
<html xmlns="http://www.w3.org/1999/xhtml"
    xmlns:h="http://java.sun.com/jsf/html"
    xmlns:ui="http://java.sun.com/jsf/facelets">
<h:head>
    <meta http-equiv="Content-Type" content="text/html;
    charset=utf-8" />
    <h:outputStylesheet   name="style.css"  />
</h:head>
<h:body>
    <div id="container">

        <div id="content">
            <ui:insert name="content">
                    [Template content will be inserted here]
            </ui:insert>
        </div>
        <div id="footer">
            <p>
                <i>JBoss AS 7 Development Ticket Booking example.
                </i><br />
            </p>
        </div>
    </div>
</h:body>
</html>
```

Next, we will add the main page view, which will be embedded into your template. For this purpose, add a JSP page named `index.xhtml` into the `webapp` folder of your Maven project:

```
<?xml version="1.0" encoding="UTF-8"?>
<ui:composition xmlns="http://www.w3.org/1999/xhtml"
  xmlns:ui="http://java.sun.com/jsf/facelets"
  xmlns:f="http://java.sun.com/jsf/core"
  xmlns:h="http://java.sun.com/jsf/html"
  template="/WEB-INF/templates/default.xhtml"> [1]
```

```
    <ui:define name="content">
      <h1>TicketBooker Machine</h1>
      <h:form id="reg">

        <h3>Money: $ #{theatreBookerBean.money}</h3> [2]
        <h:messages errorClass="error" infoClass="info"
        globalOnly="true" />
          <h:panelGrid columns="1" border="1" styleClass="smoke">
        <h:dataTable var="_seat" value="#{seats}" [3]
          rendered="#{not empty seats}" styleClass="simpletablestyle">

          <h:column>
            <f:facet name="header">Id</f:facet>
                  #{_seat.id}
          </h:column>

          <h:column>
            <f:facet name="header">Name</f:facet>
                  #{_seat.seatName}
          </h:column>
          <h:column>
            <f:facet name="header">Price</f:facet>
                  #{_seat.price}$
          </h:column>
          <h:column>
            <f:facet name="header">Booked</f:facet>
                  #{_seat.booked}
          </h:column>
          <h:column>
            <f:facet name="header">Action</f:facet>
            <h:commandButton id="book"
              action="#{theatreBookerBean.bookSeat(_seat.id)}" [4]
              disabled="#{_seat.booked}"
              value="#{_seat.booked ? 'Reserved' : 'Book'}" />
          </h:column>

        </h:dataTable>
          </h:panelGrid>
      </h:form>
    </ui:define>
  </ui:composition>
```

The `ui:composition` element is a templating tag that wraps content to be included in another Facelet. Specifically, it will be included in the template `default.xhtml[1]`.

The following sequence explains in detail what the main view will produce:

1. First, we will display the customer's money `[2]`,which is bound to a session variable called `money`.

[Notice how we directly reference CDI Beans (for example, `TheatreBookerBean`) from JSF expressions, just like we used to do with JSF Managed Beans.]

2. The next thing on the checklist is printing, via the messages element, all JSF messages `[3]` that are meant to be produced by the application.

The main task of this view is to produce a view of all tickets and let the users purchase them. This is achieved by means of a `dataTable` object `[3]` that can be used to produce a tabular list of objects, which are generally stored as `java.util.List` in your beans.

Pay attention to the value attribute of the `dataTable`:

```
<h:dataTable var="_seat" value="#{seats}"
rendered="#{not empty seats}" styleClass="simpletablestyle">
```

In this case we don't directly reference a CDI Bean, but we reference an object, which has been "produced" by a CDI Bean. To be precise it has been produced by `TheatreInfoBean`, which as we have seen, has a `@Produces` and a `@Named` annotation on our list of seats:

```
private List<Seat> seats;

@Produces
@Named
public List<Seat>getSeats() {
   return seats;
}
```

This `dataTable` will be displayed only if it contains some data in it (as dictated by the *not empty seats* EL expression). In one of the `dataTable` columns we have added a `commandButton [4]`, which will be used to book the seat that is displayed on that row. Notice one of the JSF 2 goodies here, as we are calling the `bookSeat` method of the `TheatreBookerBean` passing as argument one parameter, which is the `seatId` field.

JSF 2 facet suggestions

By enabling JSF 2 facets on your project configuration you can enjoy some additional benefits while designing your views.

Enabling JSF 2 project facets takes half a minute from you. Right-click on your project and navigate to **Properties** | **Project Facets**. Then select the **JSF 2.1 Project facets** checkbox and click on the **OK** button:

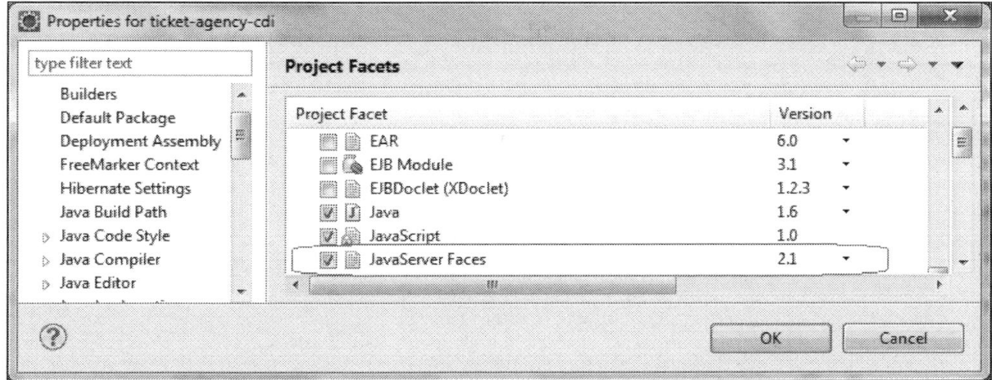

Once the JSF facet is enabled, Eclipse will notify you that JSF library configuration is missing; just disable the JSF library configuration which is a part of Maven's duty.

Once the JSF 2 facets are configured, if you press *Ctrl*+ Space bar before referencing a field or method, a suggestion popup window will let you choose the method or the attribute of the Bean you want to reference:

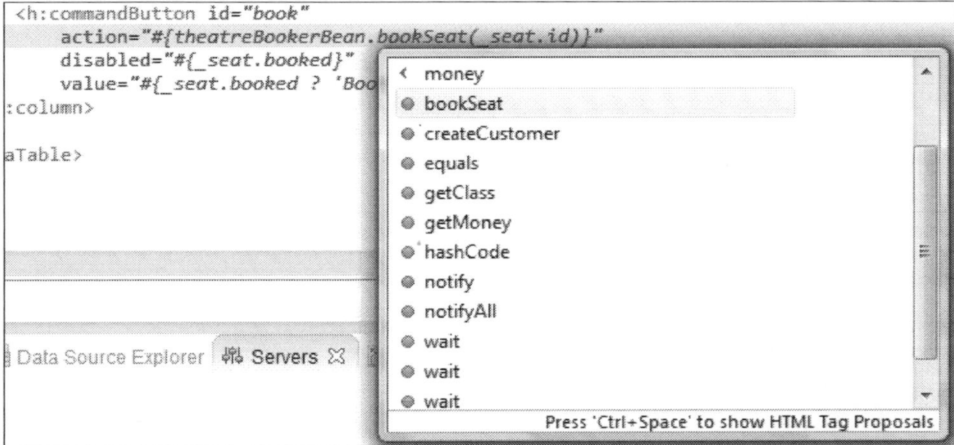

Getting ready to run the application

Ok, now your application is almost ready; we just need to add a welcome page named `index.html` that redirects to our main page, `index.xhtml`.

```
<html>
    <head>
      <meta http-equiv="Refresh" content="0; URL=index.jsf">
    </head>
</html>
```

Please note that we are triggering JSF pages by using the `*.jsf` URL pattern, as defined in `web.xml`:

```
<web-app>
  <servlet>
    <servlet-name>Faces Servlet</servlet-name>
    <servlet-class>javax.faces.webapp.FacesServlet</servlet-class>
    <load-on-startup>1</load-on-startup>
    <enabled>true</enabled>
    <async-supported>false</async-supported>
  </servlet>
  <servlet-mapping>
    <servlet-name>Faces Servlet</servlet-name>
    <url-pattern>
      *.jsf
    </url-pattern>
  </servlet-mapping>
</web-app>
```

This will then run the FacesServlet for all pages invoked with the `*.jsf` suffix.

Finally, as we stated previously, in order to activate CDI we need to add an empty `beans.xml` file in the `WEB-INF` folder of your application.

So, if you followed the same naming conventions used in this chapter, you will end up with the following project structure:

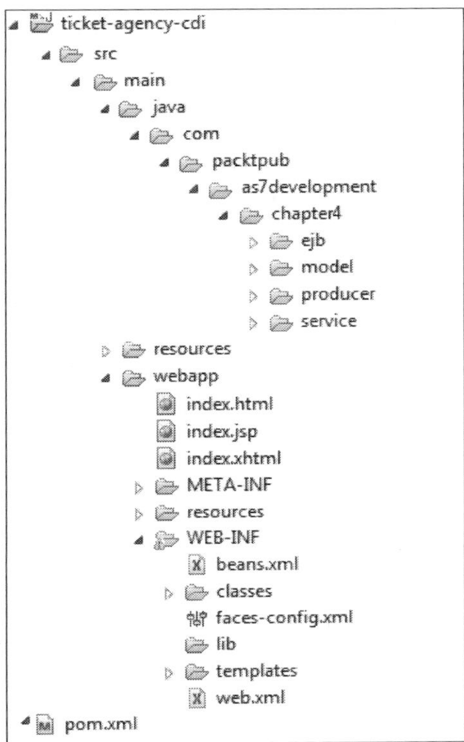

At this point you must be familiar with building and deploying your Maven applications from Eclipse or from a shell. Assuming you are managing your application from a shell—start by building up the project using:

```
mvn install
```

Then publish it as usual using JBoss' Maven plugin:

```
mvn jboss-as:deploy
```

The application will be available at the following URL:

```
http://localhost:8080/ticket-agency-cdi
```

So, after so much work, you will be pleased to have your application happily running on your browser:

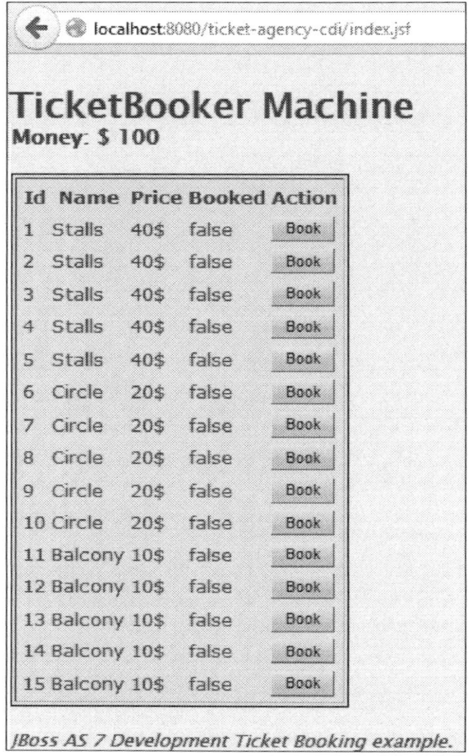

Right now, you will be able to book tickets up to the budget ($ 100) defined in your `SessionScoped` bean. So enjoy this first taste of JSF and CDI.

Combining the scheduler into our application

Up to now we have not included into our application the scheduler, which was in charge simulating other customers requesting tickets. That was not an oversight; as a matter of fact, introducing an external system in a web application poses some challenges. For example, what if the scheduler updates some data used by the application? How will the user know it?

There are several strategies to address this requirement; however, they all boil down to use some intelligence in your client application. For example, if you are familiar with web scripting languages, you can use the popular jQuery API to poll the server for some updates.

Since not all Java EE developers might be skilled with jQuery, we would rather show a simple and effective way to fulfill our requirement using **RichFaces** libraries (`http://www.jboss.org/richfaces`), which provide advanced Ajax support along with a rich set of ready-to-use components.

Installing RichFaces

Installing RichFaces requires a set of core libraries that are generally available from the RichFaces download page.

Additionally, you need to provide a set of third-party dependencies that are used by the RichFaces API. Never mind, that's what Maven is for! Start by adding the latest BOM for RichFaces API in the upper dependency management section:

```
<dependency>
   <groupId>org.richfaces</groupId>
   <artifactId>richfaces-bom</artifactId>
   <version>4.2.0.Final</version>
   <scope>import</scope>
   <type>pom</type>
</dependency>
```

Then, it's just a matter of adding the rich UI libraries and the core API:

```
<dependency>
   <groupId>org.richfaces.ui</groupId>
   <artifactId>richfaces-components-ui</artifactId>
</dependency>
<dependency>
   <groupId>org.richfaces.core</groupId>
   <artifactId>richfaces-core-impl</artifactId>
</dependency>
```

Making your application rich

Once we have installed RichFaces libraries, we will just need to reference them on each XHTML page in your project. Here's the new `index.xhtml` page using the RichFaces namespaces:

```
<ui:composition xmlns="http://www.w3.org/1999/xhtml"
  xmlns:h="http://java.sun.com/jsf/html"
  xmlns:f="http://java.sun.com/jsf/core"
  xmlns:ui="http://java.sun.com/jsf/facelets"
  xmlns:a4j="http://richfaces.org/a4j"
  xmlns:rich="http://richfaces.org/rich"
  template="/WEB-INF/templates/default.xhtml">
```

```
    <ui:define name="content">
     <f:view>
      <h:form>
        <a4j:poll id="poll" interval="2000"
          enabled="#{pollerBean.pollingActive}" render="grid" />
           <rich:panel header="TicketBooker Machine"
           style="width:350px">
          <h2>Book your Ticket</h2>
          <h3>Money: $ #{theatreBookerBean.money}</h3>
          <h:messages errorClass="error" infoClass="info"
          globalOnly="true" />
          <rich:dataTable id="grid" var="_seat" value="#{seats}"
            rendered="#{not empty seats}" styleClass="simpletablestyle">
            <h:column>
              <f:facet name="header">Id</f:facet>
                  #{_seat.id}
              </h:column>
            <h:column>
              <f:facet name="header">Name</f:facet>
                  #{_seat.seatName}
              </h:column>
            <h:column>
              <f:facet name="header">Price</f:facet>
                  #{_seat.price}
              </h:column>
            <h:column>
              <f:facet name="header">Booked</f:facet>
                  #{_seat.booked}
              </h:column>
            <h:column>
              <f:facet name="header">Action</f:facet>
              <h:commandButton id="book"
                action="#{theatreBookerBean.bookSeat(_seat.id)}"
                disabled="#{_seat.booked}"
                value="#{_seat.booked ? 'Booked' : 'Register'}" />
            </h:column>
          </rich:dataTable>
        </rich:panel>
      </h:form>
    </f:view>
    </ui:define>
  </ui:composition>
```

```
</f:view>
</ui:define>
</ui:composition>
```

We have highlighted the core enhancements added in this page. At first, as we said, we need to reference the RichFaces libraries at the top of the XHTML page.

Next, we have added a rich Ajax component, **a4j:poll**, which does a simple but an effective job of polling the server for updates, allowing re-rendering of just one component—the `grid` component—which contains the main datatable.

Additionally, this component references a JSF managed bean named `PollerBean`, which acts just as an on/off flag for our poller. We expect to turn off polling as soon as all seats are sold out:

```
package com.packtpub.as7development.chapter4.service;

import java.io.Serializable;

import javax.faces.bean.ManagedBean;
import javax.faces.bean.ViewScoped;

@ManagedBean
@ViewScoped
public class PollerBean implements Serializable{
  boolean pollingActive=true;

  public boolean isPollingActive() {
    return pollingActive;
  }
  public void setPollingActive(boolean pollingActive) {
    this.pollingActive = pollingActive;
  }
}
```

The `PollerBean` will be injected into our scheduler so that we can turn off polling, once there are no more tickets to sell:

```
@Stateless
public class AutomaticSellerBean
 {

  @Inject TheatreBox   theatreBox;
  @Inject PollerBean   pollerBean;
  private final static Logger logger = Logger.
getLogger(AutomaticSellerBean.class.getName());
```

```
    @Resource
    private TimerService timerService;

    public void cancelTimers() {
       for (Timer timer : timerService.getTimers()) {

            timer.cancel();
       }
    }
     @Schedule(dayOfWeek = "*", hour = "*", minute = "*", second =
  "*/30",year="*", persistent = false)
       public void backgroundProcessing()
        {
            int seatId = findSeat();

            if (seatId == -1) {
              pollerBean.setPollingActive(false);
              cancelTimers();
              logger.info("Scheduler gone!");
              return ; // No more seats
            }

            theatreBox.buyTicket(seatId);

            logger.info("Somebody just booked seat number "+seatId);
        }
      public int findSeat() {
            ArrayList<Seat> list = theatreBox.getSeatList();
            for (Seat s: list) {
            if (!s.isBooked()) {
            return s.getId()-1;
            }
            }

        return -1;
      }
   }
```

Running the application

With all libraries in place, you can now test run your new rich application. As you can see, every 30 seconds a ticket is sold out and buttons are turned, in real time, into **Not available**:

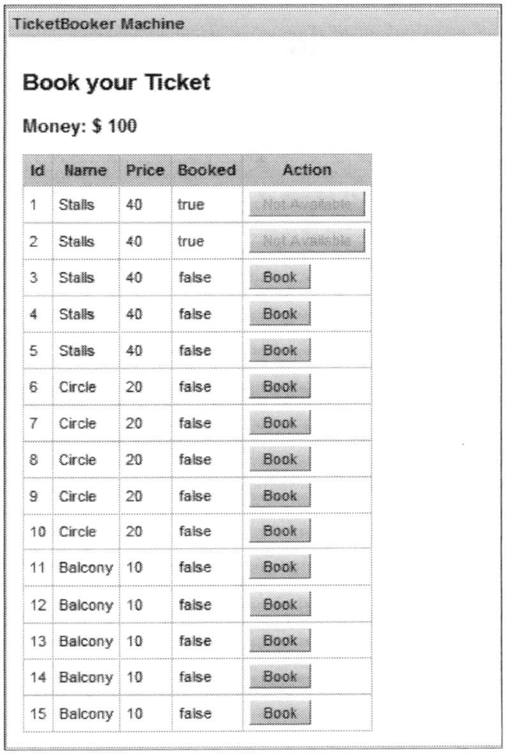

TicketBooker Machine

Book your Ticket

Money: $ 100

Id	Name	Price	Booked	Action
1	Stalls	40	true	Not Available
2	Stalls	40	true	Not Available
3	Stalls	40	false	Book
4	Stalls	40	false	Book
5	Stalls	40	false	Book
6	Circle	20	false	Book
7	Circle	20	false	Book
8	Circle	20	false	Book
9	Circle	20	false	Book
10	Circle	20	false	Book
11	Balcony	10	false	Book
12	Balcony	10	false	Book
13	Balcony	10	false	Book
14	Balcony	10	false	Book
15	Balcony	10	false	Book

Are EJBs and JSF Managed Beans obsolete?

At the end of this chapter, we would like to give our honest opinion about a common question posed by developers, that is, how EJB, JSF Managed Beans, and CDI interact and where the boundary between them lies. Are there redundancies between them? It is indeed a bit confusing since there are now multiple component models in Java EE.

JSF Managed Beans have been, for long, the actual glue between the application view and the business methods. Since the Release 2.0 of JSF, you can declare JSF Managed Beans via an annotation and the scopes are expanded with a **view scope** and the ability to create custom scopes. However, apart from the view scope, there is very little still going for JSF Managed Beans, which can be replaced by CDI Beans that are much more flexible and allow a better integration with other Java EE components.

On the other hand, EJBs, even using a less flexible injection mechanism, still maintain some unique features such as schedulable timers, asynchronous operations, declarative transactional execution, and pooling, that are essential for throttling and the prevention of denial of service attacks.

So it's likely that EJBs are not disappearing from our code. Rather it is likely (and desirable too) that they will continue to be used for some of their unique features, while for the remaining part, its functionality will be exposed via CDI instead of EJB's own annotations such as `@Stateless` and `@EJB`.

Summary

In this chapter, we provided an introduction to Contexts and Dependency Injection. We covered how JSF pages can access CDI named beans as if they were JSF Managed Beans. We also covered how CDI makes it easy to inject dependencies into our code via the `@Inject` annotation. Additionally, we explained how we can add another library of the JBoss ecosystem (RichFaces) uncovering just one aspect of its potentiality.

Until now we have worked with in-memory data, so it's time to introduce storage for our CDI applications, using the Java Persistence API, which is the theme of the next chapter.

5
Combining Persistence with CDI

In earlier chapters we covered lots of Java EE ground, combining several technologies such as the CDI API. The examples so far, however, are based on a false assumption – that all the information can be stored in memory. In this chapter, we will show how to use a persistent data store for our application in the form of a standard relational database.

The **Enterprise JavaBeans (EJB)** 3.0 specification includes a persistence specification called the **Java Persistence API (JPA)**. It is an API for creating, removing, and querying Java objects called **entities** that can be used within both a compliant EJB 3.0 Container and a standard Java SE environment.

There is a lot of ground to cover in this chapter and concepts will be coming at you from every direction. But at the end of it, you will be able to appreciate exactly how to create and deploy a complete Java EE 6 application.

Specifically, we will discuss the following topics:

- The key elements of JPA
- How to create your entities, starting with database tables
- How to manipulate the entities using CDI Beans and EJBs
- Delivering a frontend tier for our application using JSF and Facelets technology

Data persistence meets a standard

The arrival of an **Enterprise Java Persistence** standard based on the **Plain Old Java Object** (**POJO**) development model fills a substantial gap in the Java EE platform. The previous attempt (the EJB 2.x specification) missed the mark and created the stereotype of EJB entity beans being awkward to develop and too heavy for many applications. Therefore, it never achieved widespread adoption or general approval in many sectors of the industry.

Software developers knew what they wanted, but many could not find it in the existing standards, so they decided to look elsewhere. What they found was proprietary persistence frameworks, both in the commercial and open source domains.

In contrast to EJB 2.x Entity Beans, the EJB 3.0 Java Persistence API (**JPA**) is a metadata driven POJO technology. That is, to save data held in Java objects into a database, our objects are not required to implement an interface, extend a class, or fit into a framework pattern.

Another key feature of JPA is the query language, called the **Java Persistence Query Language** (**JPQL**), which gives you a way to specify the semantics of queries in a portable way, independent of the particular database you are using in an enterprise environment. JPA queries resemble SQL queries by syntax but operate against entity objects rather than directly with database tables.

Working with JPA

Inspired by ORM frameworks such as Hibernate, JPA uses annotations to map objects to a relational database. JPA entities are POJOs that do not extend any class nor implement any interface. You don't even need XML descriptors for your mapping. Actually, the JPA API is made up of annotations and only a few classes and interfaces. For example, we would mark the class `Company` as `@Entity` as follows:

```
@Entity
public class Company {
...
public Company () {   }

@Id
String companyName;
...

}
```

This little piece of code shows the minimal requirements for a class to be persistent. That is:

- It must be identified as an entity using the `@javax.persistence.Entity` annotation
- It must have an identifier attribute annotated with `@javax.persistence.Id`
- It must have a no-argument constructor

Since you will learn better with an example, we will show how to create and deploy a sample JPA application on JBoss AS 7 in the next section.

Adding persistence to our application

In order to persist data, JPA needs a relational database; we will use the MySQL database, which is pretty popular among developers and can be downloaded for free from `http://dev.mysql.com/downloads`. It is recommended to download the latest stable release of MySQL 5.x and install it using the simple installation wizard.

Setting up the database

We will create a database named `appstore`; we will then add a user named `jboss` and assign him all privileges on the schemas.

Open a shell under the `bin` folder of your MySQL installation and launch the executable `mysql`. Once logged in, execute the following commands:

```
CREATE DATABASE ticketsystem;
USE ticketsystem;
CREATE USER 'jboss'@'localhost' IDENTIFIED BY 'jboss';
GRANT ALL PRIVILEGES ON ticketsystem.* TO 'jboss'@'localhost' WITH
GRANT OPTION;
```

Our simple schema will be made up of two tables—the `SEAT` table, which contains the list of all available seats in the theatre and the `SEAT_TYPE` table, which is used to categorize the seat types. The two tables are in a *1-n* relationship and the `SEAT` table hosts a foreign key (`seat_id`) that relates to the ID of the `SEAT_TYPE` table:

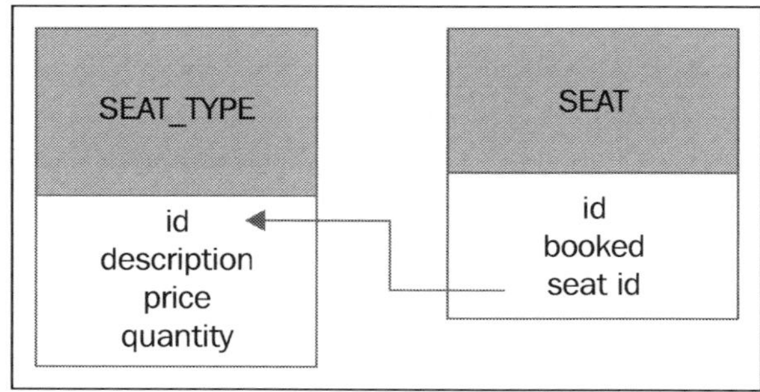

The schema is as follows:

```
CREATE TABLE seat_type (
id int(10) NOT NULL PRIMARY KEY auto_increment,
description varchar(50) NOT NULL,
price int(10) NOT NULL,
quantity int(10) NOT NULL
) ENGINE=InnoDB;

CREATE TABLE seat (
id int(10) NOT NULL PRIMARY KEY auto_increment,
booked Boolean,
seat_id int(10),
FOREIGN KEY (seat_id) REFERENCES seat_type (id) ON DELETE CASCADE)
ENGINE=InnoDB;
```

Installing the JDBC driver on JBoss AS 7

Database connectivity is carried out in Java using JDBC drivers, which are used either directly in your applications or behind the scenes in JPA or Hibernate. The MySQL JDBC driver can also be downloaded for free from `http://dev.mysql.com/downloads/connector/j/`.

Once download is complete, extract the file `mysql-connector-java-5.X.XX-bin.jar` and place it in a convenient location on your filesystem. We will show now how to install the JDBC driver on JBoss AS 7.

In JBoss AS 5 and 6, you used to install the JDBC driver into the `common/lib` folder of your server distribution. In the new modular server architecture, you have more than one option to install your JDBC driver. The recommended approach consists of installing the driver as a **module**.

The procedure for installing a new module requires creating a module path under `JBOSS_HOME/modules` and placing the `.jar` libraries and the `module.xml` file (that declares the module and its dependencies) there.

In our example, we will add the following units to our filesystem:

- `JBOSS_HOME/modules/com/mysql/main/mysql-connector-java-5.1.24-bin.jar`
- `JBOSS_HOME/modules/com/mysql/main/module.xml`

If you are using a Linux shell, enter the following commands:

```
cd $JBOSS_HOME
mkdir modules/com/mysql
mkdir modules/com/mysql/main
```

Now, in the `main` folder, add a file named `module.xml`. This file contains the actual module definition—the most interesting part of it is the module name (`com.mysql`), which corresponds to the module attribute defined in your data source.

Next, you need to state the path to the JDBC driver resource and finally the module dependencies.

```
<module xmlns="urn:jboss:module:1.0" name="com.mysql">
  <resources>
    <resource-root path="mysql-connector-java-5.1.24-bin.jar"/>
  </resources>
  <dependencies>
    <module name="javax.api"/>
    <module name="javax.transaction.api"/>
  </dependencies>
</module>
```

We are done with the module installation. Now we need to define a data source in our configuration that will use this module and hold a pool of connections to our MySQL database. In order to do this, you can edit `standalone.xml/domain.xml`, adding a driver element into the data source's subsystem.

```
<subsystem xmlns="urn:jboss:domain:datasources:1.0">
 <datasources>
  <datasource jta="false"
```

```
        jndi-name="java:jboss/datasources/jbossas7development"
        pool-name="jbossas7development" enabled="true">
            <connection-url>
             jdbc:mysql://localhost:3306/ticketsystem
            </connection-url>
            <driver-class>com.mysql.jdbc.Driver</driver-class>
            <driver>mysql</driver>
            <security>
                 <user-name>jboss</user-name>
                 <password>jboss</password>
            </security>
    </datasource>
    <drivers>
           <driver name="mysql" module="com.mysql"/>
    </drivers>
   </datasources>
  </subsystem>
```

As you can see, the new configuration file borrows the same XML schema definition from the earlier JBoss AS configurations, so it should not be difficult to migrate to the new schema. Basically, you would define the connection path to the database using the `connection-url` string and the JDBC driver class with the `driver` section.

Since JBoss AS 7.1.0, it's mandatory that the data source be bound to the `java:/` or `java:jboss/` JNDI namespace. This will standardize the resources definition among developers, avoiding bizarre JNDI bindings.

Using the command-line interface to create a new data source

The application server provides more than one option to add a data source to your configuration. We will just mention the command-line-interface approach, which can be quite useful, especially if you plan to modify your configuration using script files.

Launch the `jboss-cli.sh` script (or `jboss-cli.bat`) and connect to the application server.

```
[disconnected /] connect
[standalone@localhost:9999 /]
```

Now issue the following command, which actually creates a new data source, accomplishing the same goal we obtained by editing the configuration file:

```
/subsystem=datasources/data-source=jbossas7development:add(jndi-
name=java:jboss/datasources/jbossas7development, driver-name=mysql,
connection-url= jdbc:mysql://localhost:3306/as7development ,user-
name="jboss",password="jboss")
```

Creating the Maven project

We're now on the home stretch. The ultimate prize for us is to be able to create a Java EE 6 application using Maven and the Eclipse IDE.

In this example, we will again be using the `webapp-javaee6` archetype to keep a line of continuity with our earlier chapter; nevertheless, you are encouraged to explore some specific JBoss archetypes, such as `jboss-javaee6-webapp-archetype`, that will create a more articulate project structure including some sample classes, or the equivalent `jboss-javaee6-webapp-ear-archetype` archetype that packages your application in an enterprise archive.

For our purpose, let's start by creating a new Maven project based on the `webapp-javaee6` archetype, following the same steps exposed in *Chapter 4, Learning Context Dependency Injection*. The only difference is that we are now going to use the archetype configuration shown in the following screenshot:

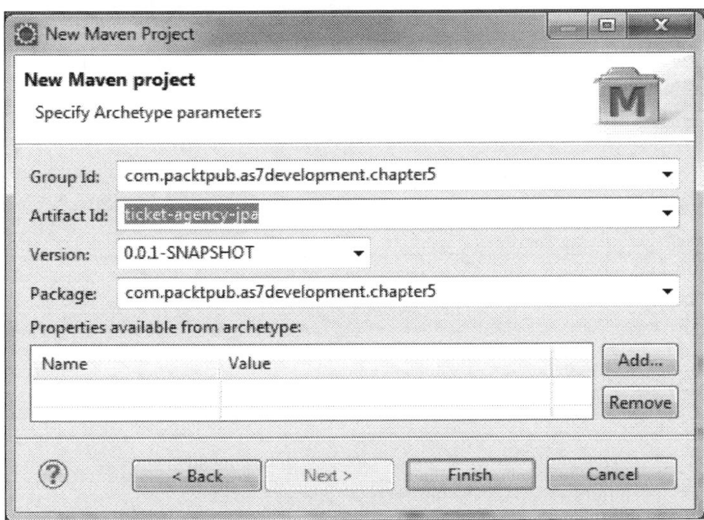

Complete the wizard by clicking on **Finish** and you will return to your Eclipse project view.

Adding Maven configuration

Now that your Maven skeleton is set up, we will include the required dependencies so that Eclipse will be able to compile your classes as you code them.

The first thing we will add is the Bill of Materials, which includes both the `jboss-javaee-6.0-with-tools` and `jboss-javaee-6.0-with-hibernate` artifacts so that Maven will be able to pick up the right enterprise stack:

```
<dependency>
   <groupId>org.jboss.bom</groupId>
   <artifactId>jboss-javaee-6.0-with-tools</artifactId>
   <version>${version.jboss.bom}</version>
   <type>pom</type>
   <scope>import</scope>
</dependency>
<dependency>
   <groupId>org.jboss.bom</groupId>
   <artifactId>jboss-javaee-6.0-with-hibernate</artifactId>
   <version>${version.jboss.bom}</version>
   <type>pom</type>
   <scope>import</scope>
</dependency>
```

Next, you will need the following dependencies to be added to your project, starting from the hibernates persistence API.

```
<dependency>
    <groupId>org.hibernate.javax.persistence</groupId>
    <artifactId>hibernate-jpa-2.0-api</artifactId>
    <scope>provided</scope>
</dependency>
```

Next, since we will be using **JSR-303 Bean Validation** in our example, we need to include the `hibernate-validator` artifact as well.

```
<dependency>
  <groupId>org.hibernate</groupId>
  <artifactId>hibernate-validator</artifactId>
  <scope>provided</scope>
  <exclusions>
    <exclusion>
      <groupId>org.slf4j</groupId>
      <artifactId>slf4j-api</artifactId>
    </exclusion>
  </exclusions>
</dependency>
```

When declaring the `hibernate-validator` dependency, we are using an **explicit exclusion** for the `slf4j` API, which will not be added to the project's classpath since we use the `java.util logging` API instead.

Finally, we will add one more hibernate dependency – the **annotation processor** that will check for compilation errors whenever constraint annotations are incorrectly used.

```
<dependency>
  <groupId>org.hibernate</groupId>
  <artifactId>hibernate-validator-annotation-processor</artifactId>
  <scope>provided</scope>
</dependency>
```

The remaining dependencies are borrowed from *Chapter 4, Learning Context Dependency Injection* (since the examples in this book grow incrementally in complexity, we would suggest referring to the latest chapter's `pom.xml` file and adding just the new dependencies).

```
<dependency>
  <groupId>javax.enterprise</groupId>
  <artifactId>cdi-api</artifactId>
  <scope>provided</scope>
</dependency>

<dependency>
  <groupId>org.jboss.spec.javax.annotation</groupId>
  <artifactId>jboss-annotations-api_1.1_spec</artifactId>
  <scope>provided</scope>
</dependency>

<dependency>
  <groupId>org.jboss.spec.javax.ejb</groupId>
  <artifactId>jboss-ejb-api_3.1_spec</artifactId>
  <scope>provided</scope>
</dependency>

<dependency>
  <groupId>org.jboss.spec.javax.faces</groupId>
  <artifactId>jboss-jsf-api_2.1_spec</artifactId>
  <scope>provided</scope>
</dependency>
```

Cooking entities

Now that we're done with the tedious configuration part, we will add our entities to the project. Some valuable options exist for auto-generating our entities, starting with the database schema. For example, Eclipse's **File** menu includes an option **JPA Entities from Table** that (once a connection has been set up to the database) allows reversing your DB schema (or part of it) into Java entities.

If you are willing to try this option, remember that you need to activate the Eclipse JPA facet in your project, from **Project Properties**, as shown in the following screenshot:

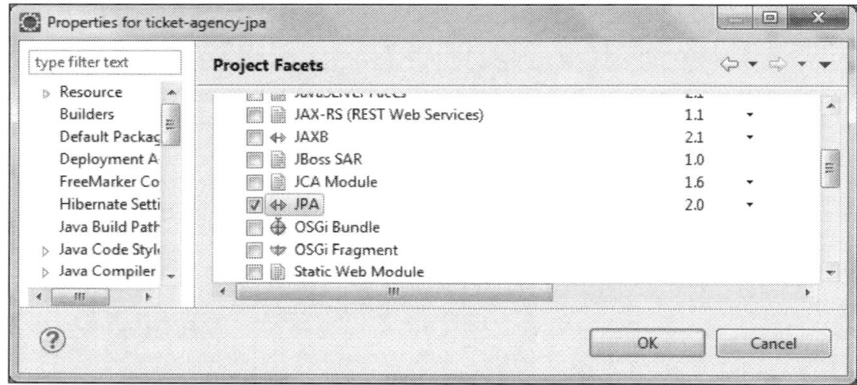

One more option is mentioned in the *Appendix, Rapid Development Using JBoss Forge*, which discusses **JBoss Forge**, a powerful, rapid application-development (aimed at Java EE 6) and project-comprehension tool.

Whatever your strategy, the expected outcome needs to conform to the following entities. Here is the first one, `SeatType`, which maps the table `SEAT_TYPE`:

```
@Entity [1]
@Table(name="seat_type) [2]
public class SeatType implements Serializable {

  @Id  [3]
  @GeneratedValue(strategy=GenerationType.IDENTITY)
  private Long id;

  private String description;

  private int price;

  private int quantity;
```

```
    //bi-directional many-to-one association to Seat
    @OneToMany(mappedBy="seatType", fetch=FetchType.EAGER) [4]
    private List<Seat> seats;
        // Getters and Setters omitted for brevity
}
```

The first meaningful annotation is `@Entity [1]`, which declares the class as `Entity`. The `@Table [2]` annotation is used to map the bean class with a database table.

The `@Id` annotation, `[3]`, is a mandatory one; it describes the primary key of the table. Along with `@Id`, there is the `@GeneratedValue` annotation. This is used to declare that the database is in charge of generating the value.

Moving along, the `@OneToMany` annotation `[4]` defines an association with one-to-many multiplicity. Actually, the `SeatType` class has many seats. The corresponding `Seat` reference is contained in a list collection.

Finally, note that we have not included here, for the sake of brevity, the field getters and setters that have been generated.

Let's have a look at the `Seat` entity.

```
@Entity
public class Seat implements Serializable {
  private static final long serialVersionUID = 1L;

  @Id
  @GeneratedValue(strategy=GenerationType.IDENTITY)
  private Long id;

  private boolean booked;

  //bi-directional many-to-one association to SeatType
  @ManyToOne [1]
  @JoinColumn(name="seat_id") [2]
  private SeatType seatType;

        // Getters and Setters omitted for brevity

}
```

As you can see, the `Seat` entity has the corresponding `@ManyToOne [1]` annotation, which naturally complements the `@OneToMany` relationship. The `@JoinColumn [2]` notifies the JPA engine that the `seatType` field is mapped through the foreign key of the database's seat ID.

Adding JavaBeans Validation

JavaBeans Validation (JSR-303 Bean Validation) is a new validation model available as part of the Java EE 6 platform. The Bean Validation model is supported by constraints in the form of annotations placed on a field, method, or class of a JavaBeans component, such as a managed bean.

In our example, the `SeatType` entity will be created using an input form; therefore, we will need to validate the data that has been entered by the user.

In our example, we will place a `@javax.validation.constraints.NotNull` constraint on every field that is part of the `SeatType` entering form, and a more complex constraint on the `description` field, which will set the maximum size for the seat description to 25 (`@javax.validation.constraints.Size` constraint) and allow just letters and spaces in it (`@javax.validation.constraints.Pattern` constraint).

```
@Entity
@Table(name="seat_type)

public class SeatType implements Serializable {
  private static final long serialVersionUID = 1L;

  @Id
  @GeneratedValue(strategy=GenerationType.IDENTITY)
  private int id;

  @NotNull
  @Size(min = 1, max = 25, message = "You need to enter a Seat
Description (max 25 char)")
  @Pattern(regexp = "[A-Za-z ]*", message = "Description must contain
only letters and spaces")
  private String description;

  @NotNull
  private int price;

  @NotNull
  private int quantity;

// Getters/Setters here
}
```

As you can see, we can also place a description on a constraint, which can be used to provide a customized error message to the JSF layer should the data fail to pass the constraint. You can check the Oracle documentation for a full list of constraints available at `http://docs.oracle.com/javaee/6/tutorial/doc/gircz.html`.

Configuring persistence

The Entity API looks great and very intuitive, but how does the server know which database is supposed to store/query the entity objects? The persistence.xml file, which will be placed under src/main/resources/META-INF of your project, is the standard JPA configuration file. By configuring this file, you can easily switch from one persistence provider to another and thus also from one application server to another (believe it, this is a huge leap towards application server compatibility).

In the persistence.xml file we will basically need to specify the persistence provider and the underlying data source used.

```
<persistence version="2.0"
  xmlns="http://java.sun.com/xml/ns/persistence" xmlns:xsi="http://
www.w3.org/2001/XMLSchema-instance"
  xsi:schemaLocation="
        http://java.sun.com/xml/ns/persistence
        http://java.sun.com/xml/ns/persistence/persistence_2_0.xsd">
  <persistence-unit name="primary">
    <jta-data-source> java:jboss/datasources/jbossas7development</jta-
data-source>
    <class>com.packtpub.as7development.chapter5.model.Seat</class>
<class>com.packtpub.as7development.chapter5.model.SeatType</class>
    <properties>
      <!-- Properties for Hibernate -->
      <property name="hibernate.hbm2ddl.auto" value="create-drop" />
      <property name="hibernate.show_sql" value="false" />
    </properties>
  </persistence-unit>
</persistence>
```

We have highlighted the attributes you need to add to persistence.xml. The attribute name is a mandatory element that will be used to reference the persistence unit from our Enterprise JavaBeans.

Then, we have specified some provider-specific properties, such as hibernate.hbm2ddl.auto, that can be used to create and drop your database tables each time you deploy your application. That can be an advantage if you want to start with a clean storage each time you deploy the application. Additionally, we have included another attribute, such as hibernate.show_sql, that (if turned on) can be useful for debugging your Hibernate queries.

Adding producer classes

Producer classes have been introduced in the earlier chapter as a means of providing some object resources to our application. In this example, we will use it to produce lots of resources, such as the **JPA Entity Manager** and the list of objects that are transferred to the JSF views. For this reason, we have provided a `Resources` class that contains some general-purpose resources and single instances of the `SeatProducer` and `SeatTypeProducer` classes, which will be used to produce collections of entities.

Here's the first `com.packtpub.as7development.chapter5.producer.Resources` class:

```
public class Resources {

    @Produces
    @PersistenceContext
    private EntityManager em;

    @Produces
    public Logger produceLog(InjectionPoint injectionPoint) {
        return Logger.getLogger(injectionPoint.getMember().
getDeclaringClass().getName());
    }

    @Produces
    @javax.enterprise.context.RequestScoped
    public FacesContext produceFacesContext() {
        return FacesContext.getCurrentInstance();
    }

}
```

As you can see, this class will be the factory for three kinds of resources:

- `EntityManager`, which will resolve to the "primary" persistence unit since there is just one persistence unit defined
- `java.util.Logger`, which will trace some information on the server console
- `FacesContext`, which will be used to output some JSF messages on the screen

Producers versus the Java EE 5 @Resource injection

If you have never used the dependency injections framework before, you might wonder what the benefit is of adding an extra layer to produce some container resources. The reason becomes evident once you need to change some configuration elements, such as the persistence unit. With the older Java EE 5 approach, you will be forced to change the `@Resource` injection's details wherever they are used; however, using a producer method for it will centralize resource creation, making changes trivial.

Next we will add some entity producers; let's add the `SeatTypeProducer` and `SeatProducer` classes:

```
@javax.enterprise.context.RequestScoped

public class SeatTypeProducer implements Serializable {

    @Inject
    private DataManager seatRepository;

    private List<SeatType> seatTypes;

    @Produces
    @Named
    public List<SeatType> getSeatTypes() {
        return seatTypes;
    }

    public void onListChanged(@Observes(notifyObserver = Reception.
IF_EXISTS) final SeatType member) {
        retrieveData();
    }

    @PostConstruct
    public void retrieveData() {
      seatTypes = seatRepository.findAllSeatTypes();
    }
}
```

If you have gone through our example in *Chapter 4, Learning Context Dependency Injection*, you will find nothing new here; as you can see, this class will merely produce a collection of `seatTypes` that are tagged as `@Named` so that they can be accessed from **JSF EL** as well. Additionally, this class contains an **Observer** handler method (`onListChanged`), which will be fired when data in the collection is changed.

The collection data is filled up using the `retrieveData` method (loaded the first and only time when the class is constructed) of the `DataManager` CDI Bean. We will define this bean in a moment; right now, we will add the last producer class used in this example, the `SeatProducer` bean:

```
@javax.enterprise.context.RequestScoped
public class SeatProducer implements Serializable {

  @Inject
  private DataManager seatRepository;
  private List<Seat> seats;

  @Produces
  @Named
  public List<Seat> getSeats() {
    System.out.println("Seattypes "+seats);
    return seats;
  }

  public void onMemberListChanged(@Observes(notifyObserver =
Reception.IF_EXISTS) final Seat member) {
    retrieveAllSeats();
  }

  @PostConstruct
  public void retrieveAllSeats() {
    seats = seatRepository.findAllSeats();
  }
}
```

This bean will be used to produce the list of `Seat` objects that will actually be available for booking.

Coding queries for your application

As you can see from the earlier code, the producer classes make use of a bean named `DataManager` to fill up their collection of data. This bean performs some simple finds on the `Seat` and `SeatType` objects, as shown by the following code:

```
@javax.enterprise.context.ApplicationScoped
public class DataManager {

  @Inject
  private EntityManager em;
```

```
    public Seat findSeatById(Long id) {
      return em.find(Seat.class, id);
    }

    public List<SeatType> findAllSeatTypes() {

      return em.createQuery("from SeatType seat").getResultList();
    }
    public List<Seat> findAllSeats() {

      return em.createQuery("from Seat seat").getResultList();
    }
    public void deleteAllData() {
      em.createQuery("delete from Seat").executeUpdate();
      em.createQuery("delete from SeatType").executeUpdate();

    }
  }
```

Besides running queries, this class will execute some other methods that are not bound to the user session, such as the `deleteAllData` method that is to be used to clean the DB data and restart the application.

Adding services to your application

Until now we have coded all the information that will be visible to the user through the application screen. What is obviously missing here is all the business logic that translates ultimately into inserting data or updating the existing data. For this reason, we will now add two classes under `com.packtpub.as7development.chapter5.service` package. The first one is `TicketService`, which is a stateless EJB that will be used to perform the core business logic of this application, and the second one is our stateful EJB's counterpart, `BookerService`. Let's start with the stateless EJB.

```
@Stateless
public class TicketService {

  @Inject
  private Logger log;

  @Inject
  private EntityManager em;

  @Inject
  private Event<SeatType> seatTypeEventSrc;
```

```
    @Inject
    private Event<Seat> seatEventSrc;

    @Inject
    private DataManager repository;

    @Inject
    private List <SeatType> seatTypes;

    public void createSeatType(SeatType seat) throws Exception {
      log.info("Registering " + seat.getDescription());
      em.persist(seat);
      seatTypeEventSrc.fire(seat);
    }

    public void createTheatre(List<SeatType> seatTypes) {

      for (SeatType type: seatTypes) {
        for (int ii=0;ii<type.getQuantity();ii++) {
          Seat seat = new Seat();
          seat.setBooked(false);
          seat.setSeatType(type);
          em.persist(seat);
        }
      }
    }

    public void bookSeat(Long seatId) {
      Seat seat = repository.findSeatById(seatId);
      seat.setBooked(true);
      em.persist(seat);
      seatEventSrc.fire(seat);
    }

    public void doCleanUp() {
      repository.deleteAllData();
    }

}
```

Why has this component been coded as an EJB instead of a CDI Bean?

One of the main advantages of using EJBs is that they are inherently **transactional components**. If we were to use CDI Beans, we would have to manually demarcate the transaction `begin()` and `commit()` (or `rollback()`) in every single method.

This service is made up of four methods. The first is the `createSeatType` method, which will be used in the first application screen to add a new `SeatType` object to our theatre. The next method, `createTheatre`, will be invoked once we are done with setting up our theatre; so we create the list of seats that will be available for booking in the next screen.

Next in the list is the `bookSeat` method that, as you might have guessed, will be used to book a seat. Finally, the `doCleanUp` is actually used to perform some clean up if you want to restart the application.

The last piece of our puzzle is the `BookerService` class, which adds a tiny session layer to your application.

```
@Named
@ConversationScoped

public class BookerService implements Serializable {

  @Inject
  private Logger logger;

  @Inject TicketService ticketService;

  int money;

  @PostConstruct
  public void createCustomer() {
    this.money=100;

  }

  public void bookSeat(Long seatId, int price)    {
    FacesContext fc = FacesContext.getCurrentInstance();

    if (price  > money) {
```

```
        FacesMessage m = new FacesMessage(FacesMessage.SEVERITY_ERROR,
"Not enough Money!", "Registration successful");
        fc.addMessage(null, m);
        return;
      }
      logger.info("Booking seat "+seatId);
      ticketService.bookSeat(seatId);
      money = money - price;

      FacesMessage m = new FacesMessage(FacesMessage.SEVERITY_INFO,
"Registered!", "Registration successful");
      fc.addMessage(null, m);
      logger.info("Seat booked.");

    }

    public int getMoney() {
      return money;
    }


}
```

As you might remember from the earlier chapter, the conversation scope is a bit like the traditional session scope, in that it holds the state associated with a user of the system and spans multiple requests to the server. However, unlike the session scope, the conversation scope is demarcated explicitly by the application. Therefore, you can set the boundaries of your conversation and unload objects from memory once your conversation has ended.

Adding a controller to drive user requests

The link between the Persistence layer and the user's view falls to the `TicketController` bean, which will drive requests to the actual services exposed by our application. Since this bean will be bound to `RequestScope` and we need to expose it to our views as well (using `@Named`), we can use the convenient `@Model` annotation for it, which is a sum of these two attributes.

```
@Model
public class TicketController {

  @Inject
  private FacesContext facesContext;
```

```
  @Inject
  private TicketService ticketService;

  @Inject
  private List <SeatType> seatTypes;

  @Inject
  private Conversation conversation;

  @Produces [1]
  @Named
  private SeatType newSeatType;

  @PostConstruct
  public void initNewSeatType() {
    newSeatType = new SeatType();
  }
  public String createTheatre() {

    ticketService.createTheatre(seatTypes);
    conversation.begin();  [2]
    return "book";
  }

  public String restart() {
    ticketService.doCleanUp();
    conversation.end(); [3]
    return "/index";    [4]
  }

  public void create() throws Exception {
    try {
      ticketService.createSeatType(newSeatType);
      FacesMessage m = new FacesMessage(FacesMessage.SEVERITY_INFO,
"Done!", "Seats Added");
      facesContext.addMessage(null, m);
      initNewSeatType();

    } catch (Exception e) {
      String errorMessage = getRootErrorMessage(e);
      FacesMessage m = new FacesMessage(FacesMessage.SEVERITY_ERROR,
errorMessage, "Error while saving data");
      facesContext.addMessage(null, m);
```

```
        }
    }

    private String getRootErrorMessage(Throwable e) {
      String errorMessage = "Registration failed. See server log for
more information";
      while (e != null) {
        errorMessage = e.getLocalizedMessage();
        e = e.getCause();
      }
      return errorMessage;
    }
}
```

The `TicketController` class is due to complete the following tasks:

1. At first it produces a `SeatType` object `[1]` and exposes it to the JSF View layer using the `@Named` annotation.

This technique is a great addition provided by CDI since it removes the need to create a boilerplate object, `SeatType`, to transport the information from the view to the services. The `SeatType` object is produced by the controller and will be populated by the JSF view and persisted by the `TicketService`.

2. Next, it is used to demarcate the user's conversation `[2]` by starting it once you've done with your theatre setup and you have chosen to restart the application `[3]`.
3. It then drives user navigation between the application screens by returning to the home page `[4]`.

As you can see from the `restart` method, JSF 2 supports **implicit navigation**, which means that you don't need to define navigation rules inside the JSF configuration file. You can simply return the page name (for example, `book`) from your methods (or set it in your form actions) and the JSF engine will look for a page named `book.xhtml` in the current directory.

We are done with the Java classes. You should now check your project structure matches the following screenshot:

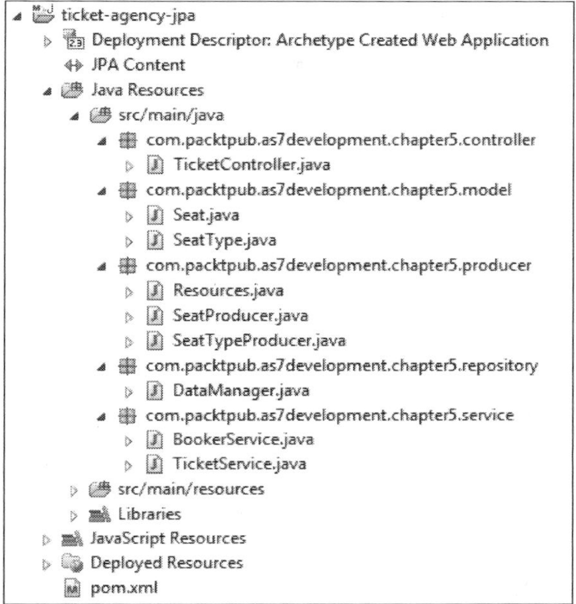

Coding the JSF view

Now that our middle tier is completed, we just need to add a couple of JSF views to our application into the `views` folder of our webapp. The first view, named `setup.xhtml`, will set up our theatre and the second one, named `book.xhtml`, will be used to book tickets, borrowing much of its code from the earlier chapter. So here's the content from `setup.xhtml`:

```
<ui:define name="content">
  <h1>Step #1: Theatre Setup</h1>

  <div>
    <p>Enter the information about Seats.</p>
    <img src="resources/gfx/seat_chart.gif" />
  </div>
```

```
    <h:form id="reg">
      <p>Add Seats.</p>
      <h:panelGrid columns="3" columnClasses="titleCell">
        <h:outputLabel for="desc" value="Description" />
        <h:inputText id="desc" value="#{newSeatType.description}" />
        <h:message for="desc" errorClass="invalid" />

        <h:outputLabel for="price" value="Price:" />
        <h:inputText id="price" value="#{newSeatType.price}" />
        <h:message for="price" errorClass="invalid" />

        <h:outputLabel for="quantity" value="Number of Seats:" />
        <h:inputText id="quantity" value="#{newSeatType.quantity}" />
        <h:message for="quantity" errorClass="invalid" />
      </h:panelGrid>
      <p>
        <h:panelGrid columns="2">
          <h:commandButton id="Add" action="#{ticketController.create}"
value="Add" />

          <h:messages styleClass="messages" errorClass="invalid"
            infoClass="valid" warnClass="warning" globalOnly="true" />
        </h:panelGrid>
      </p>
    </h:form>
    <h:form id="reg2">
      <h:panelGrid columns="1">

        <h:commandButton id="Finish"    action="#{ticketController.
createTheatre}"
          value="Finish" styleClass="register" />

      </h:panelGrid>

      <h2>Seats List</h2>
      <h:panelGroup rendered="#{empty seatTypes}">
        <em>No Seats Added.</em>
      </h:panelGroup>
      <h:dataTable var="_seatType" value="#{seatTypes}"
        rendered="#{not empty seatTypes}" styleClass="simpletablestyle">
        <h:column>
          <f:facet name="header">Id</f:facet>
          #{_seatType.id}
        </h:column>
```

```
        <h:column>
          <f:facet name="header">Name</f:facet>
          #{_seatType.description}
        </h:column>
        <h:column>
          <f:facet name="header">Price</f:facet>
          $ #{_seatType.price}
        </h:column>
        <h:column>
          <f:facet name="header">Quantity</f:facet>
          #{_seatType.quantity}
        </h:column>
      </h:dataTable>
    </h:form>
  </ui:define>
```

As you can see, this view contains in the topmost section a form for entering a new seat type. The highlighted input texts will actually pass data to the `SeatType` object, which will be transferred to the `TicketController` CDI Bean and ultimately persisted when the user clicks on the **Add** button.

Each time you add a new block of seats to your theatre, the `dataTable` contained in the lower part of the screen will be updated. When you are done with your setup, click on the **Finish** button, which will recall the `finish` method of the `TicketController` CDI Bean, creating the list of seats.

This action will also redirect you to the next view, named `book.xhtml`, which is used to book seats.

```
<ui:define name="content">
  <h1>TicketBooker Machine</h1>
  <h:form id="book">

    <h3>Money: $ #{bookerService.money}</h3>
    <h:messages errorClass="error" infoClass="info" globalOnly="true"
/>
    <h:panelGrid columns="1" border="1" styleClass="smoke">
      <h:dataTable var="_seat" value="#{seats}" rendered="#{not empty
seats}"
        styleClass="simpletablestyle">

        <h:column>
          <f:facet name="header">Id</f:facet>
          #{_seat.id}
        </h:column>
```

```
          <h:column>
            <f:facet name="header">Description</f:facet>
            #{_seat.seatType.description}
          </h:column>
          <h:column>
            <f:facet name="header">Price</f:facet>
            #{_seat.seatType.price}$
          </h:column>
          <h:column>
            <f:facet name="header">Booked</f:facet>
            #{_seat.booked}
          </h:column>
          <h:column>
            <f:facet name="header">Action</f:facet>
            <h:commandButton id="book"
              action="#{bookerService.bookSeat(_seat.id, _seat.seatType.
price)}"
              disabled="#{_seat.booked}" value="#{_seat.booked ?
'Reserved' : 'Book'}" />

          </h:column>
        </h:dataTable>

        <h:commandButton id="restart" action="#{ticketController.
restart}"
          value="Restart Application" />
      </h:panelGrid>
    </h:form>
</ui:define>
```

Finally, we will add a template page named `default.xhtml`, which acts as a container for our resources.

```
<!DOCTYPE html PUBLIC "-//W3C//DTD XHTML 1.0 Strict//EN"
    "http://www.w3.org/TR/xhtml1/DTD/xhtml1-strict.dtd">
<html xmlns="http://www.w3.org/1999/xhtml"
    xmlns:h="http://java.sun.com/jsf/html"
    xmlns:ui="http://java.sun.com/jsf/facelets">
<h:head>
    <title>Ticket Booking</title>
    <meta http-equiv="Content-Type" content="text/html; charset=utf-8"
/>
    <h:outputStylesheet name="css/screen.css" />
</h:head>
```

```
<h:body>
    <div id="container">
        <div class="dualbrand">
            <img src="resources/gfx/masks.jpg" />
        </div>
        <div id="content">
            <ui:insert name="content">
                    [Template content will be inserted here]
         </ui:insert>
        </div>

        <div id="footer">
            <p>
                A Java EE 6 application featuring CDI JPA 2.0 JSF
2.1.<br />
            </p>
        </div>
    </div>
</h:body>
</html>
```

Here's a snapshot of the project, expanded at the webapp level (as you can see, we have also included a basic `index.html` screen and an `index.xhtml` screen to redirect the user to the initial screen, `setup.xhtml`):

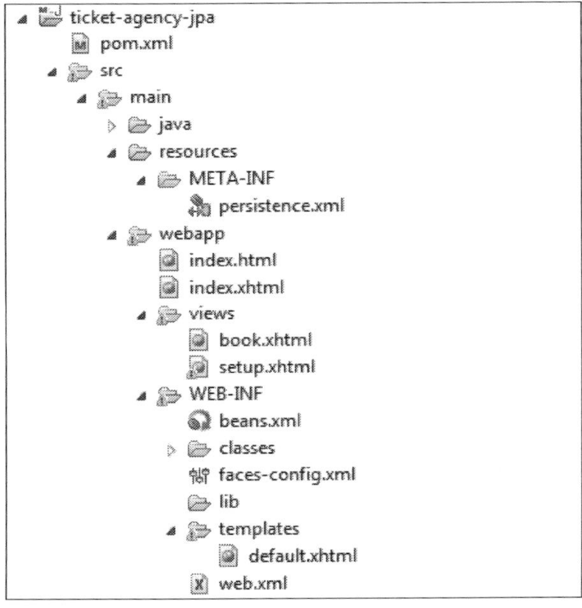

Running the example

Deploying the application requires, as usual, packaging it using the following Maven goal:

```
mvn install

[INFO] Scanning for projects...

[INFO]

[INFO] ------------------------------------------------------------------

[INFO] Building ticket-agency-jpa

[INFO] ------------------------------------------------------------------

[INFO] Building jar: C:\chapter5\ticket-agency-ejb\target\ticket-agency-jpa.jar

. . . .

[INFO] ------------------------------------------------------------------------

[INFO] BUILD SUCCESS

[INFO] ------------------------------------------------------------------------

[INFO] Total time: 5.308s
```

Finally, provided that you have installed the JBoss Maven plugin, you can deploy your application using the following command:

```
mvn jboss-as:deploy
```

Once the deployment has successfully completed, browse over to `http://localhost:8080/ticket-agency-jpa/` to view the application's welcome page.

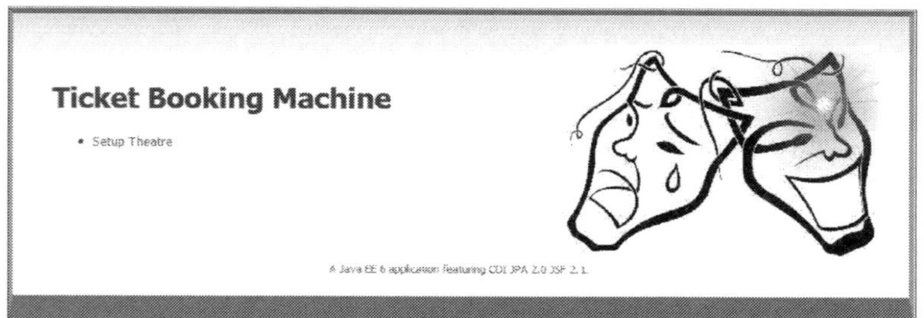

Congratulations! You're done. By clicking on the **Setup Theatre** link, you can start creating places in the `setup.xhtml` page.

Once you click on the **Finish** button, you will be redirected to the last screen, which performs the seat booking in `book.xhtml`:

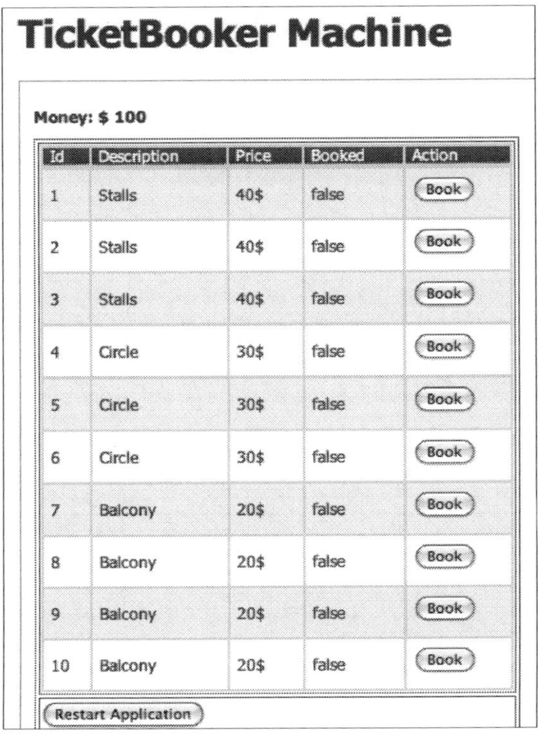

Summary

The aim of the new Java Persistence API is to simplify the development of persistent entities. It meets this objective through a simple POJO-based persistence model, which reduces the number of required classes and interfaces.

In this chapter we covered a lot of ground, starting with the database schema that we reverse engineered using the JBoss tools plugins for Eclipse. Next we coded the set of layers (producers, services, controller) that are part of the application, along with the JSF Facelets.

In the next chapter, we will further enhance our example application by introducing the Arquillian framework, which provides a simple test harness that developers can use to produce a broad range of integration tests for their Java applications.

6
Testing Your Applications

We have now reached a good mix of technologies in our example project; this includes some of the key building blocks of Java EE (except for Java Messaging, which will be discussed in the next chapter). Besides developing applications, one of the most common requests among developers is the ability to execute test cases against applications deployed on a managed (or remote) application server. In this chapter, we will describe the JBoss AS framework named **Arquillian** that promises to be the standard integration testing framework of enterprise applications.

In this chapter, we will more specifically look at:

- An introduction to enterprise testing: from mock objects to the Arquillian framework
- How to integrate an Arquillian test case for your Ticket Machine application
- How to use the Eclipse IDE and the Maven shell to run Arquillian unit testing

Unit testing and integration testing

The word "testing" offers room for several interpretations; basically, testing requires verifying the application's basic functionalities. However, there can be different types of tests depending on what you are testing and what environment you are using for testing.

The most common type of test is called a **unit test** and can be defined as a test written by the programmer to verify that a relatively small piece of code is doing what it is intended to do. Unit tests are narrow in scope; they should be easy to write and execute, and their effectiveness depends on what the programmer considers to be useful. These tests are intended for the use of the programmer; they are not directly useful to anybody else, though, if they do their job, testers and users downstream should benefit by seeing fewer bugs.

A more advanced type of test is called the **integration test**. Integration tests are done to demonstrate that different pieces of the system work together; since they cover whole applications, they require much more effort to put together. For example, they usually require resources such as database instances and hardware to be allocated for them. Integration tests do a more convincing job of demonstrating how the system works (especially to nonprogrammers), at least to the extent that the integration test environment resembles the production environment.

Instruments for testing

As you can imagine, each kind of testing uses a different approach; for example, as far as unit testing is concerned, the most common way to test is by means of **mock objects**. If you have an object whose methods you want to test, and if these methods depend on some other object, you can create a mock of the dependency rather than an actual instance of that dependency. This allows you to test your object in isolation.

As an example, one common use case might be in an MVC application, where you have a **DAO** (**data access objects**) layer and a controller that performs business logic. If you'd like to unit test the controller, and the controller has a dependency on a DAO layer, you can make a mock of the DAO that will return dummy objects to your controller.

This kind of approach, although very immediate to understand and put in to practice, has several limitations. Firstly, it relegates you into an artificial environment where you will often make invalid assumptions about the behavior and stability of that environment.

Secondly, you will end up with a hard-to-maintain mock library that will allow your tests to pass and give you the warm feeling of having done a great job.

So, even if mock objects may still provide some benefits for starting up systems, where you don't have full implementations of a particular subsystem, you should stick, as close as possible, to the target environment that the code is supposed to run in.

Arquillian is a platform that simplifies integration testing for Java middleware. It deals with all the plumbing of container management, deployment, and framework initialization so you can focus on the task of writing your tests—real tests. Arquillian minimizes the burden on you—the developer—by covering aspects surrounding test execution; some of these aspects are as follows:

- Managing the life cycle of the container (start/stop)
- Bundling the test class with the dependent classes and resources into a deployable archive

- Enhancing the test class (for example, resolving `@Inject`, `@EJB`, and `@Resource` injections)
- Deploying the archive to test applications (deploy/undeploy), and capturing results and failures

In the next section, we will show which instruments are required to run your integration tests using Arquillian.

Getting started with Arquillian

Although Arquillian does not depend on a specific build tool, it is commonly used with Maven; it offers dependency management and thus simplifies the task of including the Arquillian libraries in the application since they are distributed in the Central Maven repository.

Depending on the type of archetype you have used for generation, you might have a different folder structure in your project; that is not an issue. What is really important is that you provide the following structure under your `src` folder:

- `main/`
    - `java/`: Place all application Java source files here (under the Java package)
    - `resources/`: Place all application configuration files here
- `test/`
    - `java/`: Place all test Java source files here (under the Java package)
    - `resources/`: Place all test configuration files here (for example, `persistence.xml`)

So by now, we will be working under `test/java`, which is where we will place our first Arquillian test class.

Writing an Arquillian test

If you have been working with JUnit (`http://www.junit.org`), you will find an Arquillian test very similar, just with some extra spice in it.

In order to do that, we will use Eclipse and Maven, just as we have done so far. If you are about to add test classes to your project, there is obviously no need to create a new project for this purpose. However, for learning purposes, we have delivered this example in a separate project so that you can see exactly what to add in order to run Arquillian tests.

In order to avoid recreating the whole project from scratch, you could simply clone the `ticket-agency-jpa` project and name it `ticket-agency-test`, moving the root package from `com.packtpub.as7development.chapter5` to `com.packtpub.as7development.chapter6`. If that still seems like too much work, you could simply import the `chapter6` project from the book samples as we are going to show in a minute. From the **File** menu, navigate to **Import** | **Existing Maven Projects** from the given options.

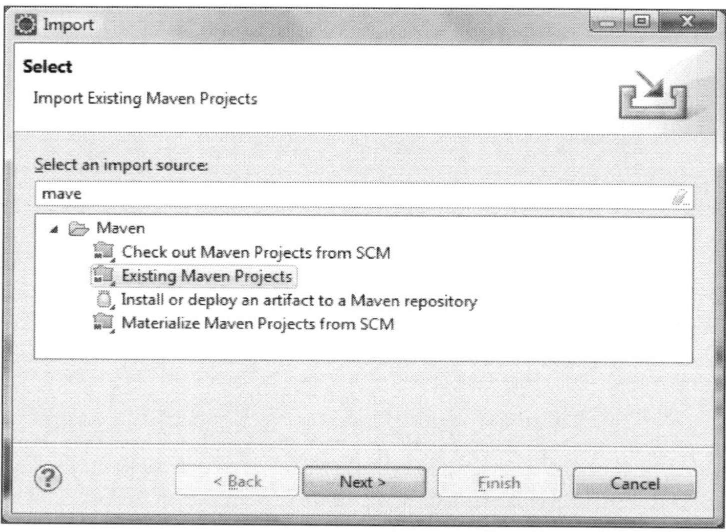

Now point to the folder where you have your Maven project for Chapter 6, and select the root folder that contains the `pom.xml` folder:

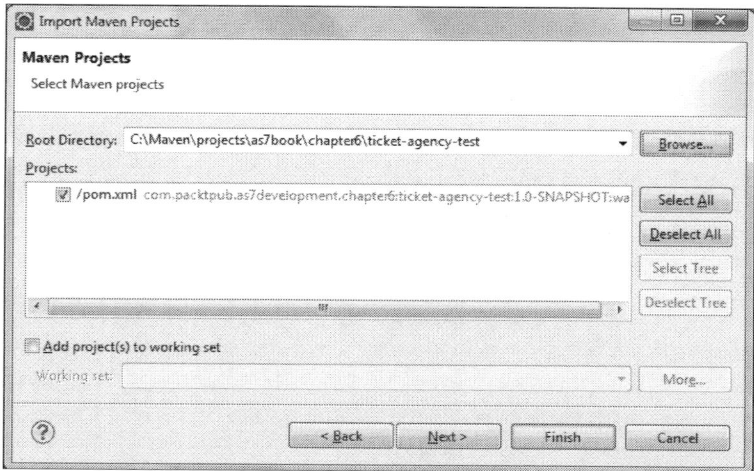

Now you can click on **Finish** and check if you have the following structure in the **Project Explorer** view:

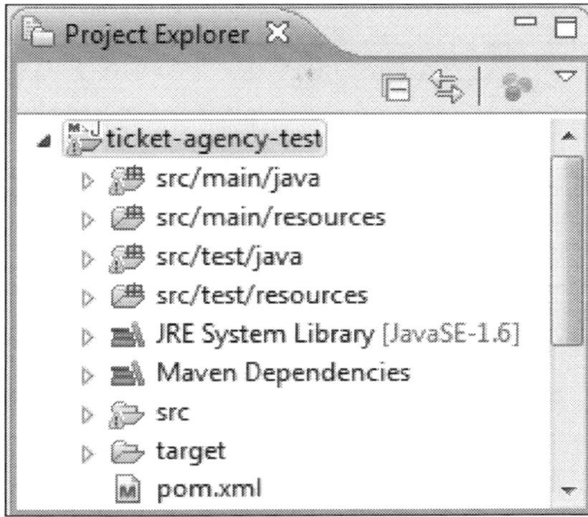

Okay, now let's see what core dependencies are needed to run the Arquillian test case.

Configuring the pom.xml file

The first thing that is necessary to include in order to run an Arquillian test is the `junit` dependency that is required to run our unit tests:

```
<dependency>
  <groupId>junit</groupId>
  <artifactId>junit</artifactId>
  <scope>test</scope>
</dependency>
```

As you can see, this dependency (just like the following ones) bears the `test` scope; this means that it will be used by Maven when running tests, so it will not add this library to the final artifact.

This dependency as part of the JBoss **Bill of Materials** (**BOM**) does not need to state the dependency version. The same applies for Arquillian-specific dependencies.

Next, if you want to test enterprise features such as EJB and the **Java Transaction API (JTA)**, you need to include the `org.jboss.arquillian.junit` dependency as well:

```
<dependency>
  <groupId>org.jboss.arquillian.junit</groupId>
  <artifactId>arquillian-junit-container</artifactId>
  <scope>test</scope>
</dependency>
```

After that, since our Arquillian test uses a protocol to communicate with the server application, we will need to add the `org.jboss.arquillian.protocol` dependency (named so as it's compatible with Servlet 2.5/3.0 specifications):

```
<dependency>
  <groupId>org.jboss.arquillian.protocol</groupId>
  <artifactId>arquillian-protocol-servlet</artifactId>
  <scope>test</scope>
</dependency>
```

The last dependency that we will add is the `weld` container dependency; this will be needed as we will test some advanced CDI techniques such as ConversationScoped communication:

```
<dependency>
  <groupId>org.jboss.weld</groupId>
  <artifactId>weld-core-test-arquillian</artifactId>
  <version>1.1.9.Final</version>
</dependency>
```

After getting done with the dependencies, we will now include two profiles into our configuration. A profile can basically be used to create different target environments for our goals; in our case, we will create two profiles:

- The first profile is named `arq-jbossas-managed`; it will start a new JBoss AS instance and execute the test, shutting it down when done:

```
<profile>
  <id>arq-jbossas-managed</id>
  <dependencies>
    <dependency>
      <groupId>org.jboss.as</groupId>
      <artifactId>jboss-as-arquillian-container-
       managed</artifactId>
      <scope>test</scope>
    </dependency>
  </dependencies>
</profile>
```

- The second profile is named `arq-jbossas-remote`; it will perform testing against a remote JBoss AS instance:

```
<profile>
  <id>arq-jbossas-remote</id>
  <dependencies>
    <dependency>
      <groupId>org.jboss.as</groupId>
      <artifactId>jboss-as-arquillian-container-
       remote</artifactId>
      <scope>test</scope>
    </dependency>
  </dependencies>
</profile>
```

Writing your first Arquillian test

Once the configuration is complete, we will finally code our test. So, create a Java class named `TicketTest` under the package `com.packtpub.as7development.chapter6.test`. The first thing that you will add to our class is the following annotation that tells JUnit to use Arquillian as the test controller:

```
@RunWith(Arquillian.class)
public class TicketTest {
}
```

Arquillian then looks for a static method with the `@Deployment` annotation; it creates a micro deployment, including all the resources, just as you would when packaging your applications with your favorite tool:

```
@Deployment
public static Archive<?> createTestArchive() {


    return ShrinkWrap.create(WebArchive.class, "ticket-agency-test.
war")
        .addPackage(SeatProducer.class.getPackage())
        .addPackage(Seat.class.getPackage())
        .addPackage(TicketService.class.getPackage())
        .addPackage(DataManager.class.getPackage())
        .addAsResource("META-INF/persistence.xml")
        .addAsWebInfResource(EmptyAsset.INSTANCE, "beans.xml");

  }
```

The fluent API provided by the **ShrinkWrap** project (`http://www.jboss.org/shrinkwrap`) makes this technique possible using the `create` method, which accepts the type of deployment unit (`WebArchive`) as the argument the deployment name (in our case, we will name it `ticket-agency-test.war`) and all the resources are included in this archive. In our case, instead of including all the single classes, we are using the `addPackage` utility method that adds all the classes that are contained in a class package (for example, by adding the `Seat.class.getPackage()` method, we will include all the classes that are in the same package as the `Seat` class):

Finally, we add one test method to it:

```
@javax.inject.Inject
TicketService ticketService;


@Inject
Logger log;

@Test
public void testTicketAgency () throws Exception {

  SeatType seatType = new SeatType();
  seatType.setDescription("description");
  seatType.setPrice(30);
  seatType.setQuantity(5);

  ticketService.createSeatType(seatType);
   log.info("Seat type created "+seatType.getDescription());
  assertNotNull(seatType.getId());
}
```

Here, the `testTicketAgency` method will create a new `SeatType` attribute using the `createSeatType` method from the `TicketService` class. Note how we inject `TicketService` just as we would if we were running this code on the server side.

Our first test case is now ready. We will just need to add an Arquillian configuration file named `arquillian.xml` into our project, under `src/test/resources`:

```
<?xml version="1.0" encoding="UTF-8"?>

<arquillian xmlns="http://jboss.org/schema/arquillian"
  xmlns:xsi="http://www.w3.org/2001/XMLSchema-instance"
  xsi:schemaLocation="http://jboss.org/schema/arquillian
        http://jboss.org/schema/arquillian/arquillian_1_0.xsd">


  <defaultProtocol type="Servlet 3.0" />

  <container qualifier="jboss" default="true">
```

```
        <configuration>
            <property name="managementAddress">localhost</property>
            <property name="managementPort">9999</property>
        </configuration>
    </container>

</arquillian>
```

The `defaultProtocol` element forces Arquillian to use the Servlet 3.0 protocol with all containers as it is the most mature option.

Besides this, you have to set the remote management address and the management port in case the container configuration differs from the default values (in our example, we have included the default values, which are `localhost` and `9999`, just to show their correct location in the configuration file).

Now before running the test, let's have a look at your project with all elements in the right place:

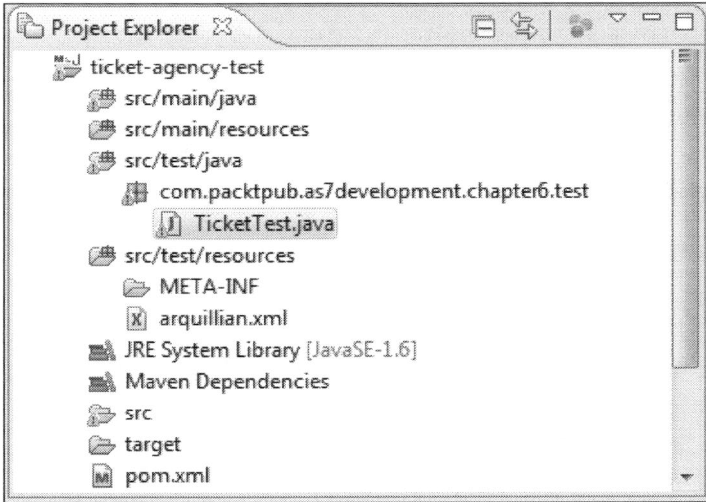

Running Arquillian TicketTest

In order to score our first goal, it's highly recommended that we perform a project clean/recompilation in order to remove all the artifacts that were part of the earlier `ticket-agency-jpa` project (if any). Therefore, issue the following Maven goal either from your Eclipse IDE or from the command line located at the root of your project:

```
mvn clean install
```

Next, we need to choose whether we want to use the remote Arquillian profile (that will be run against an existing JBoss AS 7 instance) or whether we want to start a new JBoss AS 7 instance with the managed profile. My guess is that you already have a JBoss application server running, so navigate to the project properties and select the **Maven** property. In the **Active Maven Profiles** field, enter `arq-jbossas-remote`, which we declared earlier in the `pom.xml` file:

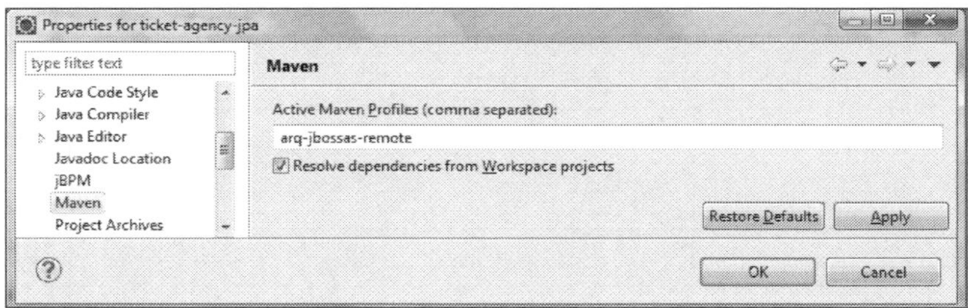

Now all you have to do is right-click on your `TicketTest` class and select **Run As JUnit Test**. The Arquillian engine will start, producing the outcome of the test in the JUnit view (you can make it appear by navigating to **Menu** | **Window** | **Show View** | **JUnit**):

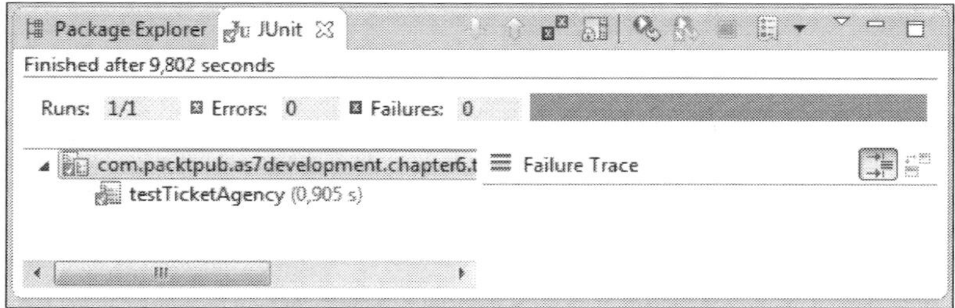

Congratulations! The JUnit console accounts for the first test that was run successfully.

Test run successful; but where is my logging?

When you run your Arquillian tests using a remote container, you may be confused as to why you are not seeing your `System.out` or `log` statements in the test output. The reason is that your test is not running in the same Java VM as the test runner. See the log or console of the JBoss application server that should contain the following statements:

```
17:40:14,728 INFO  [com.packtpub.as7development.
chapter6.test.TicketTest] (http--127.0.0.1-8080-2)
Created Seat Type Balcony
```

Running Arquillian TicketTest with a managed container

When using the remote container (for example, `arq-jbossas-remote`), Arquillian simply needs to know that the container is running and communicates with it using management instruments.

On the other hand, you can choose to use the managed container option by setting the corresponding profile into Maven's plugin properties:

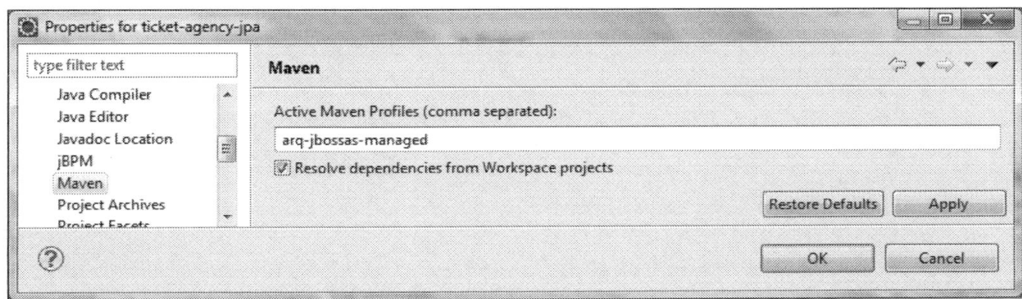

Besides this, Arquillian needs to know where JBoss AS is installed so that it can manage the lifecycle of the container using the startup script. You can configure the JBOSS HOME application into the `arquillian.xml` file shown as follows:

```
<?xml version="1.0" encoding="UTF-8"?>

<arquillian xmlns="http://jboss.org/schema/arquillian"
  xmlns:xsi="http://www.w3.org/2001/XMLSchema-instance"
  xsi:schemaLocation="http://jboss.org/schema/arquillian
        http://jboss.org/schema/arquillian/arquillian_1_0.xsd">


  <defaultProtocol type="Servlet 3.0" />

  <container qualifier="jboss" default="true">
    <configuration>

      <property name="jbossHome">C:\jboss-as-7.1.1.Final</property>
    </configuration>
  </container>

</arquillian>
```

That's all. Now your test will kick-start a JBoss AS 7 instance before deploying the application on it. This JBoss AS 7 node will be shut down as soon as the test is complete.

Enhancing your Arquillian test

You might have noticed that we have, on purpose, created just a part of the integration tests we needed. We did not reach the last mile, that is, creating seats and reserving one. As a matter of fact, if you remember, our ticket application uses `ConversationScope` to track the user's navigation. Thus, we need to bind `ConversationScope` into our test as well.

Luckily, the `weld` container provides all that you need with `org.jboss.weld.context.bound.BoundConversationContext` that needs to be injected into your test class:

```
@Inject BoundConversationContext conversationContext;

@Before
public void init() {
      conversationContext.associate(
      new MutableBoundRequest(new HashMap<String, Object>(),
                              new HashMap<String, Object>()));
      conversationContext.activate();
}
```

> Note that the `@Before` annotation is invoked before each test method and after injections have occurred. In our case, it is used to associate `conversationContext` with `MutableBoundRequest` before being activated by `conversationContext.activate`. This is needed to mimic the conversation behavior from within the Arquillian test bed.
>
> Just for completeness, you must be aware that `BoundRequest` interfaces are defined into the `weld` API to hold a conversation that spans multiple requests, but are shorter than a session.

So here's the full `TicketTest` class that also contains the `Theatre` creation and a booking seat reservation in the `testTicketAgency` method:

```
@RunWith(Arquillian.class)
public class TicketTest {

  @Inject BoundConversationContext conversationContext;

  @Before
```

```
public void init() {
  conversationContext.associate(
      new MutableBoundRequest(new HashMap<String, Object>(),
          new HashMap<String, Object>()));
  conversationContext.activate();
}
@Deployment
public static Archive<?> createTestArchive() {

  return ShrinkWrap.create(WebArchive.class, "ticket.war")
      .addPackage(SeatProducer.class.getPackage())
      .addPackage(Seat.class.getPackage())
      .addPackage(TicketService.class.getPackage())
      .addPackage(DataManager.class.getPackage())
      .addAsResource("META-INF/persistence.xml")
      .addAsWebInfResource(EmptyAsset.INSTANCE, "beans.xml");

}

@Inject
TicketService ticketService;

@Inject
BookerService bookerService;

@Inject
Logger log;

@Test
public void testTicketAgency () throws Exception {

  SeatType seatType = new SeatType();
  seatType.setDescription("Balcony");
  seatType.setPrice(20);
  seatType.setQuantity(5);

  ticketService.createSeatType(seatType);
  log.info("Created Seat Type");
  assertNotNull(seatType.getId());

  List<SeatType> listSeats = new ArrayList();
  listSeats.add(seatType);
```

```
        ticketService.createTheatre(listSeats);

        log.info("Created Theatre");
        log.info(seatType.getDescription() + " was persisted with id " +
    seatType.getId());

        bookerService.bookSeat(new Long(seatType.getId()), seatType.
    getPrice());
        log.info("Created Theatre");
        log.info("Money left: " +bookerService.getMoney());
        assertTrue(bookerService.getMoney() <100);
      }

    }
```

The expected output of the application server console should be pretty much like the following screenshot:

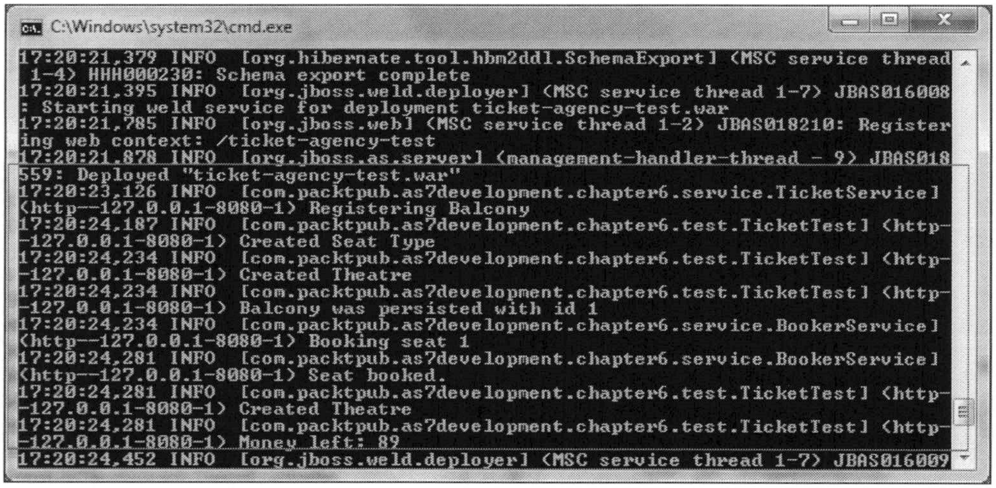

```
C:\Windows\system32\cmd.exe
17:20:21,379 INFO  [org.hibernate.tool.hbm2ddl.SchemaExport] (MSC service thread
 1-4) HHH000230: Schema export complete
17:20:21,395 INFO  [org.jboss.weld.deployer] (MSC service thread 1-7) JBAS016008
: Starting weld service for deployment ticket-agency-test.war
17:20:21,785 INFO  [org.jboss.web] (MSC service thread 1-2) JBAS018210: Register
ing web context: /ticket-agency-test
17:20:21,878 INFO  [org.jboss.as.server] (management-handler-thread - 9) JBAS018
559: Deployed "ticket-agency-test.war"
17:20:23,126 INFO  [com.packtpub.as7development.chapter6.service.TicketService]
(http--127.0.0.1-8080-1) Registering Balcony
17:20:24,187 INFO  [com.packtpub.as7development.chapter6.test.TicketTest] (http-
-127.0.0.1-8080-1) Created Seat Type
17:20:24,234 INFO  [com.packtpub.as7development.chapter6.test.TicketTest] (http-
-127.0.0.1-8080-1) Created Theatre
17:20:24,234 INFO  [com.packtpub.as7development.chapter6.test.TicketTest] (http-
-127.0.0.1-8080-1) Balcony was persisted with id 1
17:20:24,234 INFO  [com.packtpub.as7development.chapter6.service.BookerService]
(http--127.0.0.1-8080-1) Booking seat 1
17:20:24,281 INFO  [com.packtpub.as7development.chapter6.service.BookerService]
(http--127.0.0.1-8080-1) Seat booked.
17:20:24,281 INFO  [com.packtpub.as7development.chapter6.test.TicketTest] (http-
-127.0.0.1-8080-1) Created Theatre
17:20:24,281 INFO  [com.packtpub.as7development.chapter6.test.TicketTest] (http-
-127.0.0.1-8080-1) Money left: 89
17:20:24,452 INFO  [org.jboss.weld.deployer] (MSC service thread 1-7) JBAS016009
```

Additional information

The Arquillian project is an evolving framework with many other interesting topics. Describing all its extensions, however, is out of the scope of this book, but you can learn more about it from the online documentation that is available at `http://arquillian.org/guides/`.

Summary

In this chapter, we have gone through one critical part of enterprise systems: integration testing. Historically, one main downside of Java EE is its testability, but Arquillian has really solved this issue to a great extent.

Used as an extension of the JUnit framework, Arquillian excels in checking the integration layer that exposes the business logic in an enterprise Java application.

Arquillian hooks into your testing framework's life cycle and starts reacting to events to manage the container (start/stop). It also bundles the `test` class into a deployable archive with dependent classes and resources.

In the next chapter, we will discuss developing applications using JBoss Messaging Provider (HornetQ) by introducing examples with message-driven beans.

7

Developing Applications with JBoss JMS Provider

Messaging is a method of communication between software components and applications. The **Java Message Service (JMS)** documented at `http://java.sun.com/products/jms/docs.html` is a Java API designed by Sun that allows applications to create, send, receive, and read messages.

Messaging differs from other standard protocols, such as **Remote Method Invocation** (**RMI**) or **Hypertext Transfer Protocol** (**HTTP**), in two ways. First, the conversation is mediated by a messaging server, so it's not a two-way conversation between peers. Second, the sender and the receiver need to know what message format and what destination to use. This is in contrast to tightly coupled technologies, such as **Remote Method Invocation** (**RMI**), which require an application to know a remote application's methods.

In this chapter, we will cover:

- A brief introduction to message-oriented systems
- The building blocks of the JBoss messaging subsystem
- Setting up some proof of concept programming examples
- How to use JMS and resource adapters to integrate with external systems

A short introduction to JMS

JMS defines a vendor-neutral (but Java-specific) set of programming interfaces for interacting with asynchronous messaging systems. Messaging enables distributed communication that is loosely coupled. The whole messaging interchange is a two-step process: where, a component sends a message to a destination, which is in turn retrieved by the recipient with the mediation of the JMS server. In JMS, there are two types of destinations: topics and queues. These have different semantics, which are explained next.

In the **point-to-point** model, messages are sent from producers to consumers via **queues**. A given queue may have multiple receivers but only one receiver may consume each message. The first receiver to fetch the message will get it, while everyone else will not:

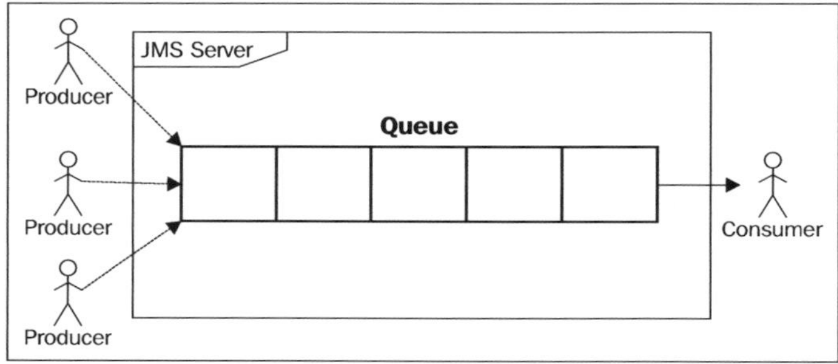

A message sent to a **topic**, on the other hand, may be received by multiple parties. Messages published on a specific topic are sent to all message consumers that have registered (subscribed) to receive messages on that topic. A subscription can be **durable** or **nondurable**. A nondurable subscriber can only receive messages that are published while it is **active**. A nondurable subscription does not guarantee the delivery of the message or may deliver the same message more than once. A durable subscription, on the other hand, guarantees that the consumer receives the message exactly once:

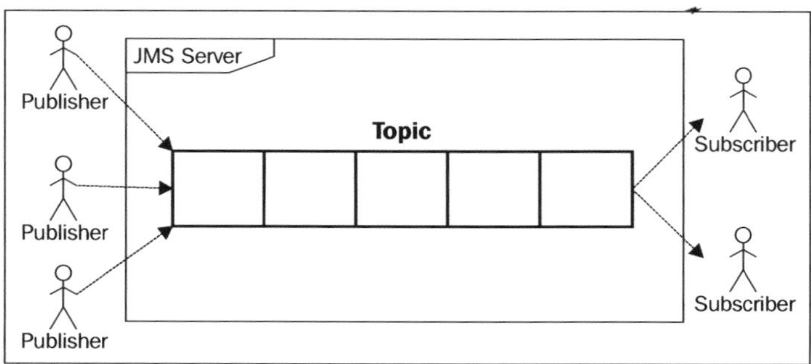

As far as message consumption is concerned, even though JMS is inherently asynchronous, the JMS specification allows messages to be consumed in either of the following two ways:

- **Synchronously**: A subscriber or a receiver explicitly fetches the message from the destination by calling the `receive()` method of any `MessageConsumer` instance. The `receive()` method can block until a message arrives or can time out if a message does not arrive within a specified time limit.
- **Asynchronously**: With the asynchronous mode, the client must implement the `javax.jms.MessageListener` interface and overwrite the `onMessage()` method. Whenever a message arrives at the destination, the JMS provider delivers the message by calling the listener's `onMessage` method, which acts on the contents of the message.

A JMS message consists of a header, properties, and a body. The message headers provide a fixed set of metadata fields describing the message, with information such as where the message is going and when it is received. The properties are a set of key-value pairs used for application-specific purposes, usually to help filter messages quickly when they have been received. Finally, the body contains whatever data is being sent in the message.

The JMS API supports two delivery modes for messages to specify whether or not the messages are lost if the JMS provider fails, indicated by the following constants:

- The **persistent** delivery mode, which is the default, instructs the JMS provider to take extra care to ensure that a message is not lost in transit in case of a JMS provider failure. A message sent with this delivery mode is logged to stable storage when it is sent.
- The **non_persistent** delivery mode does not require the JMS provider to store the message or otherwise guarantee that it is not lost if the provider fails.

The building blocks of JMS

The basic building blocks of any JMS application consists of the following:

- Administered objects—connection factories and destinations
- Connections
- Sessions
- Message producers
- Message consumers
- Messages

Some of these elements are explained as follows:

A **connection factory** object encapsulates a set of connection configuration parameters that have been defined by an administrator. A client uses it to create a connection with a JMS provider. A connection factory hides provider-specific details from JMS clients and abstracts administrative information into objects in the Java programming language.

A **destination** is the component a client uses to specify the target of messages it produces and the source of messages it consumes. In the point-to-point (PTP) messaging domain, destinations are called queues; in the **publish/subscribe (pub/sub)** messaging domain, destinations are called topics.

A **connection** encapsulates a virtual connection with a JMS provider. A connection could represent an open TCP/IP socket between a client and a provider service. You use a connection to create one or more sessions.

A **session** is a single-threaded context for producing and consuming messages. You use sessions to create message producers, message consumers, and messages. Sessions serialize the execution of message listeners and provide a transactional context with which to group a set of sends and receives into an atomic unit of work.

A **message producer** is an object created by a session and is used for sending messages to a destination. The PTP form of a message producer implements the `QueueSender` interface. The pub/sub form implements the `TopicPublisher` interface.

A **message consumer** is an object created by a session and is used for receiving messages sent to a destination. A message consumer allows a JMS client to register interest in a destination with a JMS provider. The JMS provider manages the delivery of messages from a destination to the registered consumers of the destination. The PTP form of message consumer implements the `QueueReceiver` interface. The pub/sub form implements the `TopicSubscriber` interface.

The JBoss messaging subsystem

JBoss AS has used different JMS implementations across its releases. Since JBoss AS 6.0, the default JMS provider is HornetQ (`http://www.jboss.org/hornetq`), which provides a multiprotocol, embeddable, very high performance and clusterable messaging system.

At its core, HornetQ is designed simply as a set of **Plain Old Java Objects (POJOs)**, with few dependencies on external JAR files. In fact, the only one JAR dependency is the Netty library, which leverages the **Java New Input-Output** (**NIO**) API for building high-performance network applications.

Because of its easily-adaptable architecture, HornetQ can be embedded in your own project, or instantiated in any dependency injection framework such as JBoss Microcontainer, Spring, or Google Guice.

In this book, we will cover a scenario where HornetQ is integrated into JBoss AS subsystem as a module, as shown in the following diagram. This diagram depicts how the JCA Adaptor and the HornetQ server fit in the overall picture:

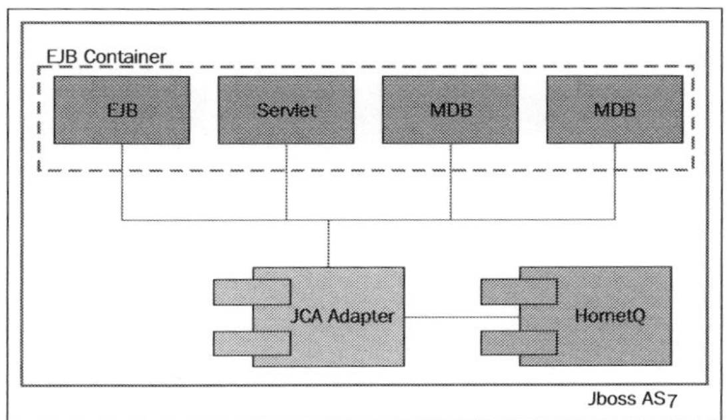

Creating and using connection factories

It is the job of the connection factory, which encapsulates the connection's parameters to create new JMS connections. A connection factory is bound in the **Java Naming Directory Index (JNDI)** and can be looked up by both local clients and remote clients, provided they supply the correct environment parameters. Since a connection factory can be reused multiple times in your code, it's the kind of object that can be conveniently cached by a remote client or a message-driven bean.

The definition of connection-factory instances is included in the `full` and `full-ha` server configurations. You can inspect them in the overall JMS configuration, which is available by surfing the admin console and navigating to **Profile** | **Messaging Provider**:

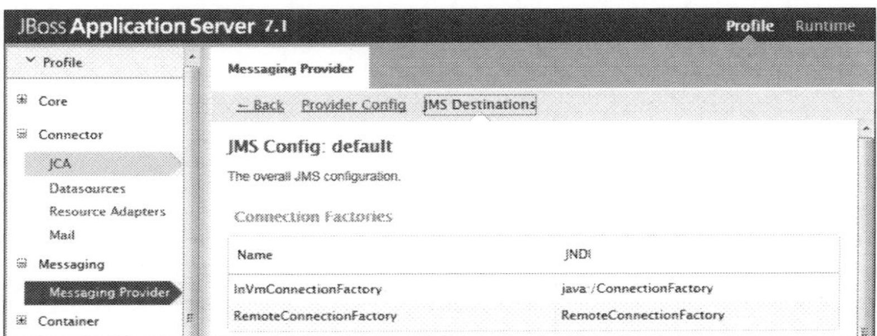

As you can see in the preceding screenshot, there are two out-of-the-box connection factory definitions:

- **InVmConnectionFactory**: This connection factory is bound under the entry `java:/ConnectionFactory`, and is used when the server and client are part of the same process (that is, they are running on the same JVM).
- **RemoteConnectionFactory**: This connection factory, as the name implies, can be used when JMS connections are provided by a remote server, using Netty as the connector.

If you want to change the connection factory's JNDI binding, the simplest choice is to go through the server configuration file (for example, `standalone-full.xml` for standalone mode):

```
<connection-factory name="InVmConnectionFactory">
   <connectors>
      <connector-ref connector-name="in-vm"
                        backup-connector-name="netty" />
      </connectors>
      <entries>
          <entry name="java:/ConnectionFactory" />
      </entries>
</connection-factory>
<connection-factory name="RemoteConnectionFactory">
   <connectors>
      <connector-ref connector-name="netty"
                      backup-connector-name="in-vm" />
      </connectors>
      <entries>
         <entry  name="java:jboss/exported/jms/
RemoteConnectionFactory"/>
      </entries>
</connection-factory>

<pooled-connection-factory name="hornetq-ra">
   <transaction mode="xa"/>
      <connectors>
         <connector-ref connector-name="in-vm"/>
      </connectors>
      <entries>
          <entry name="java:/JmsXA"/>
      </entries>
</pooled-connection-factory>
```

As you can see from the preceding code, the messaging system also contains the definition of a **pooled transacted factory**, which is bound in the JNDI at `java:/JmsXA`. We will discuss this further in the *Optimizing JMS connections* section.

The connection factory can be injected just like any other Java EE resource; the following code fragment shows how a stateless EJB gets the default connection factory injected:

```
@Stateless
public class SampleEJB {

        @Resource(mappedName = "java:/ConnectionFactory")
        private ConnectionFactory cf;
}
```

In order to use the messaging subsystem you have to start JBoss AS using a full profile, which includes the messaging subsystem. So, for example, if you want to start a standalone server instance that is JMS aware you can simply use:

```
standalone.sh -c standalone-full.xml
```

Using JMS destinations

Along with the definition of connection factories, you will need to learn how to configure the JMS destinations (queues and topics).

That can be achieved with a variety of instruments. Since we started to deal with the web console, just navigate to the **Profile** tab and pick the **Messaging** subsystem from the left panel. Select **Destinations** and click on the **View** central link, as shown in the following screenshot:

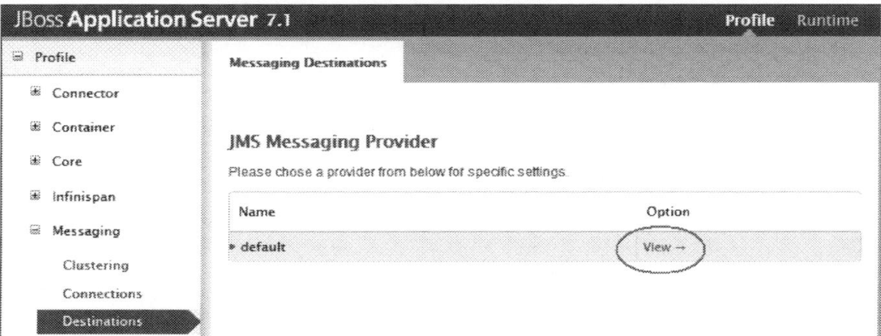

From there, you can use the upper menu tab that contains a set of options, the first one of which, named **Queues/Topics**, can be used to configure your JMS destinations:

Now click on the **Add** button and, in the preceding screen, enter the mandatory name for your destination and its JNDI. You can optionally choose to define your JMS destination as either of the following options:

- **Durable:** This option allows the JMS server to hold on to a message in case the subscriber is temporarily unavailable.
- **Selector:** This option allows a filter, to the JMS destination.

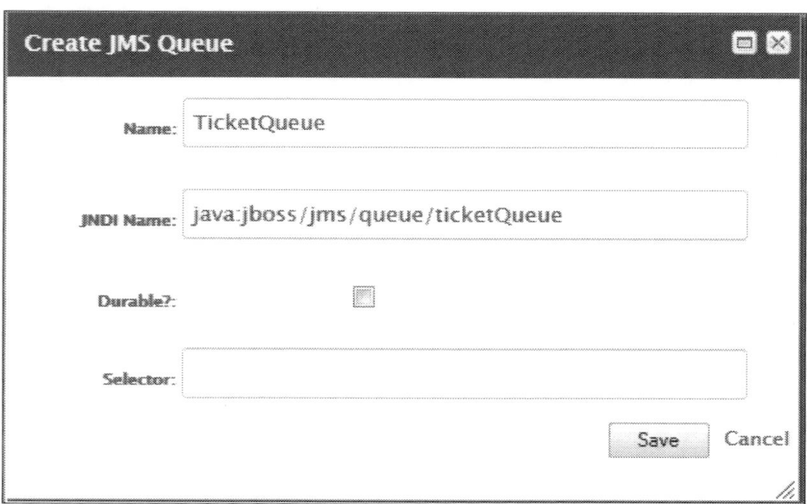

Click on the **Save** button and verify that the queue has been enlisted among the JMS destinations:

Name	JNDI
TicketQueue	java:jboss/jms/queue/ticketQueue
testQueue	queue/test

1-2 of 2

The preceding change will reflect in the server configuration file as follows:

```
<jms-destinations>
   <jms-queue name="TicketQueue">
      <entry name="java:jboss/jms/queue/ticketQueue"/>
         <durable>false</durable>
   </jms-queue>
</jms-destinations>
```

Adding message-driven beans to your application

Once we the configuration, we can start coding a JMS message consumer such as the message-driven bean.

Message-driven beans (**MDBs**) are stateless, server-side, and transaction-aware components for processing asynchronous JMS messages.

One of the most important aspects of message-driven beans is that they can consume and process messages concurrently. This capability provides a significant advantage over traditional JMS clients, which must be custom-built to manage resources, transactions, and security in a multithreaded environment. The MDB containers manage concurrency automatically, so the bean developer can focus on the business logic of processing the messages. The MDB can receive hundreds of JMS messages from various applications and process them all at the same time, because numerous instances of the MDB can execute concurrently in the container.

From the semantic point of view, an MDB is classified as an enterprise bean, just like a session or entity bean, but there are some important differences. At first, the message-driven bean does not have component interfaces. The component interfaces are absent because the message-driven bean is not accessible via the Java RMI API; it responds only to asynchronous messages.

Just as the entity and session beans have well-defined life cycles, so does the MDB bean. The MDB instance's life cycle has two states: **Does Not Exist** and **Method ready Pool**:

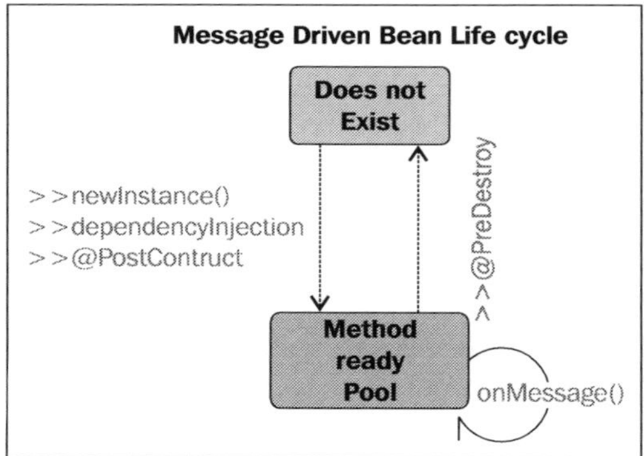

When a message is received, the EJB container checks to see if any MDB instance is available in the pool. If a bean is available in the free pool, JBoss uses that instance. After an MDB instance's `onMessage()` method returns, the request is complete, and the instance is placed back in the free pool. This results in the best response time, as the request is served without waiting for a new instance to be created.

> On the other hand, if all instances in the pool are busy, the new request will be serialized, since it's guaranteed that the same instance will not be allowed to serve multiple clients at the same time. Also, if a client sends out multiple messages to the server containing an MDB, there is no guarantee the same MDB instance will be used for each message or that the messages will be processed in the same order the client sent them. This means that the application should be designed to handle messages arriving out of order.

The amount of MDB in the pool is configured in the EJB pool, which can be reached from the console by going to **Profile** | **Container** | **EJB 3**:

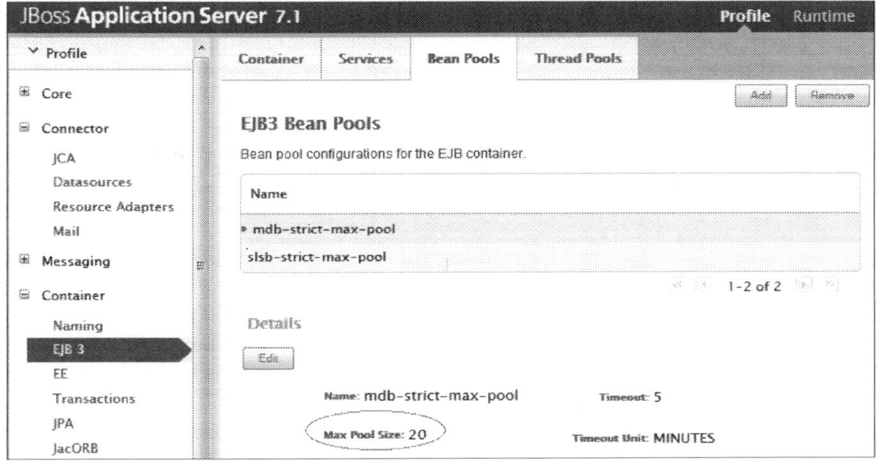

The bean pool's configuration is contained in the bean pool central tab, which holds both the stateless and MDB pool configurations. The default value for the MDB **Max Pool Size** is 20 units.

If no bean instances are available, the request will be blocked until an active MDB completes a method call or the transaction times out.

Cooking message-driven beans

We will now add a message-driven bean to our application, which will be used to intercept messages when a new Ticket has been booked. For the purpose of our example, we will just trace that the JMS message has been received; however, you can use it for more complex purposes such as notifying external systems.

So, in the Eclipse menu simply navigate to **New** | **Other** | **EJB** | **EJB 3 Message Driven Bean**. Create a new Java class `MDBService` and enter the package name as `com.packtpub.as7development.chapter7.service`. This will create a bare-bones MDB with just an empty `OnMessage` method.

Once done, let's add the MDB configuration via annotation as shown here:

```
package com.packtpub.as7development.chapter7.service;

import java.util.logging.Logger;
import javax.ejb.*;
import javax.inject.Inject;
import javax.jms.*;

@MessageDriven(name = "MDBService", activationConfig = {
                   @ActivationConfigProperty(propertyName =
"destinationType", propertyValue = "javax.jms.Queue"),
                   @ActivationConfigProperty(propertyName =
"destination", propertyValue = "java:jboss/jms/queue/ticketQueue"),
                   @ActivationConfigProperty(propertyName =
"acknowledgeMode", propertyValue = "Auto-acknowledge") }) [1]

public class MDBService implements MessageListener {

  @Inject
  private Logger logger;

  public void onMessage(Message message) {

    TextMessage tm = (TextMessage) message;
    try {
       logger.info("Received message "+tm.getText());
    }  catch (JMSException e) {

       logger.error("Error ! "+e);
    }


  }

}
```

Here we have connected the MDB to our `ticketQueue` destination `[1]` bound at `java:jboss/jms/queue/ticketQueue`. The purpose of this component will be tracing the message receipt via `java.util.Logger`.

Adding the JMS producer

Once we have finished with the JMS consumer, we need a component that will take care of sending JMS messages. For this purpose we will add an Application Scoped CDI Bean `JMSService`, which gets injected in the JMS resources:

```
package com.packtpub.as7development.chapter7.service;

import javax.annotation.Resource;
import javax.enterprise.context.ApplicationScoped;
import javax.jms.*;
import java.util.logging.Logger;

@ApplicationScoped
public class JMSService {

   @Inject
   private Logger logger;


   @Resource(mappedName = "java:/ConnectionFactory")
   private ConnectionFactory cf; [1]
   @Resource(mappedName = "java:jboss/jms/queue/ticketQueue")
   private Queue queueExample;    [2]


   private Connection connection;
   public void sendMessage(String txt) {

   try {

     connection = cf.createConnection();
     Session session = connection.createSession(false,
     Session.AUTO_  ACKNOWLEDGE);

     MessageProducer publisher = session.createProducer(queueExample);

     connection.start();
```

```
        TextMessage message = session.createTextMessage(txt);
        publisher.send(message);


      }
      catch (Exception exc) {
        logger.error("Error ! "+exc);
      }
      finally {


         if (connection != null)   {
           try {
          connection.close();
                        connection = null;
           } catch (JMSException e) { logger.error(e); }

              }
            }
         }
   }
```

Now you can use your service to notify some application-specific actions. For example, we will inject `JMSService` into the `BookerService` bean and send a message whenever a user registers:

```
   public class BookerService implements Serializable {


      @Inject JMSService jmsService;

      . . . . .

      public void bookSeat(Long seatId, int price)   {
         FacesContext fc = FacesContext.getCurrentInstance();

         if (price  > money) {

     FacesMessage m = new FacesMessage(FacesMessage.SEVERITY_ERROR, "Not
   enough Money!", "Registration successful");
     fc.addMessage(null, m);
     return;
         }
```

```
        logger.info("Booking seat "+seatId);
        ticketService.bookSeat(seatId);
        money = money - price;

        FacesMessage m = new FacesMessage(FacesMessage.SEVERITY_INFO,
"Registered!", "Registration successful");
        if (fc != null)
        fc.addMessage(null, m);

    jmsService.sendMessage("[JMS Message] User registered seat
"+seatId);
    }

}
```

Compiling and deploying the application

The preceding examples can be engineered as part of a `webapp-javaee6` Maven project, just like we have done so far in the earlier chapters. The only additional dependency we need to specify in `pom.xml` includes the JBoss messaging API as follows:

```
<dependency>
        <groupId>org.jboss.spec.javax.jms</groupId>
        <artifactId>jboss-jms-api_1.1_spec</artifactId>
        <scope>provided</scope>
</dependency>
```

Now start a JBoss AS 7 configuration, which includes the messaging subsystem such as `standalone-full.xml`:

```
standalone.sh -c standalone-full.xml
```

Remember, when switching to another server configuration you will need to recreate all the example resources, such as, data sources that were set up initially for your standalone configuration.

Now deploy your application using either Eclipse's Server view or Maven and access the application at `http://localhost:8080/ticket-agency-jms/`.

Everything should work just like the earlier JPA project; however, you should notice in your application server console the message shown in the following screenshot, which confirms that a seat has been booked:

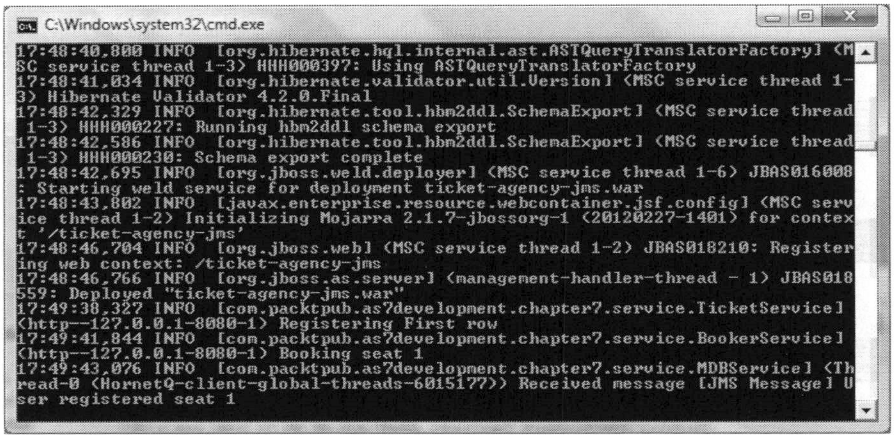

```
C:\Windows\system32\cmd.exe
17:48:40,800 INFO  [org.hibernate.hql.internal.ast.ASTQueryTranslatorFactory] (M
SC service thread 1-3) HHH000397: Using ASTQueryTranslatorFactory
17:48:41,034 INFO  [org.hibernate.validator.util.Version] (MSC service thread 1-
3) Hibernate Validator 4.2.0.Final
17:48:42,329 INFO  [org.hibernate.tool.hbm2ddl.SchemaExport] (MSC service thread
 1-3) HHH000227: Running hbm2ddl schema export
17:48:42,586 INFO  [org.hibernate.tool.hbm2ddl.SchemaExport] (MSC service thread
 1-3) HHH000230: Schema export complete
17:48:42,695 INFO  [org.jboss.weld.deployer] (MSC service thread 1-6) JBAS016008
: Starting weld service for deployment ticket-agency-jms.war
17:48:43,802 INFO  [javax.enterprise.resource.webcontainer.jsf.config] (MSC serv
ice thread 1-2) Initializing Mojarra 2.1.7-jbossorg-1 (20120227-1401) for contex
t '/ticket-agency-jms'
17:48:46,704 INFO  [org.jboss.web] (MSC service thread 1-2) JBAS018210: Register
ing web context: /ticket-agency-jms
17:48:46,766 INFO  [org.jboss.as.server] (management-handler-thread - 1) JBAS018
559: Deployed "ticket-agency-jms.war"
17:49:38,327 INFO  [com.packtpub.as7development.chapter7.service.TicketService]
(http--127.0.0.1-8080-1) Registering First row
17:49:41,844 INFO  [com.packtpub.as7development.chapter7.service.BookerService]
(http--127.0.0.1-8080-1) Booking seat 1
17:49:43,076 INFO  [com.packtpub.as7development.chapter7.service.MDBService] (Th
read-0 (HornetQ-client-global-threads-6015177)) Received message [JMS Message] U
ser registered seat 1
```

Optimizing JMS connections

Going back to our example, we have used an In-VM connection factory since our client service is a local JMS client:

```
public class JMSService {


  @Resource(mappedName = "java:/ConnectionFactory")
  private ConnectionFactory cf;
 . . . . .
}
```

The connection factory is in turn used to create new JMS connections:

```
public void sendMessage(String txt) {
   . . . .
  connection = cf.createConnection();
}
```

Although we are using an In-VM connection factory, JMS objects such as connections and sessions are pretty heavyweight objects. Therefore, a common practice for developers is to cache these objects to avoid costly object creation every time.

However, looking at the server configuration, message producers can benefit from a special connection factory such as the pooled connection factory, which is bound in the JNDI at `java:/JmsXA`:

```
<pooled-connection-factory name="hornetq-ra">
      <transaction mode="xa"/>
         <connectors>
             <connector-ref connector-name="in-vm"/>
         </connectors>
         <entries>
             <entry name="java:/JmsXA"/>
         </entries>
</pooled-connection-factory>
```

When using this connection factory, you will be able to leverage the **outbound adapter** of the HornetQ JCA Resource Adapter. This in turn translates in providing a caching layer for your connection and session objects, which will be acquired from the pool.

Therefore, in order to achieve superior performance for your local clients, the best practice is to use the pooled connection factory inside your message producers:

```
public class JMSService {

  @Resource(mappedName = "java:/JmsXA ")
  private ConnectionFactory cf;
 . . . . .
}
```

If you want a fine control over the pool size, you can specify the `min-pool-size` and `max-pool-size` elements, which determine the initial and maximum size of the connections stored in the pool:

```
<pooled-connection-factory name="hornetq-ra">
      <min-pool-size>10</min-pool-size>
      <max-pool-size>50</max-pool-size>
       ...
</pooled-connection-factory>
```

Specifying which message to receive using selectors

Message selectors allow an MDB to be more selective about the messages it receives from a particular topic or queue. Message selectors use message properties as a criteria in conditional expressions. Message properties, upon which message selectors are based, are additional headers that can be assigned to a message. They give the application developer the ability to attach more information to a message. This information can be either stored as `String` or using several primitive values (`boolean`, `byte`, `short`, `int`, `long`, `float`, and `double`).

For example, let's suppose that we want to process two kinds of messages with the same queue:

- A trace message indicating that a user booked a seat
- A warning message indicating that an error occurred

Hence, our `sendMessage` method can be changed slightly to include a `String` property that can be attached to the message:

```
public void sendMessage(String txt, String priority) {

  try {

      connection = cf.createConnection();
      Session session = connection.createSession(false, Session.AUTO_
ACKNOWLEDGE);
      MessageProducer publisher =
                  session.createProducer(queueExample);

      connection.start();

      TextMessage message =
                  session.createTextMessage(txt);
      message.setStringProperty("priority", priority);
      publisher.send(message);

  }
      . . . .
```

Now, in our application context, we might use the `sendMessage` method, attaching a `LOW` value for priority when the user registers:

```
jmsService.sendMessage("User registered seat "+seatId,"LOW");
```

On the other hand, we could attach a `HIGH` priority when an error occurs:

```
jmsService.sendMessage("Error during Transaction","HIGH");
```

From the MDB perspective, all you need to do in order to filter through messages is include the message selector as part of your `ActivationConfigProperty` as follows:

```
@MessageDriven(name = "MDBService", activationConfig = {
    @ActivationConfigProperty(propertyName = "destinationType",
propertyValue = "javax.jms.Queue"),
    @ActivationConfigProperty(propertyName = "destination",
propertyValue = "java:jboss/jms/queue/ticketQueue"),
```

```
    @ActivationConfigProperty(propertyName = "messageSelector",
propertyValue = "priority = 'HIGH'"),
    @ActivationConfigProperty(propertyName = "acknowledgeMode",
propertyValue = "Auto-acknowledge") })

public class MDBHighPriorityService implements MessageListener {
. . . . .
}
```

At the same time, you can deploy another MDB that is in charge of consuming messages which are sent with a `LOW` priority:

```
@MessageDriven(name = "MDBService", activationConfig = {
    @ActivationConfigProperty(propertyName = "destinationType",
propertyValue = "javax.jms.Queue"),
    @ActivationConfigProperty(propertyName = "destination",
propertyValue = "java:jboss/jms/queue/ticketQueue"),
    @ActivationConfigProperty(propertyName = "messageSelector",
propertyValue = "priority = 'LOW'"),
    @ActivationConfigProperty(propertyName = "acknowledgeMode",
propertyValue = "Auto-acknowledge") })

public class MDBLowPriorityService implements MessageListener {
. . . . .
}
```

Using JMS to integrate with external systems

At the beginning of this chapter, we have mentioned that the JCA Adaptor handles the communication between the application server and the HornetQ server.

As a matter of fact, one possible way to perform **Enterprise Application Integration (EAI)** is via **Java Connector Architecture (JCA)**, which can be used to drive JMS inbound and outbound connections.

Initially, Java connectors were intended to access legacy transaction servers on mainframes in a synchronous request/reply mode, and this is how the majority of the connectors worked in the beginning. The standard is currently evolving toward more asynchronous and two-way connectivity; this is exactly the case of JMS communication, which is inherently asynchronous (but also offers the capability of simulating a synchronous request/response mode). In the next section we will show you how to use a Java Resource Adapter to enable communication between JBoss' HornetQ Messaging system and Apache ActiveMQ integrated with Apache Geronimo.

JMS/JCA integration versus web services

If we are discussing EAI we cannot help but talk about the difference with web services, which is a de facto standard for integrating heterogeneous systems.

One advantage of using JMS/JCA integration is that it provides support for resource adaptation, which maps the Java EE security, transaction, and communication pooling to the corresponding EIS technology. This makes this technology fairly attractive especially if you are connecting some existing, well-consolidated, and homogeneous systems. (Remember that if you are using JMS as the driver, you are bound to Java-to-Java interaction).

On the other hand, if you are planning to connect different business partners (for example, Java and .NET applications), or you are simply building a new system from scratch with no clear interactions defined, it would be better to use web services for transport and connection.

We will learn more about web services in the *Chapter 8, Adding Web Services to Your Applications*, which should provide you with a quite complete overview of your EAI alternatives.

A real-world example – HornetQ and ActiveMQ integration

In this section we will provide an example scenario, which includes an external component such as Apache ActiveMQ (Apache 2.0 open source licensed) message broker that fully implements the Java Message Service 1.1 (JMS).

Within the ActiveMQ message broker, we have configured a JMS queue named `TicketQueue`, which can be used to buy our tickets from another Java EE web application deployed on Apache Geronimo:

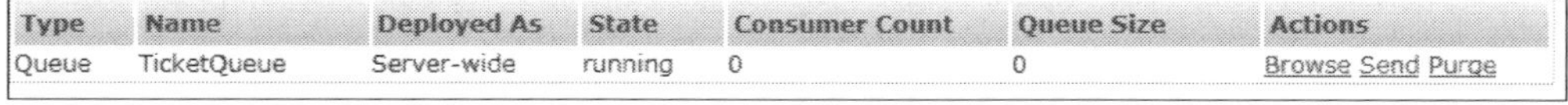

Type	Name	Deployed As	State	Consumer Count	Queue Size	Actions
Queue	TicketQueue	Server-wide	running	0	0	Browse Send Purge

In order to run this example, we would need to pick up the ActiveMQ resource adapter, `activemq-rar-5.7.0.rar`, which can be downloaded from the Maven repository at `http://repo1.maven.org/maven2/org/apache/activemq/activemq-rar/5.7.0/`.

Installing the ActiveMQ resource adapter

Resource adapters (`.rar`) can be deployed either using JBoss management instruments or, for standalone servers, by copying the resource adapter into the `deployments` directory. Before doing that, we need to configure the Resource Adapter in your server configuration. This can be done by adding the configuration in the JCA subsystem, or (suggested choice) by creating a JCA descriptor of the external resource.

JCA descriptors can be created by using an utility contained in JBoss' JCA implementation named IronJacamar (`http://www.jboss.org/ironjacamar`). Within IronJacamar 1.1 or later distributions (accessible at `http://www.jboss.org/ironjacamar/downloads`), you can find a resource adapter information tool (`rar-info.sh`) that can be used to create the resource adapter deployment descriptor by generating a report file containing all the necessary information.

The `rar-info.sh` tool can be found in the `doc/as` folder of your IronJacamar distribution. So let's move to this folder:

```
$ cd doc/as
```

And now issue the following command, which assumes that you have saved your resource adapter in the `/usr/doc` folder:

```
rar-info.sh /usr/doc/activemq-rar-5.7.0.rar
```

Troubleshooting rar-info shell

The `rar-info` command shell includes a set of libraries, which are used to execute the main utility class. In order to inspect the JMS adapter however, you need to manually edit the shell file and add `jboss-jms-api_1.1_spec-1.0.0.Final.jar` to the classpath. This JAR is contained in the `main` folder under `JBOSS_HOME/modules/javax/jms/api/`.

This will generate a file called `activemq-rar-5.7.0.txt`, which can be used to construct the JBoss' JCA configuration file that needs to be named `ironjacamar.xml`. The file `ironjacamar.xml` is pretty verbose so we will just include the core section of it with the changes required to map JMS admin objects (you can download the full `ironjacamar.xml` file along with the sources of this book):

```
<ironjacamar>

    <connection-definitions>
```

```
        <connection-definition class-name="org.apache.activemq.ra.
ActiveMQManagedConnectionFactory" jndi-name="java:jboss/activemq/
TopicConnectionFactory" pool-name="TopicConnectionFactory">
. . . .
        </connection-definition>
        <connection-definition class-name="org.apache.activemq.ra.
ActiveMQManagedConnectionFactory" jndi-name="java:jboss/activemq/
QueueConnectionFactory" pool-name="QueueConnectionFactory">
. . . .
        </connection-definition>
    </connection-definitions>

    <admin-objects>
    <admin-object class-name="org.apache.activemq.command.
ActiveMQQueue" jndi-name="java:jboss/activemq/queue/TicketQueue">
        <config-property name="PhysicalName">
               activemq/queue/TicketQueue
           </config-property>
    </admin-object>

    </admin-objects>

</ironjacamar>
```

As you can see, this file contains the definition of ActiveMQ connection factories along with the mapping of JMS administration objects, which will be imported by the resource adapter. The `ironjacamar.xml` file needs to be copied into the `META-INF` folder of `activemq-rar-5.7.0.rar`.

Along with the `ironjacamar.xml` file, there is another configuration file, which is contained in the `META-INF` folder of your `activemq-rar-5.7.0.rar` file. The file `ra.xml` is the standard JCA configuration file and describes the resource adapter-related attributes type and its deployment properties:

```
<connector xmlns="http://java.sun.com/xml/ns/j2ee"
    xmlns:xsi="http://www.w3.org/2001/XMLSchema-instance"
    xsi:schemaLocation="http://java.sun.com/xml/ns/j2ee
    http://java.sun.com/xml/ns/j2ee/connector_1_5.xsd"
    version="1.5">
```

```
    <description>ActiveMQ  inbound and outbound JMS ResourceAdapter</
description>
    <display-name>ActiveMQ JMS Resource Adapter</display-name>
    <vendor-name>activemq.org</vendor-name>
    <eis-type>JMS 1.1</eis-type>
    <resourceadapter-version>1.0</resourceadapter-version>
    <resourceadapter>
        <resourceadapter-class>org.apache.activemq.
ra.ActiveMQResourceAdapter</resourceadapter-class>

            <!--
            Configuration Properties here
            -->
        <outbound-resourceadapter>

. . . . . .

        </outbound-resourceadapter>
        <inbound-resourceadapter>

. . . . . .

        </inbound-resourceadapter>
        <adminobject>
            <adminobject-interface>javax.jms.Queue</adminobject-
interface>
            <adminobject-class>org.apache.activemq.command.
ActiveMQQueue</adminobject-class>
. . . . . .
        </adminobject>
        <adminobject>
            <adminobject-interface>javax.jms.Topic</adminobject-
interface>
            <adminobject-class>org.apache.activemq.command.
ActiveMQTopic</adminobject-class>
. . . . . .
        </adminobject>
    </resourceadapter>
</connector>
```

Now that we have completed the configuration, let's deploy the resource adapter (`activemq-rar-5.7.0.rar`) into our JBoss AS 7 and check that the JCA factories and objects have been correctly bound to the application server:

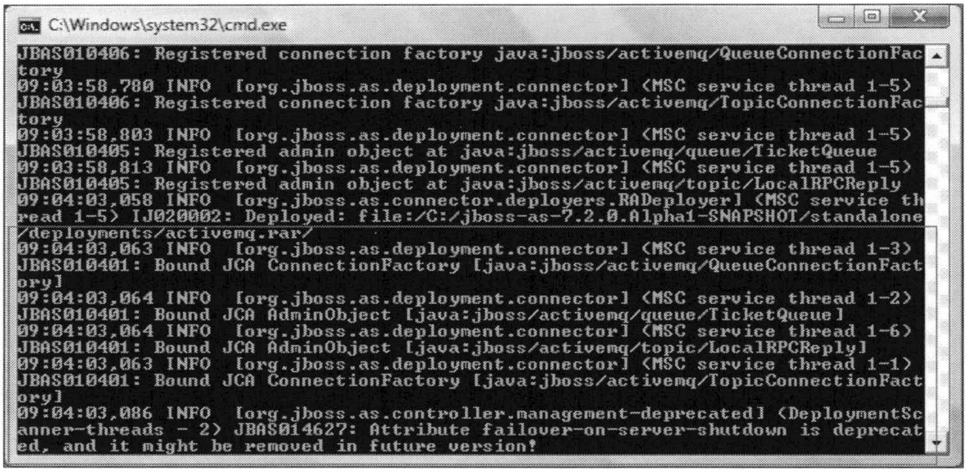

```
C:\Windows\system32\cmd.exe
JBAS010406: Registered connection factory java:jboss/activemq/QueueConnectionFac
tory
09:03:58,780 INFO  [org.jboss.as.deployment.connector] (MSC service thread 1-5)
JBAS010406: Registered connection factory java:jboss/activemq/TopicConnectionFac
tory
09:03:58,803 INFO  [org.jboss.as.deployment.connector] (MSC service thread 1-5)
JBAS010405: Registered admin object at java:jboss/activemq/queue/TicketQueue
09:03:58,813 INFO  [org.jboss.as.deployment.connector] (MSC service thread 1-5)
JBAS010405: Registered admin object at java:jboss/activemq/topic/LocalRPCReply
09:04:03,058 INFO  [org.jboss.as.connector.deployers.RADeployer] (MSC service th
read 1-5) IJ020002: Deployed: file:/C:/jboss-as-7.2.0.Alpha1-SNAPSHOT/standalone
/deployments/activemq.rar/
09:04:03,063 INFO  [org.jboss.as.deployment.connector] (MSC service thread 1-3)
JBAS010401: Bound JCA ConnectionFactory [java:jboss/activemq/QueueConnectionFact
ory]
09:04:03,064 INFO  [org.jboss.as.deployment.connector] (MSC service thread 1-2)
JBAS010401: Bound JCA AdminObject [java:jboss/activemq/queue/TicketQueue]
09:04:03,064 INFO  [org.jboss.as.deployment.connector] (MSC service thread 1-6)
JBAS010401: Bound JCA AdminObject [java:jboss/activemq/topic/LocalRPCReply]
09:04:03,063 INFO  [org.jboss.as.deployment.connector] (MSC service thread 1-1)
JBAS010401: Bound JCA ConnectionFactory [java:jboss/activemq/TopicConnectionFact
ory]
09:04:03,086 INFO  [org.jboss.as.controller.management-deprecated] (DeploymentSc
anner-threads - 2) JBAS014627: Attribute failover-on-server-shutdown is deprecat
ed, and it might be removed in future version!
```

Consuming ActiveMQ messages

Well done! The hardest part is done. Now in order to consume JMS messages sent by ActiveMQ broker, we will add a `@ResourceAdapter` annotation into a message-driven bean. This MDB will intercept bookings from the web application running on the Apache Geronimo application server:

```
@MessageDriven(name = "ActiveMqBridgeService", activationConfig = {
    @ActivationConfigProperty(propertyName = "destinationType",
propertyValue = "javax.jms.Queue"),
    @ActivationConfigProperty(propertyName = "destination",
propertyValue = " java:jboss/activemq/queue/TicketQueue"),
    @ActivationConfigProperty(propertyName = "acknowledgeMode",
propertyValue = "Auto-acknowledge") })

@ResourceAdapter(value="activemq-rar-5.7.0.rar")

public class ActiveMqBridgeService implements MessageListener {

@Inject  private Logger logger;

@Inject private BookerService bookerService;

  public void onMessage(Message message) {
        Long seatId = null;
```

```
        int price=0;

        TextMessage tm = (TextMessage) message;

        logger.info("Received message from ActiveMQ"+tm.getText());


        try {
           seatId = message.getLongProperty("seatId");
           price = message.getIntProperty("price");
        } catch (JMSException e1) {
           throw new EJBException(e1);
        }
        bookerService.bookSeat(seatId, price);

      }

    }
```

Once a message is received, the `seatId` properties and `price` value are extracted from the message header and used to issue a booking request to `BookerService`. Congratulations! If you have gone successfully through this example, you have just mastered a real-world integration scenario!

Summary

In this chapter, we have discussed JBoss' message-oriented middleware, which allows you to loosely couple heterogeneous systems together, while typically providing reliability, transactions, and many other features.

We have showed how to configure JMS destinations using the web console and how to create some message-driven beans, which are the standard way to consume messages from within the EJB container.

We will now move to another component, which is typically used for integrating heterogeneous systems—web services.

8

Adding Web Services to Your Applications

In the earlier chapter, we discussed the Java Messaging Service API that is commonly used to develop loosely coupled applications and also to develop a common integration pattern for Java-to-Java systems. In this chapter, we will learn about web services that are defined by W3C as software systems, and are designed to support interoperable machine-to-machine interaction over a network.

What makes web services different from other forms of distributed computing is that information is exchanged using only simple and nonproprietary protocols. This means the services can communicate with each other regardless of location, platform, or programming language. Essentially, web services protocols provide a platform-independent way to perform **Remote Procedure Calls (RPCs)**.

The focus of this chapter will be on the two chief web services standards, **JAX-WS** (JSR 224) and **JAX-RS** (JSR 311), and how they are implemented into JBoss AS 7. As you can imagine, there is a lot of ground to cover, so we will quickly get our hands dirty with the following topics:

- A short introduction to SOAP web services
- Creating, deploying, and testing web services using the JBoss JAX-WS implementation (Apache CXF)
- A quick overview of REST web services
- How to create, deploy, and test RESTful services using the JBoss JAX-RS implementation (RESTEasy)

Developing SOAP-based web services

As stated, web services are based on the exchange of messages using nonproprietary protocol messages. The messages themselves are not sufficient to define the web service platform. We actually need a list of standard components, including the following:

- A language used to define the interfaces provided by a web service in a manner that is not dependent on the platform on which it is running or the programming language used to implement it
- A common standard format for exchanging messages between web service **providers** and web service **consumers**
- A registry within which service definitions can be placed

The **Web Service Description Language**, also known as WSDL, (`http://www.w3.org/TR/wsdl`) is the de facto standard for providing a description of a web service contract exposed to clients. In particular, a WSDL document describes a web service in terms of the operations that it provides, and the data types that each operation requires as inputs and can return in the form of results.

Communication between the service provider and service consumer happens by means of XML messages that rely on the **SOAP** specification.

A basic SOAP message consists of an envelope that may contain any number of headers and a body. These parts are delimited by XML elements called `envelope`, `header`, and `body` that belong to a namespace defined by the SOAP specification. The following figure depicts the basic structure of a SOAP message:

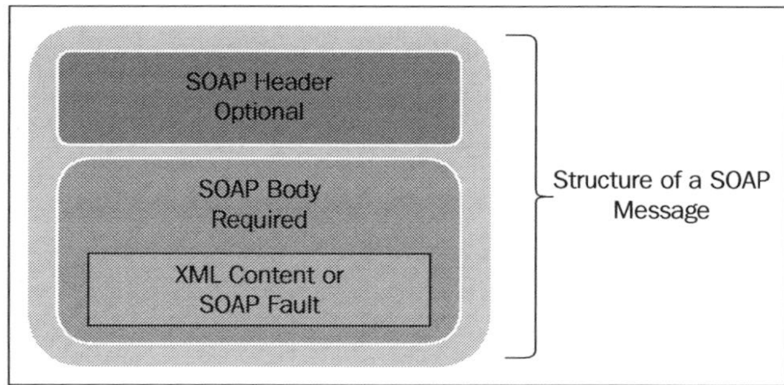

Strategies for building SOAP web services

As we have just learned, the service description is provided by a commonly-used document interface named **WSDL** that exposes the services as a collection of networks, endpoints, and ports, using the XML format.

You may logically be inclined to think that it is necessary to state the corresponding programming interfaces at the beginning of the contract of the service and then produce them.

Actually, you can follow two approaches for developing your SOAP web services:

- **Top-down**: This development strategy involves creating a web service from a WSDL file. The top-down approach is likely to be used when creating web services from scratch. It is the preferred choice of "purist" web service engineers because it's business driven, that is, the contract is defined by business people and so the software is designed to fit the web service contract.
- **Bottom-up**: This approach requires the WSDL file to be generated by the programming interfaces. It is likely to be used when we have existing applications that we want to expose as web services. As it does not require a deep knowledge of the WSDL syntax, it is the easiest choice if you want to turn your Java classes or EJB into web services.

As the audience of this book is composed mainly of Java developers with little or no knowledge at all of WSDL basics, we will focus primarily on the bottom-up approach.

Designing top-down web services, on the other hand, will require you to integrate the basic web services notions provided with this chapter with a comprehensive awareness of the WSDL standard.

JBoss SOAP web services stack

All JAX-WS functionalities provided on top of JBoss Application Server are currently served through a proper integration of the JBoss web services stack with most of the **Apache CXF** project.

Apache CXF is an open source web service framework that provides an easy-to-use, standard-based programming model for developing both SOAP and REST web services. The integration layer (JBossWS-CXF in short hereafter) allows us to:

- Use standard web services APIs (including JAX-WS) on a JBoss Application Server; this is performed internally by leveraging Apache CXF, without requiring the user to deal with it
- Leverage Apache CXF's advanced native features on top of a JBoss Application Server without the need for the user to deal with all the required integration steps for running the application in such a container

Therefore, the focus of the next section will be developing JAX-WS web services using the built-in Apache CXF configuration. If you want to further expand your knowledge about Apache CXF's native features, you can refer to the official documentation that is available at `http://cxf.apache.org/`.

A brief look at the JAX WS architecture

When a SOAP message sent by the client enters the web service runtime environment, it is captured by a component named **Server endpoint listener** that, in turn, uses the **Dispatcher** module to deliver the SOAP message to that Service.

At this point, the HTTP request is converted internally into a SOAP Message. The message content is extracted from the transport protocol and is processed through the handler chain configured for the web service.

SOAP message handlers are used to intercept SOAP messages as they make their way from the client to the endpoint service and vice versa. These handlers intercept SOAP messages for both the request and response of the web service.

The next step is unmarshalling the SOAP message into Java objects. This process is governed by WSDL to Java Mapping and XML to Java Mapping. The former is performed by the JAX-WS engine, and it determines which endpoint to invoke from the SOAP message. The latter, performed by the JAXB libraries, deserializes the SOAP message so that it is ready to invoke the endpoint method.

Finally, the deserialized SOAP message reaches the actual web service implementation and the method is invoked.

Once the call is completed, the process is reversed. The return value from the web service method is marshalled into a SOAP response message using JAX-WS WSDL to Java mapping and JAXB 2.0 XML to Java mapping.

The **Java Architecture for XML Binding (JAXB)** provides a fast and convenient way to bind XML schemas and Java representations, making it easy for Java developers to incorporate XML data and process functions in Java applications. As part of this process, JAXB provides methods for unmarshalling XML instance documents into Java content trees, and then marshalling Java content trees back into XML instance documents. JAXB also provides a way to generate XML schema from Java objects.

Then, the outbound message is processed by handlers before returning it to the dispatcher and endpoint listener that will transmit the message as an HTTP response.

The following diagram describes how data flows from a web service client to a web service endpoint and back:

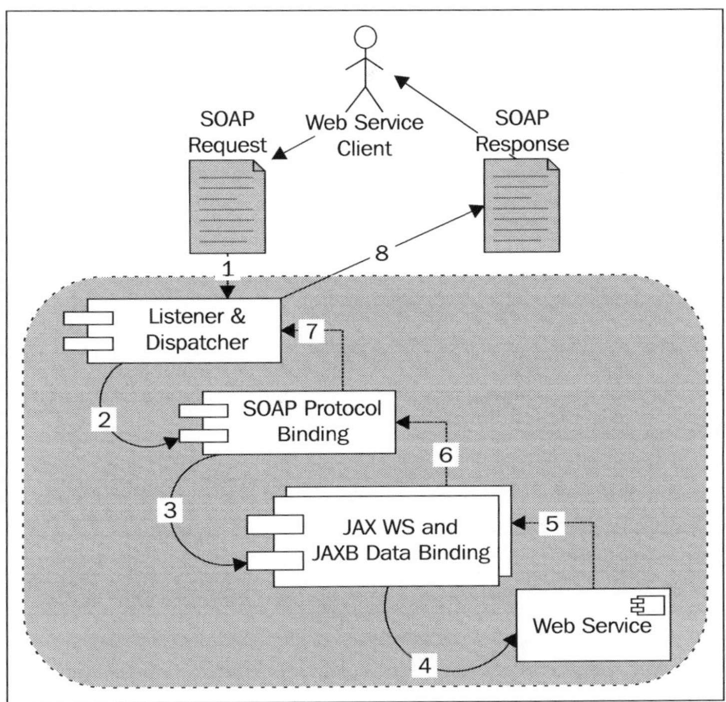

Coding SOAP web services with JBoss AS 7

In the first deliverable, we will show how easily you can turn a plain Java class into a web service. The newly created Service will be then tested using a simple Eclipse-based testing GUI. The second part of this section will draw your attention to how EJBs can be exposed as web service endpoints by enhancing your Ticket application with a web service.

Developing a POJO web service

We will start developing web services, using a Maven project named `ticket-agency-ws` as a template based on the `webapp-javaee6` archetype and `com.packtpub.as7development.chapter8` base package.

Our first class will not be related to our Ticket application, but it will just demonstrate how to create a web service from a POJO class named `POJOWebService`. This class has a method named `calculatePower` that returns the power of an argument as shown in the following highlighted code:

```
package com.packtpub.as7development.chapter8.webservice;

public class POJOWebService
{
    public double calculatePower(double argument,
    double power)
    {
       return Math.pow(argument,power);
    }
}
```

Now we will turn this simple class into a web service by adding the mandatory `@WebService` annotation.

```
package com.packtpub.as7development.chapter8.webservice;
import javax.jws.WebMethod;
import javax.jws.WebParam;
import javax.jws.WebResult;
import javax.jws.WebService;
import javax.jws.soap.SOAPBinding;
import javax.servlet.annotation.*;

@WebService(targetNamespace = "http://www.packtpub.com/",
serviceName = "CalculatePowerService")
@SOAPBinding(style = SOAPBinding.Style.RPC)
@WebServlet(name="POJOService", urlPatterns={"/pojoService"} )
public class POJOWebService
{

  @WebMethod
  @WebResult(name="result")   [1]
  public double calculatePower(@WebParam(name="base")  [2]
                               double base,
                               @WebParam(name="exponent")
                               double exponent {
             return Math.pow(base,exponent);
  }
}
```

Inside the `@WebService` annotation, you can specify additional elements, such as the `targetNamespace` element, that declares the namespace used for the WSDL elements generated by the web service. If you don't specify this element, the web service container will use the Java package name to generate a default XML namespace.

You can also use the `serviceName` element to specify the Service name. The name specified using `serviceName` is used for generating the name attribute in the Service element in the WSDL interface. If you don't specify the `serviceName` element, the server will generate it using the default, which is the bean class name appended with the Service.

In the next row, we have stated that the web service is of the type Remote Procedure Call using the `@javax.jws.SOAPBinding` annotation. The possible values are `DOCUMENT` and `RPC`, the first one being the default value.

> The choice between the RPC and Document style boils down to the different ways we can construct Services using these two styles. The body of an RPC-style SOAP message is constructed in a specific way, which is defined in the SOAP standard. This is built around the assumption that you want to call the web service just like you would call a normal function or method that is part of your application code.
>
> Therefore, the RPC is more tightly coupled because if you make any changes in the message structure, you'll need to change all the clients and servers processing that kind of message.
>
> A document-style web service, on the other hand, contains no restrictions for how the SOAP body must be constructed. It allows you to include whatever XML data you want and also to include a schema for this XML. Therefore, the Document style is probably more flexible, but the effort for implementing the web service and clients may be slightly larger.
>
> In the end, the likeliness of change is a factor that one has to consider when choosing whether to use either RPC- or Document-style web services.

Attaching the `@WebMethod` attribute to a public method indicates that you want the method exposed as part of the web service.

The `@WebParam` annotation is used to specify the parameter's name that needs to be exhibited in the WSDL. You should always consider using a `WebParam` annotation, especially when using multiple parameters, else the WSDL will use the default argument parameter (in this case `arg0`), which is meaningless for web service consumers.

The `@WebResult` annotation is quite similar to `@WebParam` in the sense that it can be used to specify the name of the value returned by the WSDL.

Your web service is now complete. In order to deploy your web service, run the following Maven goal that will package and deploy your web service to your running JBoss AS 7 instance.

```
mvn install jboss-as:deploy
```

JBoss AS will provide a minimal output on the console; this will inform you that the web service project has been deployed and the WSDL file has been generated:

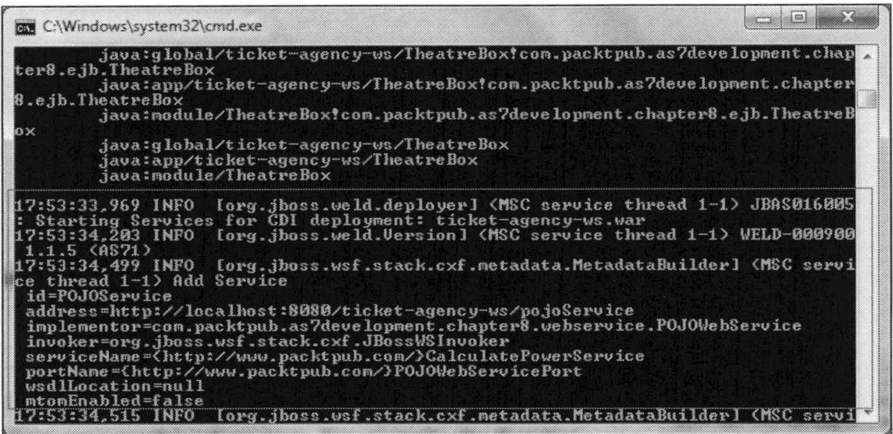

From the short log shown in the previous screenshot, you can pick up some useful information. For example, the first line states that the web service has been bound in the endpoint registry as `POJOService`. Next is the information about the web context path that, by default, has the same name as your project, that is, `ticket-agency-ws`. The last piece of information is about the web service address that is `http://localhost:8080/ticket-agency-ws/pojoService`. By appending the `?wsdl` suffix at the end of the address, you can inspect the web service contract.

The `data` directory contains a versioned list of all generated WSDLs. So, you might find all the history of your web services published by `ticket-agency-ws` in `JBOSS_HOME/standalone/data/wsdl/ticket-agency-ws.war`.

Inspecting the web service from the console

You can inspect the web services subsystem by moving to the web admin console and navigating to **Runtime** | **Deployments** | **Web Services**.

Here, you can gather some useful information about the services deployed. In fact, its most useful option is the list of endpoint contracts available that is needed when developing our clients. The following screenshot shows a view of the web service endpoints from the console:

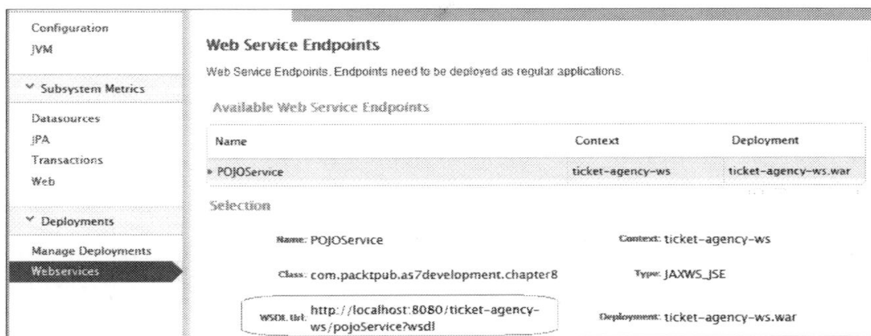

Particularly in the lower part of the screen, you can read the web service endpoint address that bears the web application context name and the registered name for the web service. In our case, it is `http://localhost:8080/ticket-agency-ws/pojoService?wsdl`.

Testing our simple web service

Since our first web service is not yet connected with our Ticketing System, we will use an external client application to test our web service. One of my favorite tools for testing web services is **soapUI**.

SoapUI is a free, open source, cross-platform functional testing solution with an easy-to-use graphical interface and enterprise-class features. This tool allows you to easily and rapidly create and execute automated, functional, regression, compliance, and load tests. SoapUI is available as an Eclipse plugin at the site, `http://www.soapui.org/eclipse/update`.

Install the plugin by navigating to **Help** | **Install New Software** from the menu. Now add the previous location and install the plugin as shown in the following screenshot. Once completed, Eclipse will need restarting.

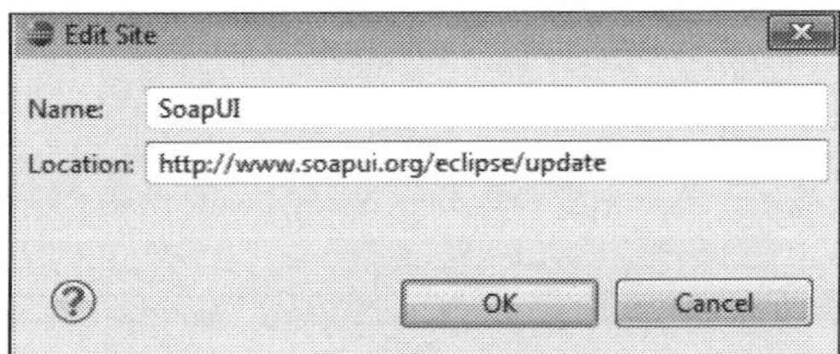

Open the soapUI perspective; then, navigate to **Window | Open Perspective | Other...** and select **soapUI** from the list. The perspective will open two views as follows:

- A **soapUI Navigator** view to the left containing the same navigator and details tab as the standalone soapUI version
- A **soapUI Logs** view at the bottom containing the same log tabs as the standalone soapUI version

Now in the **soapUI Navigator** view, right-click on your project and choose **New soapUI Project**. Fill in the next dialog with the WSDL information available on the JBoss AS server as shown in the following screenshot:

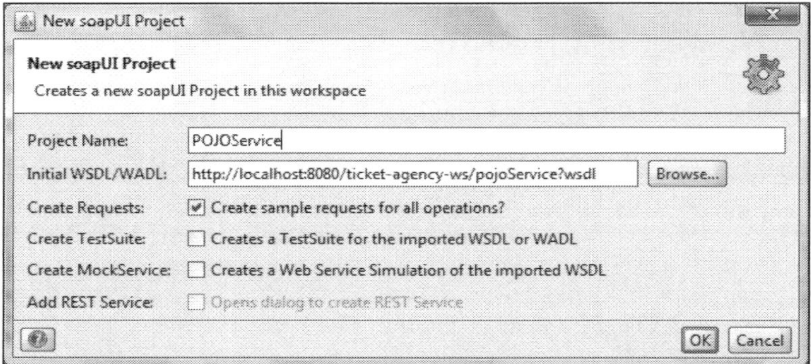

You will see that the project automatically discovers the operations exposed by the web service:

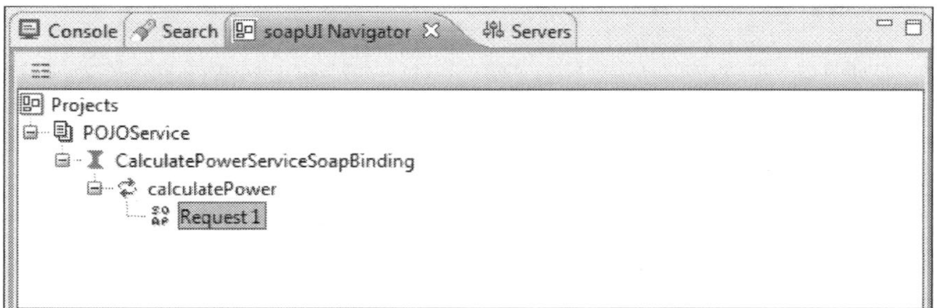

Double-click on the **Request 1** tree element; the soapUI request perspective will appear, where you can enter the named parameters. Enter the two arguments for the web service as shown in the following screenshot:

```
<soapenv:Envelope xmlns:soapenv="http://schemas.xmlsoap.org/soap/envelope/"
   <soapenv:Header/>
   <soapenv:Body>
      <pac:calculatePower>
         <base>3</base>
         <exponent>2</exponent>
      </pac:calculatePower>
   </soapenv:Body>
</soapenv:Envelope>
```

Click on the **Submit** button on the toolbar and check the result in the SOAP response window:

```
<soap:Envelope xmlns:soap="http://schemas.xmlsoap.org/soap/envelope/">
   <soap:Body>
      <ns1:calculatePowerResponse xmlns:ns1="http://www.packtpub.com/">
         <result>9.0</result>
      </ns1:calculatePowerResponse>
   </soap:Body>
</soap:Envelope>
```

EJB3 Stateless Session Beans (SLSB) web services

The JAX-WS programming model supports the same set of annotations on EJB3 Stateless Session Beans as on POJO endpoints. Now that we already have some web service muscle, we will engineer one of the examples introduced in this book.

Our main web service class will be named `TicketSOAPService` and will use some of the core classes that we described in *Chapter 3, Beginning Java EE 6 – EJBs*, such as `TheatreBox` that will keep in memory the ticket bookings and the `Seat` class as the model. The business methods of our web service will be described by a **Service Endpoint Interface (SEI)** named `TicketSOAPServiceItf`.

Writing the service interface is always good practice as it gives a proper client-side view of our Service methods. The implementation class can then implement the methods defined in the interface.

```
package com.packtpub.as7development.chapter8.webservice;
import java.util.List;
import javax.jws.WebService;
import com.packtpub.as7development.chapter8.model.Seat;
```

```
@WebService
public interface TicketSOAPServiceItf {
  public  List<Seat>  getSeats();

  public boolean bookSeat(int seatId);
}
```

We will now implement the interface by providing the business logic to the interface methods in the `TicketSOAPService` class:

```
package com.packtpub.as7development.chapter8.webservice;

import java.io.Serializable;
import java.util.List;

import javax.inject.Inject;
import javax.jws.*;

import com.packtpub.as7development.chapter8.ejb.TheatreBox;
import com.packtpub.as7development.chapter8.exception.*;
import com.packtpub.as7development.chapter8.model.Seat;
import com.packtpub.as7development.chapter8.producer.*;

@WebService(targetNamespace = "http://www.packtpub.com/", serviceName
= "TicketWebService")
public class TicketSOAPService implements TicketSOAPServiceItf,
Serializable {
  @Inject TheatreBox theatreBox;
  @Inject TheatreInfoBean infoBean;

  @WebMethod
  @WebResult(name="listSeats")
  public  List<Seat>  getSeats() {
     return infoBean.getSeats();
  }

  @WebMethod
  public boolean bookSeat(@WebParam(name="seatId") int seatId) {
    try {
         theatreBox.buyTicket(seatId);
         return true;
    } catch (SeatBookedException e) {
         System.out.println("Error! "+e.getException());
         return false;
```

```
        }

      }
    }
```

As you can see, the implementation class contains the `getSeats` method that returns the list of seats that are self generated when the `InfoBean` object is initialized. The `bookSeat` method will be able to book seats for your web service clients as well.

Now deploy your web service and verify on the Console that it has been correctly registered:

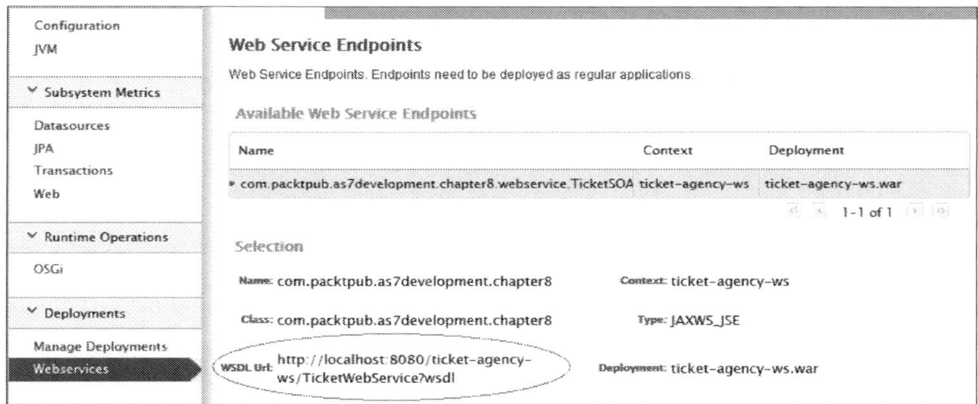

Developing a web service consumer

The web service consumer of the `TicketSOAPService` class will be coded using the Apache CXF utility classes; we will use a factory class named `JaxWsProxyFactoryBean` that, as the name suggests, can be used to create proxies for your JAX-WS interfaces. This `factory` is peculiar to Apache CXF, however it provides a greater control over your web services in terms of logging and debugging.

Right, now add a class named `TicketWebServiceIT` to your project in the package `com.packtpub.as7development.chapter8.test`:

```
package com.packtpub.as7development.chapter8.test;

import static org.junit.Assert.*;

import java.util.List;

import javax.xml.ws.BindingProvider;
```

```
import org.apache.cxf.interceptor.*;

import org.apache.cxf.jaxws.JaxWsProxyFactoryBean;
import org.junit.Test;

import com.packtpub.as7development.chapter8.model.Seat;
import com.packtpub.as7development.chapter8.webservice.*;


public class TicketWebServiceIT {

  @Test
  public void testSOAP() {


        JaxWsProxyFactoryBean factory = new
        JaxWsProxyFactoryBean();
        factory.setServiceClass(TicketSOAPServiceItf.class);
        factory.setAddress("http://localhost:8080/ticket-agency-
        ws/TicketWebService?wsdl");
        factory.getInInterceptors().add(new
        LoggingInInterceptor());
        factory.getOutInterceptors().add(new
        LoggingOutInterceptor());

        TicketSOAPServiceItf infoService = (TicketSOAPServiceItf)
        factory.create();
        System.out.println("Got the Service: "+infoService);

        infoService.bookSeat(1);

        List<Seat>  list = infoService.getSeats();

        dumpSeatList(list);

        assertTrue(list.size() > 0);
        assertTrue(list.get(1).isBooked());



  }
}
```

As you can see, the native Apache CXF client is pretty short in code and requires just one class named `JaxWsProxyFactoryBean` to get instantiated. This class handles the hard job of binding the SEI to a local proxy using the `setProxyClass` method. In order to read the web service contract, you need to provide the WSDL location (in our example, it is `http://localhost:8080/ticket-agency-ws/TicketWebService?wsdl`) using the `setAddress` method.

Optionally, you can bind a set of **logging interceptors** to your web service endpoint to debug your web services.

> Apache CXF uses Java SE logging for both the client and server-side logging of SOAP requests and responses behind the scenes. Logging is activated by the use of separate in/out interceptors that can be attached to the client and/or service as shown in the previous code.

Finally, the `create` method of your JAX-WS factory will return a proxy to your web service that can be used for testing two basic operations: booking a seat and checking from the `Seat` list if the seat has actually been reserved.

Compiling the example

In order to compile this client, you need to add the following Apache CXF dependencies to your `pom.xml` file:

```
<properties>
  <cxf.version>2.2.3</cxf.version>
</properties>

<dependency>
  <groupId>org.apache.cxf</groupId>
  <artifactId>cxf-rt-frontend-jaxws</artifactId>
  <version>${cxf.version}</version>
  <scope>provided</scope>
</dependency>
<dependency>
  <groupId>org.apache.cxf</groupId>
  <artifactId>cxf-rt-transports-http</artifactId>
  <version>${cxf.version}</version>
  <scope>provided</scope>
</dependency>
```

Also, since we are using JUnit for testing, we need to include the JUnit stack in the list of dependencies as well:

```
<dependency>
  <groupId>junit</groupId>
  <artifactId>junit</artifactId>
  <scope>test</scope>
</dependency>
```

Since we are building an integration test, we will use the `maven-failsafe-plugin` that has specifically been designed for running integration tests and decouple the failing builds if there are test failures from actually running the tests. (On the other hand, the maven-surefire-plugin we have learned of so far has been designed for running unit tests; if any of the tests fail, it will fail the build immediately.)

Here's the plugin declaration that needs to be added in the build section:

```
<build>
  <plugins>
    <plugin>
      <artifactId>maven-failsafe-plugin</artifactId>
      <version>2.6</version>
      <executions>
        <execution>
          <goals>
            <goal>integration-test</goal>
            <goal>verify</goal>
          </goals>
        </execution>
      </executions>
    </plugin>
  </plugins>
</build>
```

You can run the test on your application using the previous profile.

Now you can execute the integration test with:

```
mvn install jboss-as:deploy
mvn verify
```

The expected output is pretty verbose since it includes all the activity that is performed behind the scenes by the Apache CXF Bus and the SOAP exchange data. The most interesting part, however, is at the bottom of the maven output where the Ticket list is dumped after booking one seat, as depicted in the following screenshot:

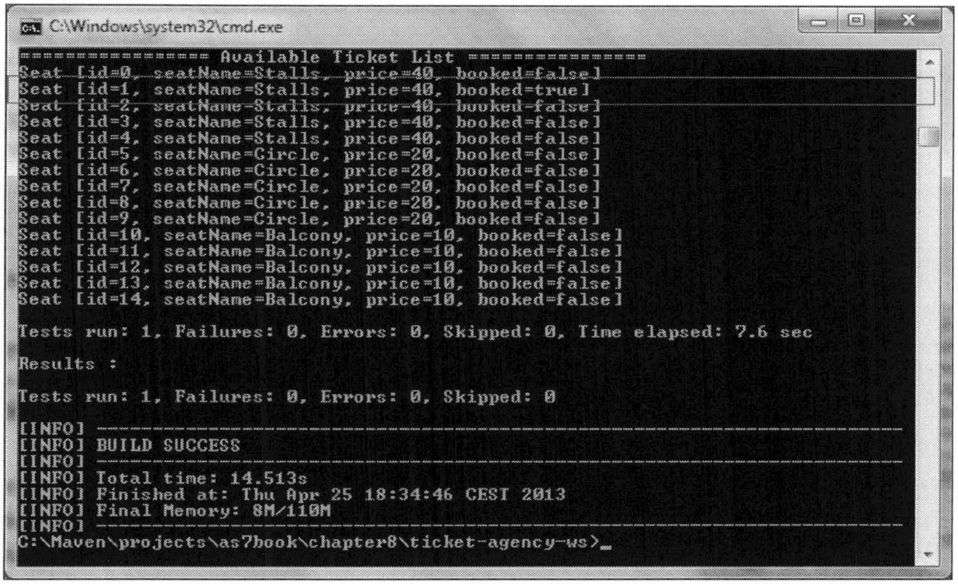

```
C:\Windows\system32\cmd.exe
================== Available Ticket List =================
Seat [id=0, seatName=Stalls, price=40, booked=false]
Seat [id=1, seatName=Stalls, price=40, booked=true]
Seat [id=2, seatName=Stalls, price=40, booked=false]
Seat [id=3, seatName=Stalls, price=40, booked=false]
Seat [id=4, seatName=Stalls, price=40, booked=false]
Seat [id=5, seatName=Circle, price=20, booked=false]
Seat [id=6, seatName=Circle, price=20, booked=false]
Seat [id=7, seatName=Circle, price=20, booked=false]
Seat [id=8, seatName=Circle, price=20, booked=false]
Seat [id=9, seatName=Circle, price=20, booked=false]
Seat [id=10, seatName=Balcony, price=10, booked=false]
Seat [id=11, seatName=Balcony, price=10, booked=false]
Seat [id=12, seatName=Balcony, price=10, booked=false]
Seat [id=13, seatName=Balcony, price=10, booked=false]
Seat [id=14, seatName=Balcony, price=10, booked=false]

Tests run: 1, Failures: 0, Errors: 0, Skipped: 0, Time elapsed: 7.6 sec

Results :

Tests run: 1, Failures: 0, Errors: 0, Skipped: 0

[INFO] ------------------------------------------------------------------------
[INFO] BUILD SUCCESS
[INFO] ------------------------------------------------------------------------
[INFO] Total time: 14.513s
[INFO] Finished at: Thu Apr 25 18:34:46 CEST 2013
[INFO] Final Memory: 8M/110M
[INFO] ------------------------------------------------------------------------
C:\Maven\projects\as7book\chapter8\ticket-agency-ws>_
```

Developing REST-based web services

JAX-RS (JSR-311) is a new JCP specification that provides a Java API for RESTful web services in the HTTP protocol.

In their simplest form, RESTful web services are networked applications that manipulate the state of system resources. In this context, resource manipulation means resource creation, retrieval, update, and deletion (CRUD). However, RESTful web services are not limited to just these four basic data manipulation concepts. On the contrary, RESTful web services can execute logic at the server level, but, remember that every result must be a resource representation of the domain.

The main difference with SOAP web services is that REST asks developers to use HTTP methods explicitly and in a way that's consistent with the protocol definition. This basic REST design principle establishes a **one-to-one** mapping between CRUD operations and HTTP methods.

Therefore, with the delineated roles for resources and representations, we can now map our CRUD actions to the HTTP methods `POST`, `GET`, `PUT`, and `DELETE` as follows:

Action	HTTP protocol equivalent
`RETRIEVE`	`GET`
`CREATE`	`POST`

Action	HTTP protocol equivalent
UPDATE	PUT
DELETE	DELETE

Accessing REST resources

As we said, REST resources can be accessed using actions that map an equivalent HTTP request. In order to simplify the development of REST applications, you can use simple annotations to map your actions; for example, in order to retrieve some data from your application, you can use something similar to the following:

```
@Path("/users")
public class UserResource {

@GET
public String handleGETRequest() { . . .}
}
@POST
public String handlePOSTRequest(String payload) {
}
```

The first annotation, `@Path`, used in our example is used to specify the URI that is assigned to this web service. Subsequent methods have their specific `@Path` annotation so that you can provide a different response according to the URI requested.

Then, we have an `@GET` annotation that maps an HTTP `GET` request and an `@POST` annotation that handles an HTTP `POST`. So in this example, if we were to request for a web application bound to the web context `example`, an HTTP `GET` request to the URL `http://host/example/users` would trigger the method `handleGETRequest`; while on the other hand, an HTTP `POST` request to the same URL would conversely invoke the `handlePOSTRequest` method.

JBoss REST web services

Having understood the basics of REST services, let's see how we can develop a RESTful web service using JBoss AS 7. The application server includes an out-of-the-box **RESTEasy** library that is a portable implementation of the JSR-311 specification. RESTEasy is able to run in any servlet container; however, it is perfectly integrated with JBoss Application Server, thus making the user experience nicer in that environment.

Besides the server-side specification, RESTEasy has been innovative in bringing JAX-RS to the client through the RESTEasy **JAX-RS Client Framework**. This client-side framework allows you to map outgoing HTTP requests to remote servers using JAX-RS annotations and interface proxies.

Activating RESTEasy

RESTEasy is bundled with JBoss AS 7, so you need very little effort to get started. At first, you must at least provide an empty `web.xml` file:

```
<web-app version="3.0" xmlns="http://java.sun.com/xml/ns/javaee"
        xmlns:xsi="http://www.w3.org/2001/XMLSchema-instance"
        xsi:schemaLocation="http://java.sun.com/xml/ns/javaee http://
java.sun.com/xml/ns/javaee/web-app_3_0.xsd">
</web-app>
```

Once you have completed the `web.xml` file, you just need to activate the JAX-RS resources by declaring the application path used by your REST service, using the `@ApplicationPath` annotation in a class that extends `javax.ws.rs.core.Application`:

```
@ApplicationPath("/rest")
public class JaxRsActivator extends Application {

}
```

This simply means that if we were to deploy our former example, the HTTP `GET` method, `http://host/example/rest/users` would trigger our `getUser` business method; while the same URL would place a request through the `handlePOSTRequest` method using a `POST` request.

Adding REST to our Ticket example

With all the configurations in place, we can now add a simple REST web service to our `Ticket Web Service` project that will provide the same functionalities of our SOAP web service.

So add a new class to your project and name it `TicketRESTService`. The code for this is as follows:

```
package com.packtpub.as7development.chapter8.webservice;

import java.util.*;

import javax.enterprise.context.RequestScoped;
import javax.inject.Inject;
```

```
import javax.ws.rs.*;
import javax.ws.rs.core.*;

import com.packtpub.as7development.chapter8.ejb.TheatreBox;
import com.packtpub.as7development.chapter8.model.Seat;


@Path("/seat")
@RequestScoped
public class TicketRESTService {


  @Inject TheatreBox service;
  @Inject TheatreInfoBean infoBean;

  @GET
  @Produces(MediaType.APPLICATION_JSON)
  public List<Seat> getSeatList() {
    return infoBean.getSeatList();
  }

  @POST
  @Path("/{id:\\d+}")
  @Produces(MediaType.APPLICATION_JSON)
  public Response buyTicket(@PathParam("id") int id) {
    Response.ResponseBuilder builder = null;
    try {
      service.buyTicket(id);
      builder = Response.ok("Ticket booked");
    }
    catch (Exception e) {
      // Handle generic exceptions
      Map<String, String> responseObj = new HashMap<String,
      String>();
      responseObj.put("error", e.getMessage());
      builder = Response.status(Response.Status.BAD_REQUEST)
      .entity(responseObj);
    }
    return builder.build();
  }

}
```

If you have understood our earlier section well, this code will be almost intuitive to you. We have included two methods here, just like the SOAP alter ego; the former one is named `getSeatList`, which is bound to an HTTP `GET` request and produces the list of `Seats`. The list is returned using a **JSON** representation that is pretty common when returning Java objects to the client.

> The grammar for JSON objects is simple and requires the grouping of the data definition and data values, it is as follows:
>
> - Elements are enclosed with curly brackets ({ and })
> - Values of elements come in pairs having the structure of `name:value` and are comma separated
> - Arrays are enclosed with square brackets ([and])
>
> That's all there is to it. (For the full JSON grammar description, see `http://www.json.org/`.)

The second method included in this class is `buyTicket` that will be used to invoke the corresponding `buyTicket` class of our EJB. This method, on the other hand, is bound to the following HTTP `POST` method:

```
@POST
@Path("/{id:\\d+}")
@Produces(MediaType.APPLICATION_JSON)
public Response buyTicket(@PathParam("id") int id)
```

You might be thinking that this `Path` expression seems a bit weird, but all it does is map a URI numeric parameter (included in the `Path` expression) to a method parameter. In short, the parameter that is included in the URL will be passed to the method in the ID variable.

The previous method also returns a JSON-formatted string that we will get decoded on the client side using a simple Java library.

Now the REST service is complete and we can start deploying it in the usual way:

```
mvn install jboss-as:deploy
```

If you followed all the steps so far, the following `GET` method issued by your browser should print out the list of available seats:


```
[{"id":0,"seatName":"Stalls","price":40,"booked":false},{"id":1,"seatN
ame":"Stalls","price":40,"booked":false},{"id":2,"seatName":"Stalls","
price":40,"booked":false},{"id":3,"seatName":"Stalls","price":40,"book
ed":false},{"id":4,"seatName":"Stalls","price":40,"booked":false},
. . . . . .
```

Consuming our REST service

Connecting to a RESTful web service takes no more work than directly connecting to the service through an HTTP connection. For this reason, you can use plenty of APIs to access your REST services, such as the JDK `URLConnection` class or Jakarta Commons HttpClient API. However, since we are already using RESTEasy in our project, we suggest using its great client API that helps you to easily consume REST web services in the way JAX-RS is consumed.

A simpler way to create an individual HTTP request is using the `org.jboss.resteasy.client.ClientRequest` class. Therefore, if you want to retrieve the list of `Seats` from your REST service, you just need to issue the following `ClientRequest` class:

```
ClientRequest cr = new ClientRequest("http://localhost:8080/ticket-
agency-ws/rest/seat");
String result = cr.get(String.class).getEntity();
System.out.println(result);
```

The previous code will simply perform a `GET` action to the REST service that is deployed as part of the `ticket-agency-ws` web application. Once that `ClientRequest` class is returned, we cast the result as a string, which in our case will be a list of JSON-formatted `Seat` objects.

Here's a quick recap of what the `ClientRequest` class is made up of:

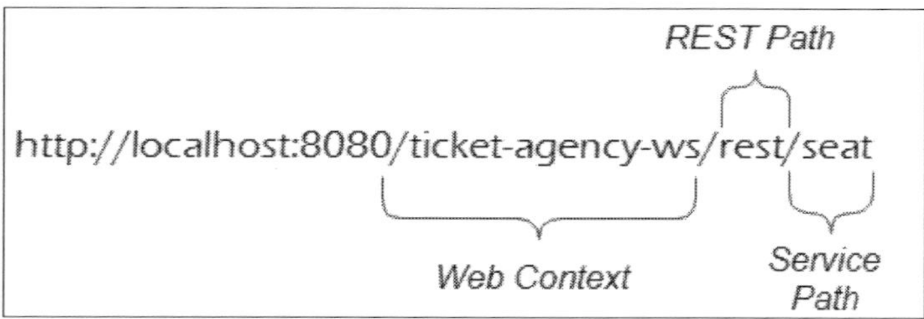

As you can see, besides the **Web Context** string, you need to include the JAX-RS application path (`rest`) we discussed earlier. Next, you need to include the `@Path` annotation of your `TicketRESTService` (the seat) and eventually the ID of the seat booking if you are trying to book a seat.

The previous approach works well if you are issuing a single request; on the other hand, if you have lots of URIs to consume, you can use the `ClientRequestFactory` class to encapsulate your URIs. This approach has two main benefits:

- It allows the initial request to be reused by just changing the `query` parameter or a `Path` element

- It allows the REST interceptor to be registered so that any future `client.get` calls or `client.createRequest` will use that interceptor

So, let's see the full test method using the `ClientRequestFactory` class:

```
@Test
  public void testREST() {
    System.out.println("Testing Ticket REST Service");

    ClientRequestFactory crf = new
    ClientRequestFactory(UriBuilder.fromUri(
       "http://localhost:8080/ticket-agency-
       ws/rest/seat").build());


    ClientRequest bookRequest = crf
      .createRelativeRequest("/4");

    String entity=null;
    try {
      entity = bookRequest.post(String.class).getEntity();

      assertTrue(entity.equals("Ticket booked"));
      System.out.println("Ticket Booked with REST Service");
      ClientRequest request = crf
        .createRelativeRequest("/");
      String seatList=null;

      seatList = request.get(String.class).getEntity();
    } catch (Exception e1) {

      e1.printStackTrace();
    }
    System.out.println("SEAT List \n" + seatList);

    Object obj=JSONValue.parse(seatList);
    JSONArray array=(JSONArray)obj;

    JSONObject seat =(JSONObject)array.get(4);

    Boolean isbooked = (Boolean)seat.get("booked");

    assertTrue(isbooked);
  }
```

So in our test, we are first creating the `ClientRequestFactory` class from the URI `http://localhost:8080/ticket-agency-ws/rest/seat`. The factory is then used to issue two `ClientRequest`; the first one will be used to book a Ticket, adding the URI `/4`, that will be translated on the server side as an invocation of `buyTicket`, passing as the ID value of `4`.

Next, another `ClientRequest` is issued to retrieve the list of `Seats` which will be returned in the JSON format. The last piece of code uses a utility library named JSON.simple (`http://code.google.com/p/json-simple/`) that adds a thin wrapper over your JSON objects so that they can conveniently be converted from/to Java objects.

Once we have got a reference to the fourth element in the `JSONArray`, we'll simply check the Boolean value of the field booked, asserting that it has actually been booked.

Compiling our Ticket example

In order to compile our project with the REST web service, we need to import the JAX-RS API that is included in the application server libraries. This ensures that we will use the `provided` scope for our `dependency` class, which means that we will not include it in the target artifact:

```
<dependency>
   <groupId>org.jboss.spec.javax.ws.rs</groupId>
   <artifactId>jboss-jaxrs-api_1.1_spec</artifactId>
   <scope>provided</scope>
</dependency>
```

Then since we are using the RESTEasy native client API, we'll need to include its `dependency` class as well:

```
<dependency>
   <groupId>org.jboss.resteasy</groupId>
   <artifactId>resteasy-jaxrs</artifactId>
   <version>2.2.1.GA</version>
   <scope>test</scope>
</dependency>
```

Finally, the JSON.simple library from `googlecode` needs to be declared in your `pom.xml` file as well, using a `test` scope, just like the RESTEasy client:

```
<dependency>
  <groupId>com.googlecode.json-simple</groupId>
  <artifactId>json-simple</artifactId>
  <version>1.1</version>
  <scope>test</scope>
</dependency>
```

You can test your application using the JUnit profile which you created previously:

```
mvn verify
```

You should be able to see an output similar to the following screenshot; it is confirmation that the Ticket has been sold and verified via JUnit's assertion:

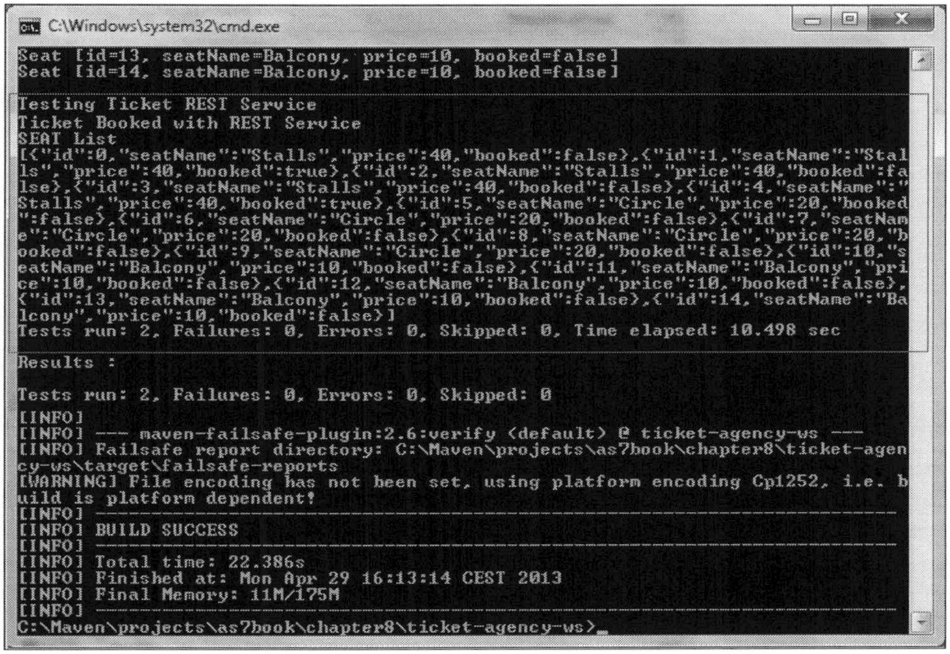

```
C:\Windows\system32\cmd.exe
Seat [id=13, seatName=Balcony, price=10, booked=false]
Seat [id=14, seatName=Balcony, price=10, booked=false]

Testing Ticket REST Service
Ticket Booked with REST Service
SEAT List
[{"id":0,"seatName":"Stalls","price":40,"booked":false},{"id":1,"seatName":"Stal
ls","price":40,"booked":true},{"id":2,"seatName":"Stalls","price":40,"booked":fa
lse},{"id":3,"seatName":"Stalls","price":40,"booked":false},{"id":4,"seatName":"
Stalls","price":40,"booked":true},{"id":5,"seatName":"Circle","price":20,"booked
":false},{"id":6,"seatName":"Circle","price":20,"booked":false},{"id":7,"seatNam
e":"Circle","price":20,"booked":false},{"id":8,"seatName":"Circle","price":20,"b
ooked":false},{"id":9,"seatName":"Circle","price":20,"booked":false},{"id":10,"s
eatName":"Balcony","price":10,"booked":false},{"id":11,"seatName":"Balcony","pri
ce":10,"booked":false},{"id":12,"seatName":"Balcony","price":10,"booked":false},
{"id":13,"seatName":"Balcony","price":10,"booked":false},{"id":14,"seatName":"Ba
lcony","price":10,"booked":false}]
Tests run: 2, Failures: 0, Errors: 0, Skipped: 0, Time elapsed: 10.498 sec

Results :

Tests run: 2, Failures: 0, Errors: 0, Skipped: 0
[INFO]
[INFO] --- maven-failsafe-plugin:2.6:verify (default) @ ticket-agency-ws ---
[INFO] Failsafe report directory: C:\Maven\projects\as7book\chapter8\ticket-agen
cy-ws\target\failsafe-reports
[WARNING] File encoding has not been set, using platform encoding Cp1252, i.e. b
uild is platform dependent!
[INFO] ------------------------------------------------------------------------
[INFO] BUILD SUCCESS
[INFO] ------------------------------------------------------------------------
[INFO] Total time: 22.386s
[INFO] Finished at: Mon Apr 29 16:13:14 CEST 2013
[INFO] Final Memory: 11M/175M
[INFO] ------------------------------------------------------------------------
C:\Maven\projects\as7book\chapter8\ticket-agency-ws>_
```

Choosing between SOAP and REST services

The choice of adopting SOAP rather than REST depends on your application's requirements. SOAP web services are exposed using its own well-defined protocol and focus on exposing pieces of application logic as services. So if your requirement is to consume business services that are exposed using a well-defined and negotiated contract (between the service consumer and the service provider), SOAP web services are a perfect match.

On the other hand, if you need to access some server resources using stateless HTTP invocations and as little as the navigation bar of your browser, you should probably go with RESTful web services.

That being said, there may still be some scenarios that could fit both the options, and you are free to choose whichever web service suits your requirements the best. Since I have never been able to cure my adversity for SOAP-based Java clients (which are inherently more complex to code than other languages), I'd go for REST web services; however, that's just one man's opinion!

Summary

In this chapter, we have introduced some of the basic web services concepts so that you could get acquainted with these technologies before using them to enhance your Ticket application.

Then, we went through SOAP-based web services that are based on a contract between the service and the client defined by the WSDL file. SOAP web services are an excellent option for integrating systems when you have well-defined, abstract operations exposed using standard XML files.

Then we discussed REST services. The key to the REST methodology is to write web services using an interface that is already well known and widely used: the URI. The twist here is to identify the key system resources (this can be entities, collections, or anything else the designer thinks is worthy of having its own URI) and expose them using standard methods that are mapped to standard methods. In this case, the HTTP verbs are mapped to resource-specific semantics.

We have discussed a lot about application server resources. In the next chapter, we will see how to manage them using the Command Line Interface and JBoss client libraries.

9
Managing the Application Server

So far we have covered many Java Enterprise examples and deployed them on the application server. We will now dive headlong into the vast and varied ocean of instruments that are available for managing the application server. The ultimate purpose of this chapter is to learn how to use these instruments to administer and monitor all the resources available on the application server.

Here is the list of topics we will cover:

- An introduction to the JBoss **Command Line Interface** (CLI)
- How to create scripts with the CLI
- How to programmatically manage your server resources using scripting languages and the JBoss' client API

Entering the JBoss Command Line Interface (CLI)

The CLI is a complete management tool, which can be used to start and stop servers, deploy and undeploy applications, configure system resources, and perform other administrative tasks. Operations can be performed in an atomic way or in batch modes, allowing multiple tasks to be run as a group.

Launching the CLI

You can start the CLI by entering the following command from the `JBOSS_HOME/bin` folder if you are using Windows:

```
jboss-cli.bat
```

Or enter the following command if you are using Linux:

```
./jboss-cli.sh
```

Once the CLI has started, you can connect to the managed server instance using the `connect` command, which by default connects to `localhost` and the `9999` port:

```
[disconnected /] connect
Connected to domain controller at localhost:9999
```

If you want to connect to another address or port, you can simply pass it to the `connect` command shown as follows:

```
[disconnected /] connect 192.168.1.1
Connected to domain controller at 192.168.1.1:9999
```

It is also possible to launch the CLI in the connected mode, which allows it to connect automatically, and possibly to specify commands to execute. For example, the following shell command automatically connects to an AS 7 instance and issues a `shutdown` command:

```
jboss-cli.bat --connect command=:shutdown
```

Connecting from remote hosts

Starting from the 7.1.0 Beta release of the application server, security is enabled by default on the AS management interfaces to prevent unauthorized remote access to the application server. Although local clients of the application server are still allowed to access the management interfaces without any authentication, remote clients need to enter a username/password pair to access the CLI. Here's an example session that successfully connects to a remote host with the IP address, `10.13.2.255`:

```
[disconnected /] connect 10.13.2.255
Authenticating against security realm: ManagementRealm
Username: administrator
Password:
[standalone@10.13.2.255:9999 /]
```

Please refer to *Chapter 2, What's New in JBoss AS 7* for more information about creating a user with the `add-user.sh` shell command.

Using the CLI in the graphical mode

A useful option available for the Command Line Interface is the graphical mode, which can be activated by adding the `--gui` parameter to the shell script:

```
jboss-cli.bat --gui
```

Here's how the CLI looks in the graphical mode:

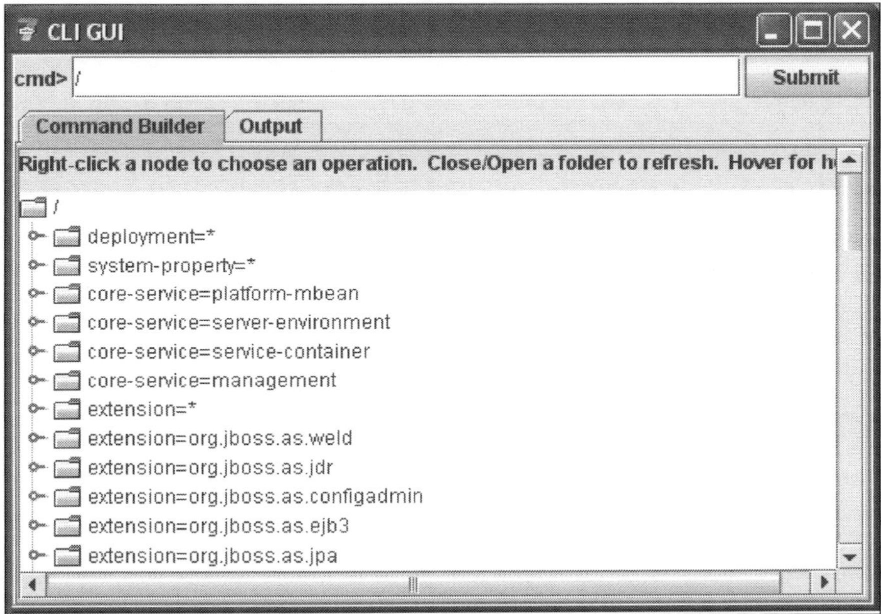

As described in the label, the resource will expand by clicking on a folder; on the other hand, if you can right-click on a node, you can fire an operation on it. The next section discusses constructing CLI commands, which can be executed either in the terminal mode or in the graphical mode.

Constructing the CLI commands

All CLI operation requests allow for low-level interactions with the server management model. They provide a controlled way to edit server configurations. An operation request consists of three parts:

- An address, which is prefixed with a slash (/)
- An operation name, which is prefixed with a colon (:)
- An optional set of parameters contained within parentheses (())

Determining the resource address

The server configuration is presented as a hierarchical tree of addressable resources. Each resource node offers a different set of operations. The address specifies the resource node on which to perform the operation. An address uses the following syntax:

```
/node-type=node-name
```

The notations are explained as follows:

- `node-type`: This is the resource node type. This maps to an element name in the server configuration.
- `node-name`: This specifies the resource node name. This maps to the name attribute of the element in the server configuration.

Separate each level of the resource tree with a slash (/). So, for example, the following CLI expression identifies the HTTP connector, which is part of the web subsystem:

```
/subsystem=web/connector=http
```

Performing operations on resources

Once you have identified a resource, you can perform operations on the resource. An operation uses the following syntax:

```
:operation-name
```

So in the previous example, you can query the list of available resources for your nodes by adding the `read-resource` command at the end of it:

```
/subsystem=web/connector=http/:read-resource()
{
    "outcome" => "success",
    "result" => {
        "enable-lookups" => false,
        "enabled" => true,
        "executor" => undefined,
        "max-connections" => undefined,
        "max-post-size" => 2097152,
        "max-save-post-size" => 4096,
        "name" => "http",
        "protocol" => "HTTP/1.1",
        "proxy-name" => undefined,
```

```
        "proxy-port" => undefined,
        "redirect-port" => 8433,
        "scheme" => "http",
        "secure" => false,
        "socket-binding" => "http",
        "ssl" => undefined,
        "virtual-server" => undefined
    }
}
```

If you want to query for a specific attribute of your node, you can use the `read-attribute` operation instead. For example, the following code shows how to read the `enabled` attribute from the HTTP connector:

```
/subsystem=web/connector=http/:read-attribute(name=enabled)
{
    "outcome" => "success",
    "result" => true
}
```

Apart from the operations on a specific resource, you can also perform a set of commands, which are available on every path of your AS 7 subsystem, such as the `cd` or `ls` commands. These commands are pretty much equivalent to their Unix shell counterparts, and allow navigation through the AS 7 subsystems. Other important additions are the `deploy` and `undeploy` commands, which as you might guess, allow you to manage the deployment of applications. These key commands are discussed in the *Deploying applications using the CLI* section.

The CLI is not however just about querying attributes from the JBoss AS 7 subsystems; you can also set attributes or create resources. For example, if you were to set the HTTP port of the HTTP connector, you have to use the corresponding `write-attribute` on HTTP's socket binding interface, shown as follows:

```
/socket-binding-group=standard-sockets/socket-binding=http/:write-
attribute(name=port,value=8080)
{
    "outcome" => "success",
    "response-headers" => {
        "operation-requires-reload" => true,
        "process-state" => "reload-required"
    }
}
```

Apart from the operations that we have seen so far, (which can be performed on every resource of your subsystems), there can be special operations that can be performed *exclusively* on one resource. For example, within the `naming` subsystem, you are able to issue a `jndi-view` operation that will display the list of JNDI bindings, as shown in the following code snippet:

```
/subsystem=naming/:jndi-view
{
    "outcome" => "success",
    "result" => {"java: contexts" => {
        "java:" => {
            "TransactionManager" => {
                "class-name" => "com.arjuna.ats.jbossatx.jta.
                TransactionManagerDelegate",
                "value" => "com.arjuna.ats.jbossatx.jta.
                TransactionManagerDelegate@afd978"
            },
    . . . .
}
```

Using the tab completion helper

Getting to know all the available commands in CLI is a pretty hard task; however, since its first release, this management interface includes an essential feature, the tab completion. Suppose the cursor is positioned at the beginning of an empty line, if you type in / and press the *Tab* key, you will get a list of all the available node types:

```
[standalone@localhost:9999 /] /

core-service          deployment          extension
interface             path                socket-binding-group
subsystem             system-property
```

After selecting the node type, you want to enter into the tree of resources, so type = and press the *Tab* key again. This will result in a list of all the node names available for the chosen node type:

```
[standalone@localhost:9999 /] /subsystem=

configadmin           datasources          deployment-scanner
ee                    ejb3                 infinispan
jaxrs                 jca                  jdr
```

```
jmx                     jpa                     logging
mail                    naming                  osgi
pojo                    remoting                resource-adapters
sar                     security                threads
transactions            web                     webservices
weld
```

After you have finished with the node path, adding a `:` at the end of the node path and pressing the *Tab* key will print all the available operation names for the selected node:

```
[standalone@localhost:9999 /] /subsystem=deployment-scanner/
scanner=default:

add                             read-attribute
read-children-names             read-children-resources
read-children-types             read-operation-description
read-operation-names            read-resource
read-resource-description       remove
undefine-attribute              whoami
write-attribute
```

To see all the parameters of the operation, add a `(` after the operation name and press the *Tab* key:

```
[standalone@localhost:9999 /] /subsystem=deployment-
scanner/scanner=default:read-attribute(

include-defaults=   name=
```

Choose the parameter you want and specify its value after `=`. Finally, when all the parameters have been specified, add `)` and press *Enter* to issue the command.

Deploying applications using the CLI

Deploying an application (in the standalone mode) can be easily performed by copying the application's archives into the `deployment` folder of your server distribution. That's a pretty handy option; however, we would like to stress on the advantage of using the CLI interface, which offers a wide choice of additional options when deploying, and also provides the opportunity to deploy applications remotely.

All it takes to deploy an application's archive is a connection to the management instance, either local or remote, and by issuing the `deploy` shell command. When used without arguments, the `deploy` command provides the list of applications that are currently deployed, as shown in the following command:

```
[disconnected /] connect
Connected to standalone controller at localhost:9999
[localhost:9999 /] deploy
ExampleApp.war
```

If you feed a resource archive such as a WAR file to the shell, it will deploy it on the standalone server right away:

```
[standalone@localhost:9999 /] deploy ../MyApp.war
'MyApp.war' deployed successfully.
```

By default, the CLI uses the `JBOSS_HOME/bin` file as a source for your deployment archives. You can however, use absolute paths when specifying the location of your archives; the CLI expansion facility (using the *Tab* key) makes this option fairly simple:

```
[standalone@localhost:9999 /] deploy c:\deployments\MyApp.war
'MyApp.war' deployed successfully.
```

Redeploying the application requires an additional flag to the `deploy` command. Use the `-f` argument to force the application's redeployment:

```
[localhost:9999 /] deploy -f ../MyApp.war
'MyApp.war' re-deployed successfully.
```

Undeploying the application can be done through the `undeploy` command, which takes as an argument the application that is deployed:

```
[localhost:9999 /] undeploy MyApp.war
'MyApp.war' undeployed successfully.
```

By checking the AS 7 configuration file (for example `standalone.xml` or `domain.xml`), you will notice that the deployment element for your application has been removed.

Deploying applications to a JBoss AS 7 domain

When you are deploying an application using the domain mode, you have to specify to which server group the deployment is associated. The CLI lets you choose between two options:

- Deploy to all server groups
- Deploy to a single server group

We will discuss these choices in two separate sections.

Deploy to all server groups

If this option is chosen, the application will be deployed to all the available server groups. The `--all-server-groups` flag can be used for this purpose. For example:

```
[domain@localhost:9999 /] deploy ../application.ear --all-server-groups
Successfully deployed application.ear
```

If, on the other hand, you want to undeploy an application from all server groups belonging to a domain, you have to issue the `undeploy` command, as shown in the following command:

```
[domain@localhost:9999 /] undeploy application.ear --all-relevant-server-groups
Successfully undeployed application.ear
```

> You might have noticed that the `undeploy` command uses the `--all-relevant-server-groups` instead of `--all-server-groups`. The reason for this difference is that the deployment may not be enabled on all server groups, so by using this option, you will actually undeploy it just from all the server groups in which the deployment is enabled.

Deploy to a single server group

The other option lets you perform a selective deployment of your application only on the server groups you have indicated:

```
[domain@localhost:9999 /] deploy application.ear --server-groups=main-server-group
Successfully deployed application.ear
```

You are not limited to a single server group, and you can separate multiple server groups with a comma (`,`). For example:

```
[domain@localhost:9999 /] deploy application.ear --server-groups=main-server-group,other-server-group
Successfully deployed application.ear
```

Tab completion will help complete the value for the list of `--server-groups` selected for deployment.

Now, suppose we want to undeploy the application from just one server group. There can be two possible outcomes. If the application is available just on that server group, you will successfully complete the undeployment:

```
[domain@localhost:9999 /] undeploy as7project.war --server-groups=main-server-group
Successfully undeployed as7project.war.
```

On the other hand, if your application is available on other server groups, the following error will be returned by the CLI:

```
Undeploy failed: {"domain-failure-description" => {"Composite operation failed and was rolled back. Steps that failed:" => {"Operation step-3" => "Cannot remove deployment as7project.war from the domain as it is still used by server groups [other-server-group]"}}}
```

It seems that something went wrong. As a matter of fact, when you are removing an application from a server group, the domain controller checks that the application is **not** referenced by any other server group, otherwise the previous command will fail.

You can however, instruct the domain controller to undeploy the application without deleting the content also, as shown in the following command:

```
[domain@localhost:9999 /] undeploy application.ear --server-groups=main-server-group --keep-content
Successfully undeployed application.ear.
```

Creating CLI scripts

As a program developer, you might be interested to know that the CLI is able to execute commands in a non-interactive way, by adding them in a file, just as a shell script. In order to execute the script, you can launch the CLI with the `--file` parameter as in the following example (for Windows):

```
jboss-cli.bat --file=test.cli
```

The equivalent command for Unix users will be:

```
./jboss-cli.sh --file=test.cli
```

In the next section, we will add some useful scripts that can be added to your administrator toolbox.

Deploying an application to several JBoss AS 7 nodes

The earlier JBoss AS releases used to ship with a `farm` folder, which would trigger a deployment to all nodes that are part of a JBoss cluster. This option is not included anymore with JBoss AS 7, but resurrecting a farm deployment is just a matter of a few CLI instructions.

In the following example, we are deploying an application to the default server address (`127.0.0.1` and port `9999`) and to another server instance that is bound to the same address but to port `10199`:

```
connect
deploy /usr/data/example.war
connect 127.0.0.1:10199
deploy /usr/data/example.war
```

Restarting servers in a domain

A common requirement for the domain administrator is to restart the application server nodes, for example, when some server libraries are updated. The CLI provides a handy shortcut for stopping and starting all the servers that are part of a server group:

```
connect
/server-group=main-server-group:start-servers
/server-group=main-server-group:stop-servers
```

If you prefer a more granular approach, you can start the single server nodes as shown in the following example, which shows how you can apply a conditional execution logic in your CLI scripts:

```
connect
if (result == "STARTED") of /host=master/server-config=server-one:read-attribute(name=status)
/host=master/server-config=server-one:stop
end-if

if (result == "STARTED") of /host=master/server-config=server-two:read-attribute(name=status)
/host=master/server-config=server-two:stop
end-if
```

```
/host=master/server-config=server-one:start

/host=master/server-config=server-two:start
```

In the `if end-if` section, we are checking for the server's `status` attribute. If the `status` is `"STARTED"`, the application servers are stopped and then restarted.

The CLI conditional execution is available since the release 7.2.0 Alpha of the application server.

Installing a datasource as a module

Since the 7.2.0 Alpha release of the application server (downloadable as a snapshot at the time of writing at `https://ci.jboss.org/jenkins/job/JBoss-AS-7.x-latest/`), you can use the `module` command in order to install a new module. Therefore, you can fully automate a data source creation as shown in the following example:

```
connect

module add --name=org.mysql --resources=mysql-connector-java-5.1.18-
bin.jar --dependencies=javax.api,javax.transaction.api

/subsystem=datasources/jdbc-driver=mysql:add(driver-module-
name=org.mysql,driver-name=mysql,driver-class-
name=com.mysql.jdbc.Driver)

/subsystem=datasources/data-source=MySQLDS:add(jndi-
name=java:jboss/datasources/MySQLDS, driver-name=mysql, connection-
url=jdbc:mysql://localhost:3306/as7development,user-
name=root,password=admin)
```

The first line of the script, after the connection, installs a new module named `org.mysql` in your server modules' directory, including the MySQL JDBC driver and the required dependencies.

The second line installs the JDBC driver for the `org.mysql` module into the `datasources/jdbc-driver` subsystem.

Finally a datasource is added at the `jndi java:jboss/datasources/MySQLDS` with the required URL and credentials.

Adding JMS resources

Adding a new JMS destination is quite easy since it does not require a lengthy set of commands. However, it is sometimes your application that needs to set up lots of JMS destinations in order to work, so why not create a script for it too? The following is a tiny script that adds a JMS queue to the server configuration:

```
connect
jms-queue add  --queue-address=queue1 --entries=queues/queue1
```

And the following is the corresponding script for creating a JMS topic:

```
connect
jms-topic add  --topic-address=topic1 --entries=topics/topic1
```

Using advanced languages to create powerful CLI scripts

So far, we have learnt how to write CLI shell commands to manage the application server's resources. This approach has the advantage that you can easily access every server resource easily and quickly, thanks to the built-in autocompletion feature. If, on the other hand, you want to perform some sophisticated logic around your commands, then you need to find some other alternatives.

If you are a shell guru, you might easily resort to some bash scripting in order to capture the output of the CLI, and use the rich set of Unix/Linux tools to perform some administrative actions.

Supplying a short overview of the bash functionalities might be an amusing exercise; however, we would move away from the scope of this book. We will instead document some built-in functionalities, such as:

- In the first section, we will show how to use the CLI remote client API from within a Python script
- In the next section we will use the raw management API to execute CLI commands from within Java applications

Using scripting languages to wrap CLI execution

JBoss AS 7 has introduced a new CLI remote API that acts as a façade for the CLI public API. The core class that acts as a bridge between these two APIs is the `scriptsupport.CLI` class, which is contained in the `JBOSS_HOME/bin/client/jboss-client.jar` file.

In order to use these new functionalities, you need to grab one of the latest 7.2.0 snapshots available at `https://ci.jboss.org/jenkins/job/JBoss-AS-7.x-latest/`, or use the RedHat EAP 6.1.0 that is now available for nonproduction use at `http://www.jboss.org/jbossas/downloads`.

Thanks to this API, you can execute CLI commands using lots of different languages such as **Jython**, **Groovy**, or **Rhino**. Since Jython is also the de facto management standard for other application servers (such as Oracle WebLogic and WebSphere), we will use it to perform some basic management tasks.

Jython is an implementation of Python for the JVM. Jython is extremely useful because it provides productivity features of a mature scripting language while running on a JVM. Unlike a Python program, a Jython program can run in any environment that supports a JVM.

Jython is invoked using the `jython` script, which is a short script that invokes your local JVM, running the Java class file, `org.python.util.jython`.

The first thing you have to do in order to get started is, download Jython installer from `http://www.jython.org/downloads.html`.

Run the installer with:

```
java -jar jython_installer-2.5.2.jar
```

Next, add the `JYTHON_HOME/bin` folder (for example, `C:\jython2.5.3\bin`) to the system path and add the `jboss-cli-client.jar` file to the system, `CLASSPATH`. For example, on Windows, follow the given command:

```
set PATH=%PATH%;C:\jython2.5.3\bin


set CLASSPATH=%CLASSPATH%;C:\jboss-as-7.2.0.Alpha1-SNAPSHOT\bin\client\jboss-cli-client.jar;.
```

And here follows the same command on Linux:

```
export PATH=$PATH:/usr/data/ jython2.5.3/bin
export CLASSPATH=$CLASSPATH$:/usr/data/jboss-as-7.2.0.Alpha1-
SNAPSHOT/bin/client/jboss-cli-client.jar
```

Ok, now we will create our first script that will basically return the JNDI view of our application server.

Be aware that Jython, just like Python, uses indentation to determine the code structure instead of using braces or keywords. Therefore, do not use them randomly!

Create a file named `script.py` containing the following code:

```
from org.jboss.as.cli.scriptsupport import CLI


cli = CLI.newInstance()
cli.connect()


cli.cmd("cd /subsystem=naming")


result = cli.cmd(":jndi-view")
response = result.getResponse()


print 'JNDI VIEW ====================== '
print response
cli.disconnect()
```

Now execute the script with the following code:

```
jython script.py
```

As you can see, the code is very self explanatory; we are importing the `org.jboss.as.cli.scriptsupport.CLI` class, which is used to send commands and read the response. Then we are connecting to the local AS 7 instance and issuing a `":jndi-view"` command.

The `connect` command can be used for connecting to a remote AS 7 host as well by adding the following parameters: `connect, (String controllerHost, int controllerPort, String username, String password)`.

The response variable is an `org.jboss.dmr.ModelNode` type, which can be further inspected, as shown in the following example, which goes in to some depth about platform MBeans, to get some memory statistics:

```
from org.jboss.as.cli.scriptsupport import CLI


cli = CLI.newInstance()
cli.connect()


cli.cmd("cd /core-service=platform-mbean/type=memory/")


result = cli.cmd(":read-resource(recursive=false,proxies=false,include-
runtime=true,include-
defaults=true)")


response = result.getResponse()
enabled = response.get("result").get("heap-memory-usage")


used = enabled.get("used").asInt()


if used > 512000000:
    print "Over 1/2 Gb Memory usage "
else:
    print 'Low usage!'


cli.disconnect()
```

In the previous example, we are tracking the resources contained in `/core-service=platform-mbean/type=memory`. The available resources are however child resources of the two kinds of available heap memory areas (`heap-memory-usage` and `non-heap-memory-usage`), as shown by the following code:

```
[standalone@localhost:9999 /] /core-service=platform-mbean/
type=memory:read-resource(recursive=false,proxies=false,
include-runtime=true,include-defaults=true)
{
    "outcome" => "success",
    "result" => {
```

```
        "heap-memory-usage" => {
            "init" => 67108864L,
            "used" => 59572256L,
            "committed" => 170852352L,
            "max" => 477233152L
        },
        "non-heap-memory-usage" => {
            "init" => 24313856L,
            "used" => 90491328L,
            "committed" => 90701824L,
            "max" => 369098752L
        },
        "object-pending-finalization-count" => 0,
        "verbose" => false
    }
}
```

By using just the `get` command of the `ModelNode` object, you can reference the child resources of the memory type, and reach all the single attributes. Once you have got the attributes, it's easy to cast them to an integer using the `asInt()` function of the `ModelNode` object, and use the cool Python constructs to alert your administrator.

Using the raw management API to manage the application server

If you don't feel like learning a scripting language to manage the application server, you can still use the raw management API from within your Java classes. Don't be influenced by the fact that we left this option as the last one; in fact, using the native management API is not difficult at all since it is based on very few classes and has little compile-time and runtime dependencies on the JBoss API.

For this reason, you can use the management API as well from any Java EE application, by simply adding the following dependencies in the `META-INF/MANIFEST.MF` file of your application:

```
Dependencies: org.jboss-as-controller-client,org.jboss.dmr
```

The core API named **detyped management API** is quite simple; the primary class is `org.jboss.dmr.ModelNode`, which we already mentioned in the Jython section. A `ModelNode` is essentially just a wrapper around a value; the value is typically a basic JDK type, which can be retrieved using the `getType()` method of `ModelNode`.

In addition to the `jboss-dmr` API, the other module that is used to connect to the management API is `jboss-as-controller-client`.

You don't need to download any of these libraries, since both of these modules are included in the application server release 7.

Reading management model descriptions via the raw management API

Using the detyped management API is not too different from the scripting language counterpart; at first, you need to create a **management client** that can connect to your target process's native management socket (which can be an individual standalone mode server, or in a domain mode environment, the domain controller):

```
ModelControllerClient client = ModelControllerClient.Factory.
create(InetAddress.getByName("localhost"), 9999);
```

Next, you need to create an operation request object using the `org.jboss.dmr.ModelNode` class, as shown in the following command:

```
ModelNode op = new ModelNode();
op.get("operation").set("jndi-view");

ModelNode address = op.get("address");
address.add("subsystem", "naming");

op.get("recursive").set(true);
op.get("operations").set(true);

ModelNode returnVal = client.execute(op);
out.println(returnVal.get("result").toString());
```

As you can see, the `ModelNode` objects can be chained in order to reach an operation (in the example, the JNDI view), which is available on a node path (in our case the naming subsystem).

Once you have added the `ModelNode` attributes, you can issue the `execute` commands on your node, which will in turn return `ModelNode`, where the result of the operation will be stored.

Creating your resource watches using the detyped API

Now that you have learned the basics of the detyped management API, we will illustrate a concrete example; our goal will be monitoring a server resource (the number of active JDBC connections for a datasource) using an EJB. You can use this pattern to create your own server watches, which can be integrated with your application environment:

```
import java.io.IOException;
import java.net.*;
import java.util.logging.Logger;

import javax.annotation.Resource;
import javax.ejb.*;

import org.jboss.as.controller.client.ModelControllerClient;
import org.jboss.dmr.ModelNode;

@Stateless
public class WatchMyDB
{

  private final static Logger logger = Logger.getLogger(WatchMyDB.class.
getName()  );());

  @Resource
  private TimerService timerService;

  @Schedule(dayOfWeek = "*", hour = "*", minute = "*", second =
  "*/30",year="*", persistent = false)
  public void backgroundProcessing()
  {
    ModelControllerClient client=null;
    try {
      client =
      ModelControllerClient.Factory.create
      (InetAddress.getByName("localhost"), 9999);
```

```
      ModelNode op = new ModelNode();
      op.get("operation").set("read-resource");
      op.get("include-runtime").set(true);

      ModelNode address = op.get("address");
      address.add("subsystem", "datasources");
      address.add("data-source", "ExampleDS");
      address.add("statistics", "pool");
      ModelNode returnVal=null;
      returnVal = client .execute(op);

      ModelNode node2 = returnVal .get("result");
      String _activeCount = node2.get("ActiveCount").asString();

      if (_activeCount.equals("undefined")) {
        return; // Connection unused
      }
      int activeCount = Integer.parseInt(_activeCount);

      if (activeCount > 50) {
        alertAdministrator(); // Implement it !
      }
    }
    catch (Exception exc) {
      logger.info("Excepton ! "+exc.getMessage());
    }
    finally {
      safeClose(client);

    }
  }
  public static void safeClose(final Closeable closeable) {
    if (closeable != null) try {
      closeable.close();
```

```
    } catch (Exception e) {
      logger.info("Excepton closing the client! "+e.getMessage());
    }
  }

}
```

We will not rehash the basic concepts about EJB Timers, which have been discussed in *Chapter 3, Beginning Java EE 6 – EJBs*. We suggest that you have a look at the highlighted section of the code, which shows how you can chain your `ModelNode` objects in order to reach the attribute that we are going to monitor (the `activeCount` attribute of the `ExampleDS` datasource).

Once you have the value of the `activeCount` attribute, we leave to your imagination all the possible actions you can undertake!

Summary

In this chapter, we have covered the application server's management API from a developer's perspective, which will enable you to write your own scripts to monitor the health of your application server.

The most effective tool for monitoring the application server is the Command Line Interface. However, if you want to spice it up with some typical programming logic, you can resort to some other alternatives such as scripting languages or the raw management API.

We have now completed our review of management, in the next chapter we are going to discuss clustering, which is the environment where critical applications are deployed.

10
Clustering JBoss AS 7 Applications

In the former chapters, we went through the most interesting aspects of Java Enterprise development. Once you are ready to rollout your applications, it is mandatory that you guarantee your customers a responsive and reliable environment. This requirement is usually achieved through application server clustering.

JBoss clustering is not the product of a single library or specification, but rather a blend of technologies. In this chapter, we will first introduce some basics about clustered programming. Next, we will quickly move to the cluster configuration and setup, which will be required to deploy some clustered applications.

Here is a preview of what we will learn from this unit:

- What clustering is, and how JBoss AS implements it
- Setting up a standalone and a domain of application server clusters
- Developing clustered Java EE 6 applications in order to achieve load balancing and high availability

Clustering basics

A cluster of application servers consists of multiple server instances (cluster nodes) running simultaneously and working together to provide increased scalability and reliability. The nodes that make up the cluster can be located either on the same machine or on different machines. From the client's point of view, this is irrelevant because the cluster appears as a single server instance.

Introducing clustering in your applications will produce the following benefits:

- **Scalability**: Adding a new node to a cluster should allow the overall system to service a higher client load than that provided by the simple basic configuration. Ideally, it should be possible to service any given load simply by adding the appropriate number of servers or machines.
- **Load balancing**: In a clustered environment, the individual nodes composing the cluster should each process a fair share of the overall client load. This can be achieved by distributing client requests across multiple servers, which is also known as load balancing.
- **High availability**: Applications running in a cluster can continue when a server instance fails. This is achieved because applications are deployed on multiple nodes of the cluster, and so if a server instance fails, another server instance on which that component is deployed can continue application processing.

JBoss AS 7 clustering

JBoss AS comes out of the box with clustering support. There is no all-in-one library that deals with clustering, but rather a set of libraries that cover different kinds of aspects.

The following diagram shows the basic clustering architecture adopted by JBoss AS 7:

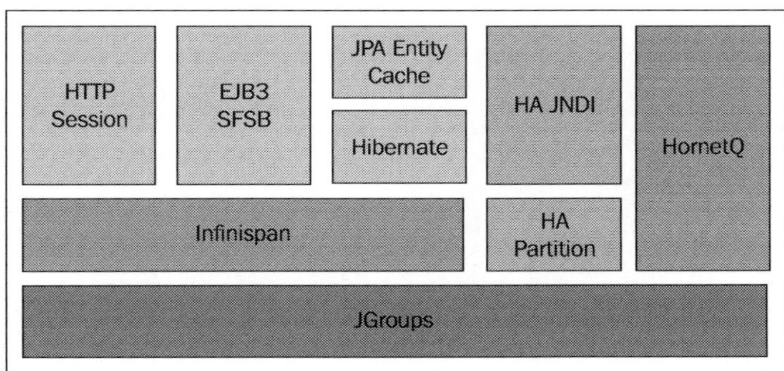

The backbone of JBoss clustering is the **JGroups** library, which provides communication between members of the cluster using a multicast transmission.

Multicast is a protocol where data is transmitted simultaneously to a group of hosts that have joined the appropriate multicast group. You can think about multicast as a radio or television streaming, where only those tuned to a particular frequency receive the streaming.

The next building block is **Infinispan**, which handles the consistency of your application across the cluster by means of a replicated and transactional JSR-107-compatible cache.

JSR-107 specifies the API and semantics for temporary, in-memory caching of Java objects, including object creation, shared access, spooling, invalidation, and consistency across JVMs.

Before getting started with some cluster examples, we will first need to describe how to set up a cluster of JBoss AS 7 nodes using the two available nodes: **standalone cluster** and **domain cluster**.

Starting a cluster of standalone nodes

A standalone server starts as a single JVM process; therefore, we need to start each server using the `standalone.bat/standalone.cmd` command, passing all the required parameters. In the following example, we are starting a cluster of two server nodes on two different boxes that are bound to the IP addresses `192.168.1.1` and `192.168.1.2` respectively:

```
./standalone.sh -c standalone-ha.xml -b 192.168.1.1
./standalone.sh -c standalone-ha.xml -b 192.168.1.2
```

The `-c` parameter specifies the server configuration to be used; out of the box, the application server includes two standalone clustering configurations: `standalone-ha.xml` and `standalone-full-ha.xml`. The latter one also includes the messaging subsystem; therefore, it has been named the "full" configuration.

The other parameter (`-b`) should sound familiar to the older JBoss users, as it's still used to specify the server-bind address, which needs to be unique in order to avoid port conflicts.

In this other example, we are starting another cluster of two nodes on the same box using some additional parameters in order to avoid port conflicts:

```
./standalone.sh -c standalone-ha.xml -Djboss.node.name=node1
./standalone.sh -c standalone-ha.xml -Djboss.node.name=node2 -Djboss.
socket.binding.port-offset=200
```

As you can see, we had to specify two additional parameters: `jboss.node.name`, in order to assign a unique server name to each node, and a socket-binding port, which uses an offset of `200`. So for example, the second node would respond to the HTTP channel on port `8280` instead of port `8080`.

Don't be surprised if you don't see any message about clustering on your server console. Clustering modules are activated on demand, so at first you need to deploy an application that is cluster-aware. In a few minutes, we will show you how.

Starting a cluster of domain nodes

In order to configure a cluster running on a domain of server nodes, you need to configure the main `domain.xml` file for your domain controller, and then, for every AS 7 host that is a part of the cluster, you need to provide a `host.xml` configuration file, which describes the configuration of a single-server distribution.

The domain configuration has been enhanced in the latest AS 7 builds and in the current EAP 6 platform. It is available for download at `http://www.jboss.org/jbossas/downloads`; therefore, you need to upgrade your current AS 7.1.1 release in order to be able to complete the following steps.

The domain controller configuration

The `domain.xml` file is located at `JBOSS_HOME/domain/configuration/`. It includes the main domain configuration, which is shared by all server instances. In the `domain.xml` file, we will define the server group configurations, specifying a profile that is compatible with clustering. Out of the box, a JBoss AS 7 domain ships with four different profiles:

- `default`: This profile has the support of Java EE Web Profile and some extensions, such as RESTful web services or support for EJB 3 remote invocations

- `full` :This profile supports all the default subsystems contained in the default profile and the messaging subsystem
- `ha`: This profile corresponds to the default profile with clustering capabilities
- `full-ha`: This is the full profile with clustering capabilities

So, first specify in your `domain.xml` file a cluster-aware profile for your server groups. In our example, we have adopted the `full-ha` profile for both server groups so that you can run the full Java EE stack on all your domain servers:

```
<server-groups>
        <server-group name="main-server-group" profile="full-ha">
            <jvm name="default">
                <heap size="64m" max-size="512m"/>
            </jvm>
            <socket-binding-group ref="full-sockets"/>
        </server-group>
        <server-group name="other-server-group" profile="full-ha">
            <jvm name="default">
                <heap size="64m" max-size="512m"/>
            </jvm>
            <socket-binding-group ref="full-sockets"/>
        </server-group>
</server-groups>
```

In addition to the `domain.xml` file, you need to check that your domain controller's `host.xml` file contains a reference to the local domain controller, as shown in the following code snippet:

```
<host name="master" xmlns="urn:jboss:domain:1.3">
    ...
    <domain-controller>
       <local/>
    </domain-controller>
    ...
</host>
```

In case your domain controller is located on a remote host, the preceding configuration requires to specify the remote domain controller host and its port (in this example we have added some variables as placeholders):

```
<host name="master" xmlns="urn:jboss:domain:1.3">
    ...
    <domain-controller>
       <remote host="${jboss.domain.master.address}"  port="${jboss.
       domain.master.port}" />
```

```
    </domain-controller>
    ...
</host>
```

Finally, you need to create a management user that will be used to establish a connection between the slave nodes and the domain controller. For this purpose, launch the `add-user.sh/add-user.cmd` script, which is located in `JBOSS_HOME/bin` of your distribution:

```
C:\Windows\system32\cmd.exe
What type of user do you wish to add?
 a) Management User (mgmt-users.properties)
 b) Application User (application-users.properties)
(a): a

Enter the details of the new user to add.
Realm (ManagementRealm) :
Username : admin1234
Password :
Re-enter Password :
About to add user 'admin1234' for realm 'ManagementRealm'
Is this correct yes/no? yes
Added user 'admin1234' to file 'C:\jboss\jboss-eap-6.1\standalone\configuration\
mgmt-users.properties'
Added user 'admin1234' to file 'C:\jboss\jboss-eap-6.1\domain\configuration\mgmt
-users.properties'
Is this new user going to be used for one AS process to connect to another AS pr
ocess?
e.g. for a slave host controller connecting to the master or for a Remoting conn
ection for server to server EJB calls.
yes/no? yes
To represent the user add the following to the server-identities definition <sec
ret value="QWxlc3NhbmRybzIh" />
Press any key to continue . . .
```

As you can see from the preceding screenshot, you have to create a management user by specifying a username and a password for it. You should answer the previous question with `yes` or `y` to indicate that the user will be used to connect to the domain controller from the host controller. The generated secret value is the Base64-encoded password of the newly created user.

> Please note that in the earlier example we have used a latest snapshot of JBoss AS 7.2. The current JBoss AS 7.1.1 release will not display the secret key, which is a Base64-encoded version of your password. You can use any free Base64 utility such as `http://www.motobit.com/util/base64-decoder-encoder.asp` to convert your password into a Base64-encoded password.

Now we can start the domain controller by specifying the address that will be used for the public and management interfaces (in our example `192.168.1.1`) with the following command:

```
domain.sh -b 192.168.1.1 -Djboss.bind.address.management=192.168.1.1
```

We have set the physical network bind address to the host configuration with the jboss.bind.address.management property. The management interface must be reachable for all hosts in the domain in order to establish a connection with the domain controller.

Host configurations

After the domain controller is configured and started, the next step is to set up the other hosts that will connect to the domain controller. On each host, we also need an installation of JBoss AS 7, where we will configure the host.xml file (as an alternative you can name the host file as you like, and start the domain with the -host-config parameter. For example, ./domain.sh -host-config=host-slave.xml.)

The first thing is to choose a unique name for each host in our domain in order to avoid name conflicts. Otherwise, the default is the hostname of the server.

```
<host name="server1" xmlns="urn:jboss:domain:1.4">
    ...
</host>
```

And for the other host:

```
<host name="server2" xmlns="urn:jboss:domain:1.4">
    ...
</host>
```

Next, we need to specify that the host controller will connect to a remote domain controller. We will not specify the actual IP address of the domain controller, but leave it as a property named jboss.domain.master.address.

Additionally, we need to specify the username that will be used to connect to the domain controller. So let's add the user admin1234, which we have created on the domain controller machine:

```
<domain-controller>
        <remote host="${jboss.domain.master.address}"
port="${jboss.domain.master.port:9999}"
        username="admin1234"
        security-realm="ManagementRealm"/>
</domain-controller>
```

Finally, we need to specify the Base64 password for the server identity that we have included in the remote element:

```
<management>
   <security-realms>
      <security-realm name="ManagementRealm">
```

```
            <server-identities>
               <secret value="QWxlc3NhbmRybzIh" />
            </server-identities>
            <authentication>
               <properties path="mgmt-users.properties"
               relative-to="jboss.domain.config.dir" />
            </authentication>
         </security-realm>
         <security-realm name="ApplicationRealm">
            <authentication>
               <properties path="application-users.properties"
               relative-to="jboss.domain.config.dir" />
            </authentication>
         </security-realm>
      </security-realms>
      <management-interfaces>
         <native-interface security-realm="ManagementRealm">
            <socket interface="management" port="${jboss.management.
   native.port:9999}" />
         </native-interface>
      </management-interfaces>
   </management>
```

The final step is to configure the server nodes inside the `host.xml` file on both hosts. So, on the first host, we will configure `server-one` and `server-two` to belong to `main-server-group`:

```
<servers>
        <server name="server-one" group="main-server-group"/>
        <server name="server-two" group="main-server-group"
        auto-start="false">
            <socket-bindings port-offset="150"/>
        </server>
</servers>
```

And on the second host, we will configure `server-three` and `server-four` to belong to `other-server-group`:

```
<servers>
     <server name="server-three" group="other-server-group"/>
     <server name="server-four" group="other-server-group">
     auto-start="false">
            <socket-bindings port-offset="150"/>
     </server>
</servers>
```

Please note that the `auto-start` flag indicates that the server instances will not be started automatically if the host controller is started.

For `server-two` and `server-four`, a `port-offset` value of `150` is configured to avoid port conflicts. Okay, now we are done with our configuration. Assuming that the first host has an IP address of `192.168.1.2`, we can then start the first host with the following code snippet:

```
domain.sh \
-b 192.168.1.2
-Djboss.domain.master.address=192.168.1.1
-Djboss.bind.address.management=192.168.1.2
```

The second host(`192.168.1.3`) can be started with the following code snippet:

```
domain.sh \
-b 192.168.1.3
-Djboss.domain.master.address=192.168.1.1
-Djboss.bind.address.management=192.168.1.3
```

Deploying clustered applications

If you have tried starting your standalone or domain set of cluster nodes, you will be surprised that there is no information at all about clustering in your server logging. Believe it, it is not a bug, but a feature! One of the key features of JBoss AS 7 is that only a minimal set of services is started; therefore, in order to see a cluster's live demonstration, you need to deploy a cluster-aware application. In order to trigger clustering libraries in your application, you can follow two approaches:

- If your application uses Enterprise JavaBeans, you can tag it as clusterable by adding a JBoss proprietary annotation, (`@org.jboss.ejb3.annotation.Clustered`), or via the EJB configuration file (`jboss-ejb3.xml`)
- If your application includes a web application archive, you can use the portable `<distributable />` element in your `web.xml` file. Let's see both the approaches, starting from clustering EJBs.

Clustering EJBs

All that is necessary to cluster an EJB is to mark (annotate) the EJB component explicitly as `clustered` by adding the `@org.jboss.ejb3.annotation.Clustered` annotation to your EJB at the class level. You can apply this annotation on your stateless EJB, enabling load balancing over the cluster nodes for a remote client:

```
@Stateless
@Clustered
public class StatelessLBBean
{
public void doSomething()
{
// Do something
}
}
```

On the other hand, marking a stateful EJB enables, in addition to load balancing, the replication of session data between the cluster nodes:

```
@Stateful
@Clustered
public class StatefulHABean
{
public void doSomething()
{
// Do something
}
}
```

If you prefer to keep your code "neutral" from this point of view, you can use the clustered element into the `jboss-ejb3.xml` file, as shown in the following code snippet:

```
<jboss xmlns="http://www.jboss.com/xml/ns/javaee"
       xmlns:jee="http://java.sun.com/xml/ns/javaee"
       xmlns:c="urn:clustering:1.0">


    <jee:assembly-descriptor>
        <c:clustering>
            <jee:ejb-name>StatefulHABean</jee:ejb-name>
            <c:clustered>true</c:clustered>
        </c:clustering>
    </jee:assembly-descriptor>
</jboss>
```

Creating HA Stateful Session Beans

Clustered SFSB have built-in failover capabilities. This means that the state of the `@Stateful` and `@Clustered` EJBs are replicated across the cluster nodes so that if one of the nodes in the cluster goes down, some other node will be able to take over the invocations.

The following diagram depicts a typical exchange of information between the EJB client application and the remote EJB component:

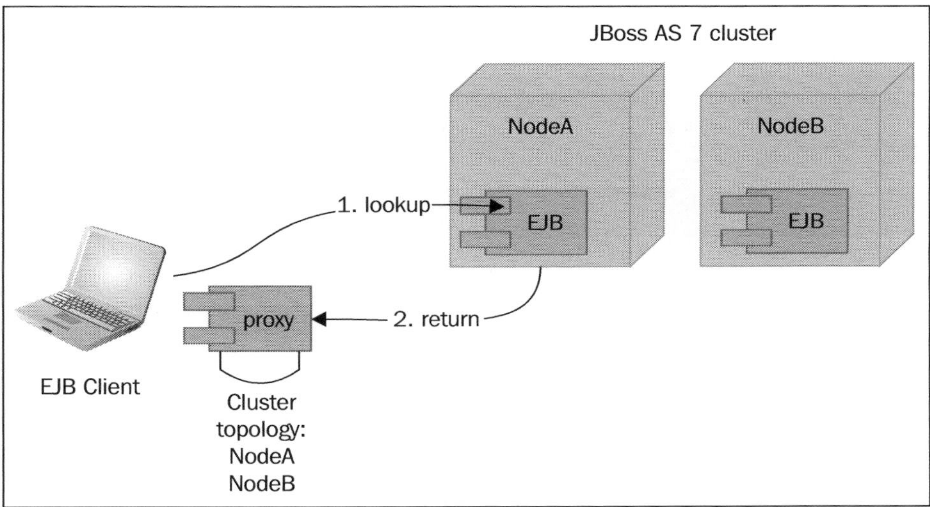

As you can see, after a successful lookup of an SFSB via JNDI, a proxy is returned to the client for subsequent method invocations.

Since the EJB is clustered, it will return back a session ID and along with it the "affinity" of that session, that is, the name of the cluster to which the stateful bean belongs on the server side. This affinity will later help the EJB client to route the invocations on the proxy appropriately to a specific node in the cluster.

While this session creation request is going on, **NodeA** will also send back an asynchronous message that contains the cluster topology. The JBoss **EJB client** implementation will take note of this topology information, and will later use it for creation of connections to nodes within the cluster and routing invocations to those nodes, whenever necessary.

Now let's assume that **NodeA** goes down, and the client application subsequently invokes on the proxy. At this stage the JBoss **EJB client** implementation will be aware of the cluster topology; therefore, it knows that the cluster has two nodes: **NodeA** and **NodeB**. When the invocation now arrives, it detects that the **NodeA** is down; so it uses a selector to fetch a suitable node from among the cluster nodes.

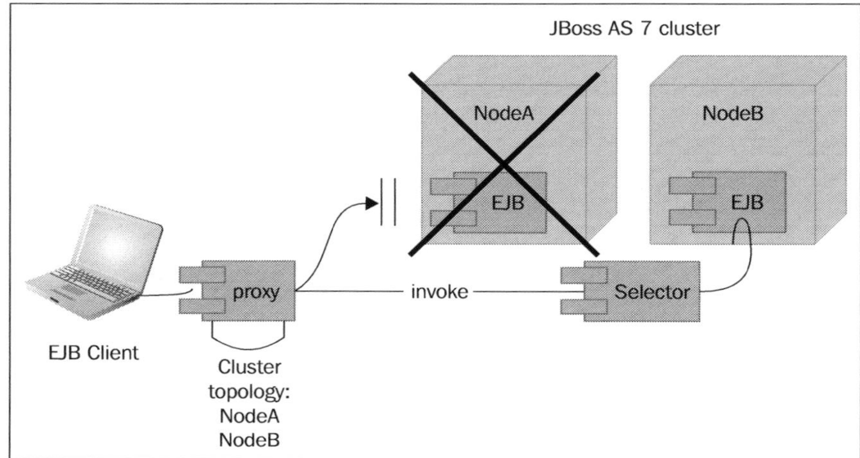

If a suitable node is found, the JBoss **EJB client** implementation creates a connection to that node (in our case **NodeB**) and creates an EJB receiver out of it. At the end of this process, the invocation has now been effectively failed over to a different node within the cluster.

Clustering the Ticket example

In *Chapter 3, Beginning Java EE 6 – EJBs*, we have shown our Ticket System example, which was built around the following:

- A stateful EJB to hold the session data
- A singleton EJB to store the cache of data
- A stateless EJB to perform some business methods

Let's see how to apply the necessary changes to move our application in a cluster context.

So let's start from our stateful EJB:

```
@Stateful
@Remote(TheatreBooker.class)
@Clustered
public class TheatreBookerBean implements TheatreBooker {
```

```
    private static final Logger logger =
        Logger.getLogger(TheatreBookerBean.class);

    int money;
    @EJB TheatreBox theatreBox;

    @PostConstruct
    public void createCustomer() {
      this.money=100;
    }



    public String bookSeat(int seatId) throws SeatBookedException,NotEno
ughMoneyException {
        // Unchanged method
    }
  }
```

As you can see, the only relevant change to our stateful EJB is the `@org.jboss.ejb3.annotation.Clustered` annotation, which is added at the class level. We can also apply this annotation in the stateless EJB, which will add load-balancing capabilities to your business methods, there by improving its scalability:

```
@Clustered
@Stateless
@Remote(TheatreInfo.class)
public class  TheatreInfoBean implements TheatreInfo  {
@EJB TheatreBox box;

@Override
public StringBuffer printSeatList() {
// Unchanged method

}


}
```

As it is, our Ticket application is ready to be deployed in a cluster; however, there's a last pitfall. As a matter of fact, the singleton EJB used to hold the cache of seat will be instantiated once in each JVM of the cluster. This means that if there's a server failure, the data in the cache will be lost and a new one (unsynchronized) will be used.

There are several alternatives to set up a cache in a clustered environment:

- Use a JBoss proprietary solution that is deploying a clustered version of `SingletonService`, which exposes an HA-singleton of `org.jboss.msc.service.Service` (An example of this approach is contained in the JBoss quickstart demo at `https://github.com/jboss-jdf/jboss-as-quickstart/tree/master/cluster-ha-singleton`)
- Move your cache to a persistent storage, which means using JPA to store and read data from the cache (See *Chapter 5, Combining Persistence with CDI*, which includes a JPA-based example of our application)
- Use a distributed data cache such as Infinispan to store our data, providing a failover and data consistency to your cache

Showing all possible solution implementations would, however, make this section excessively long; therefore, we will illustrate how to pursue the last option, which can provide a good architectural pattern with the least amount of effort.

Turning your cache into a distributed cache

Infinispan is a distributed data grid platform that exposes a JSR-107-compatible cache interface in which you can store data and enhance it by providing additional APIs and features (such as transactional cache, data eviction and expiration, asynchronous operations on the cache, and more). Its primary interface is `javax.cache.Cache`, which is similar to the Java SE `java.util.ConcurrentMap`, with some modifications for distributed environments. In particular, it adds the ability to register, deregister, and list event listeners, and it defines a `CacheLoader` interface for loading/storing cached data. Cache instances can be retrieved using an appropriate `CacheManager`, which represents a collection of caches.

So here's our singleton `TheatreBox` class rewritten using the Infinispan API:

```
@Singleton
@Startup
public class TheatreBox {
  @Resource(lookup="java:jboss/infinispan/container/cluster")
  private org.infinispan.manager.CacheContainer container;
  private org.infinispan.Cache<Integer, Seat> cache;
  private static final Logger logger =
      Logger.getLogger(TheatreBox.class);
  @PostConstruct  public void start() {
     try {
         cache = container.getCache();
         logger.info("Got Infinispan cache");
            setupTheatre();
```

```
        } catch ( Exception e) {
              logger.info("Error! "+e.getMessage());


        }

      }
   public void setupTheatre(){

     int id = 0;
     for (int i=0;i<5;i++) {
       int cacheid=++id;
       Seat seat = new Seat(cacheid,"Stalls",40);
       cache.put(new Integer(cacheid), seat);
     }
     for (int i=0;i<5;i++) {
       int cacheid=++id;
       Seat seat = new Seat(cacheid,"Circle",20);
       cache.put(new Integer(cacheid), seat);
     }
     for (int i=0;i<5;i++) {
       int cacheid=++id;
       Seat seat = new Seat(cacheid,"Balcony",10);
       cache.put(new Integer(cacheid), seat);
     }
     logger.info("Seat Map constructed.");

   }
   public List<Seat> getSeatList() {
     List<Seat> dataList = new ArrayList<Seat>();
     dataList.addAll(cache.values());
     return dataList;
   }

   public Seat getSeat(int seatId) {
     return cache.get(seatId);
   }

   public void buyTicket(int seatId )      {
     Seat seat = cache.get(seatId);
     seat.setBooked(true);
     cache.put(seatId,seat);
   }
}
```

```
    public Seat getSeat(int seatId) {

        return cache.get(seatId);
    }


    public void buyTicket(int seatId )      {

        Seat seat = cache.get(seatId);
        seat.setBooked(true);
        cache.put(seatId,seat);

    }

    }
```

The first thing we want to stress is the `@Resource` annotation, which injects a `org.infinispan.manager.CacheContainer` instance; when the JBoss AS deployer encounters this annotation, your application will include a dependency on the requested cache container. Consequently, the cache container will automatically start deploying and stop (including all caches) undeploying of your application.

> Please notice that the `@Resource` annotation bears a `lookup` attribute, which is not included in the default JDK implementation of the `@javax.annotation.Resource` annotation. In order to solve this issue and avoid a compilation problem, you need to copy the JAR file `jboss-annotations-api_1.X_spec-1.X.X.Final.jar` (contained in `JBOSS_HOME/modules/javax/annotation/api/main`) into `JAVA_HOME/jre/lib/endorsed` of your JDK distribution. As an alternative, you can pass `-Djava.endorsed.dirs` to the JVM parameters, indicating the folder where the JBoss API is located.

Subsequently, when the EJB is instantiated (see the method `start`, which is annotated as `@PostConstruct`), `org.infinispan.Cache` is created using `CacheContainer` as a factory. This cache will be used to store our highly available set of data.

The operations performed against the distributed cache are quite intuitive: the `put` method is used to store instances of the `Seat` object in the cache and the corresponding `get` method is used to retrieve elements from it, just what you would do from an ordinary hashtable.

As far as application deployment is concerned, you need to state a dependency to the Infinispan API explicitly, which is not included as an implicit dependency in the AS 7 class loading policy. This is most easily done by adding the following line to your application's `META-INF/MANIFEST.MF`:

```
Dependencies: org.infinispan export
```

Coding the cluster-aware remote client

The remote EJB client will not need any particular change in order to be able to achieve high availability. We have added a `pressAKey` method between each ticket transaction so that you will be able to shut down the application server that is pinned to our EJB client, and thus test failover on the other server node:

```
private static void testRemoteEJB() throws NamingException {


    final TheatreInfo theatreInfo = lookupTheatreInfoEJB();
    final TheatreBooker theatreBook = lookupTheatreBookerEJB();

    try {
      String retVal = theatreBook.bookSeat(5);
      logger.info(retVal);
      logger.info(theatreInfo.printSeatList().toString());
    }

    catch ( Exception e) {
      logger.info(e.getMessage());
    }
    logger.info("Press [Enter] to continue");
      // Await for key press. Not included for brevity
    pressAKey();

    try {
      String retVal = theatreBook.bookSeat(7);
      logger.info(retVal);
      logger.info(theatreInfo.printSeatList().toString());
    }

    catch ( Exception e) {
      logger.info(e.getMessage());
    }
}
```

Now that we are done with the client, our last effort would be deploying a `jboss-ejb-client.properties` file, which will contain the list of servers that will be initially contacted (via remoting) by our client application:

```
remote.connectionprovider.create.options.org.xnio.Options.SSL_
ENABLED=false
remote.connections=node1,node2
remote.connection.node1.host=localhost
remote.connection.node1.port = 4447
remote.connection.node1.connect.options.org.xnio.Options.SASL_POLICY_
NOANONYMOUS=false

remote.connection.node2.host=localhost
remote.connection.node2.port = 4647
remote.connection.node2.connect.options.org.xnio.Options.SASL_POLICY_
NOANONYMOUS=false
```

As you can see from this file, we assume that you are running a two-node cluster on the `localhost` address, the first one running the default port settings and the second one using an offset of `200` (just as shown in the second paragraph of the *Starting a cluster of standalone nodes* section).

Replace the `remote.connection.nodeX.host` variable value with the actual IP or host if you are running your server nodes on different machines from your client.

Deploying and testing high availability

Deploying an application to a cluster can be achieved in several ways; if you prefer automation instead of copying each archive into the `deployments` folder, you can re-use the CLI deployment script contained in the earlier chapter.

Alternatively, if you are using JBoss'Maven plugin to deploy, you can parameterize its configuration, including the hostname and the port as variables, which will be passed to the command line:

```
<plugin>
      <groupId>org.jboss.as.plugins</groupId>
      <artifactId>jboss-as-maven-plugin</artifactId>
      <version>${version.org.jboss.as.plugins.maven.plugin}</version>
      <configuration>
          <filename>${project.build.finalName}.jar</filename>
          <hostname>${hostname}</hostname>
          <port>${port}</port>
      </configuration>
</plugin>
```

Therefore, you will use the following shell to compile the package and deploy the application on the first node:

```
mvn install jboss-as:deploy -Dhostname=localhost -Dport=9999
```

For the second node, you will use the following:

```
mvn install jboss-as:deploy -Dhostname=localhost -Dport=10199
```

> Deploying in the domain node works the same as in the preceding example, except that you need to add the `domain` tag in your configuration, and you also need to specify at least one server group. Visit `https://docs.jboss.org/jbossas/7/plugins/maven/latest/examples/deployment-example.html` for more information about it.

Once you have deployed both applications on your server node, you should be able to see the cluster view in the server console logs, and also see that the Infinispan cache has been started. The following is the expected log for the first node:

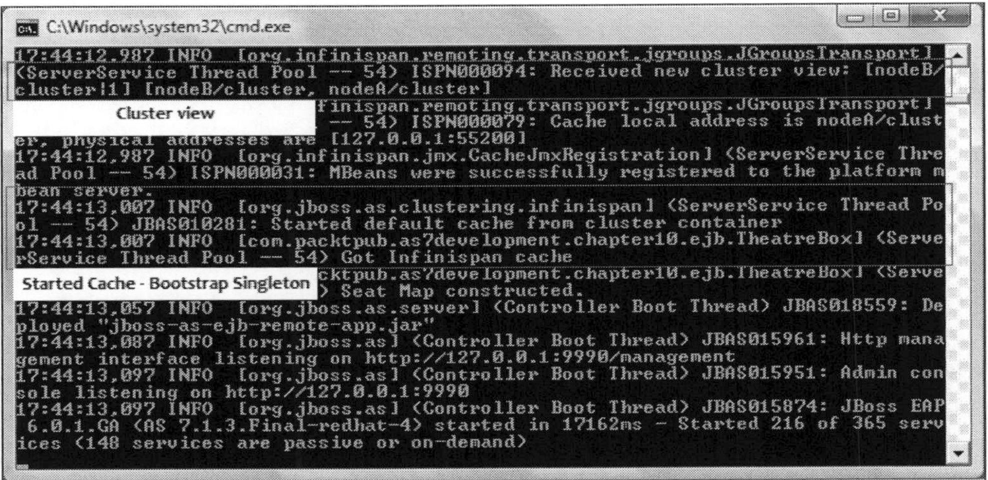

The following is the corresponding log for the second node, which is bound to the same server address (`localhost`) with a port offset of `200`:

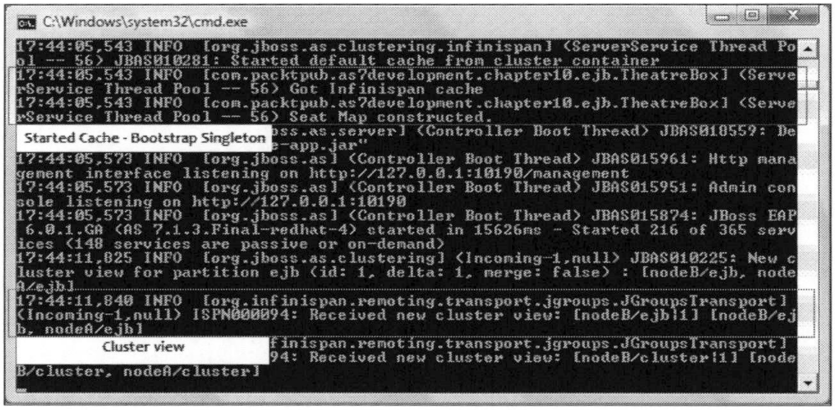

Before launching your application, update Maven's exec plugin information, which should now reference our remote EJB client application, as shown in the highlighted section of the following code snippet:

```
<plugin>
   <groupId>org.codehaus.mojo</groupId>
   <artifactId>exec-maven-plugin</artifactId>
   <version>${version.exec.plugin}</version>
   <executions>
     <execution>
         <goals>
            <goal>exec</goal>
         </goals>
     </execution>
   </executions>
   <configuration>
     <executable>java</executable>
     <workingDirectory>${project.build.directory}/
     exec-working-directory</workingDirectory>
     <arguments>
       <argument>-classpath</argument>
       <classpath>
       </classpath>
       <argument>com.packtpub.as7development.chapter10.client.
       RemoteEJBClient</argument>
     </arguments>
   </configuration>
</plugin>
```

You can run it using the following command:

```
mvn exec:exec
```

The first part of the client will show the evidence that we have successfully completed the first transaction. On the client console, you will see the return value from the booking transaction and the `Seat` list:

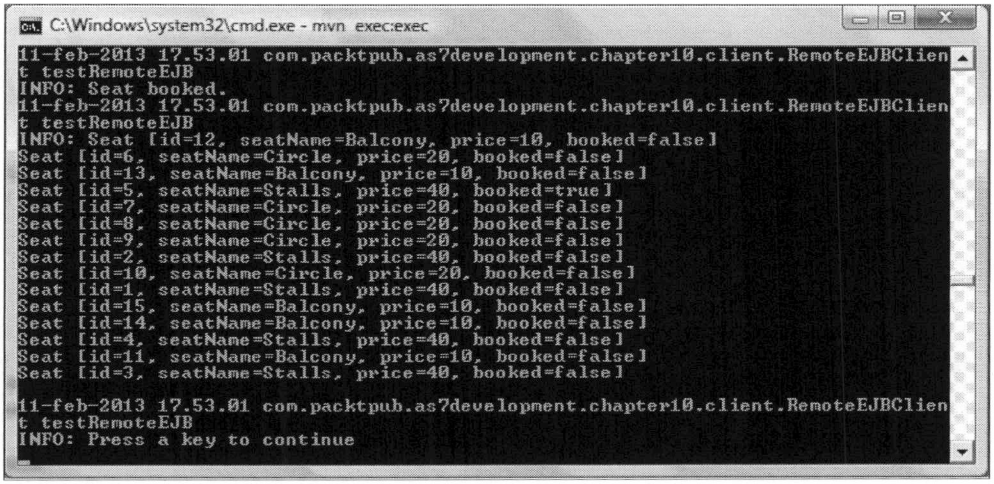

The following screenshot shows the server node where our EJB client landed:

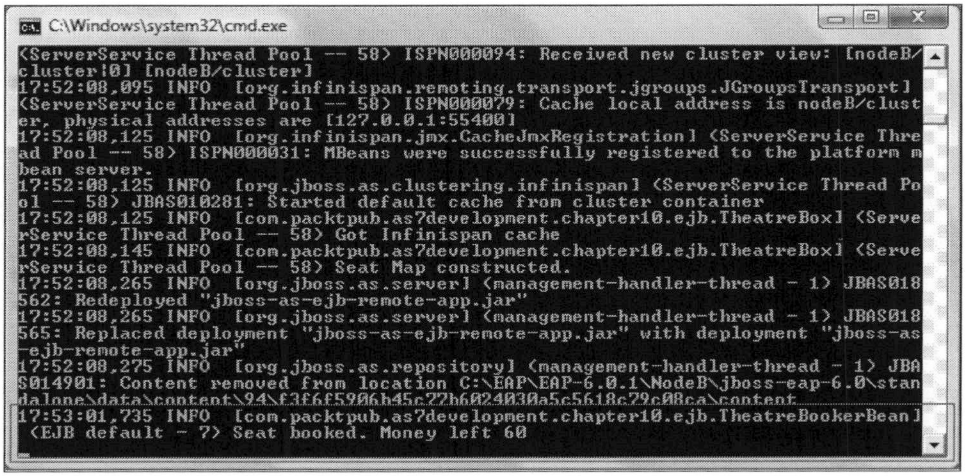

Now shut down the preceding server node (*Ctrl* + *C* would suffice if you are starting it as a foreground process), and press *Enter*(or *Return* in Mac) on the client application.

As you can see from the following screenshot, you should see that the session continues to run on the survivor node and correctly displays the session values (the money left). Your client window should also display the updated cache information.

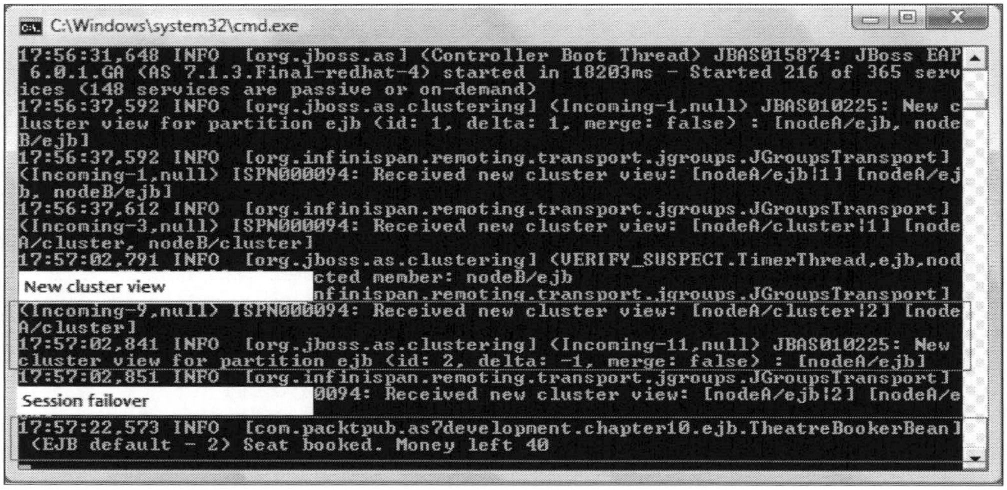

Web application clustering

Web application clustering involves two aspects: setting up an HTTP load balancer, and telling JBoss to make the application's user sessions HA. How to do the former depends on what load balancer you choose (`mod_cluster` is our suggested choice); the latter could not be simpler—just add the `<distributable/>`tag to your application's `web.xml` file.

Let's see in concrete how to pursue both steps.

Load balancing your web applications

You have several choices available in order to achieve load balancing of your HTTP requests; you can opt for a hardware load balancer that sits in front of your cluster of servers, or you can choose from the many available software solutions for JBoss AS, which include the following:

- Use ApacheTomcat's `mod_jk` to route your requests to your nodes
- Use Apache `mod_proxy` that configures Apache to act as a proxy server and forwards requests to JBoss AS nodes
- Use JBoss' built-in solution `mod_cluster` to achieve dynamic load balancing of your requests.

Here we will illustrate how to get started with `mod_cluster`. The advantage of using `mod_cluster` against other options can be summarized in the following key points:

- Dynamic clustering configuration
- Server-side pluggable load metrics
- Lifecycle notifications of the application status

As a matter of fact, when using a standard load balancer such as `mod_jk`, you have to provide a static list of nodes that are used to spread the load. This is a very limiting factor, especially if you have to deliver upgrades to your configuration by adding or removing nodes or you simply need to upgrade releases used by single nodes. Besides this, using a flat cluster configuration can be tedious and prone to errors, especially if the number of cluster nodes is high.

When using `mod_cluster`, you can dynamically add or remove nodes to your cluster, because cluster nodes are discovered through an advertising mechanism.

In practice, the `mod_cluster` libraries on the httpd side send UDP messages on a multicast group, which is subscribed by AS7 nodes. This allows AS7 nodes the automatic discovery of httpd proxies where application lifecycle notifications are sent.

The next diagram illustrates this concept better:

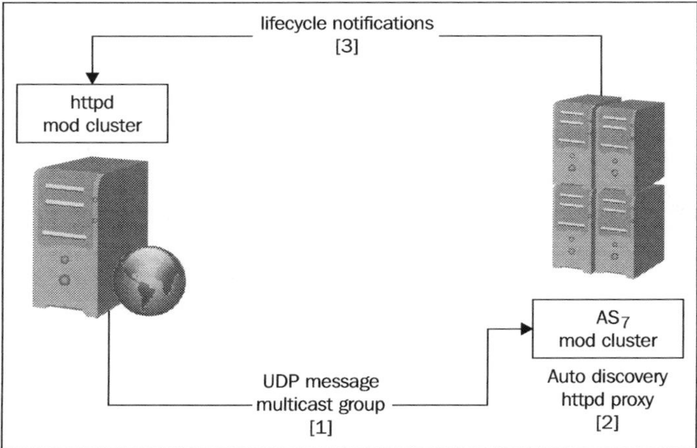

Installing mod_cluster

The `mod_cluster` module is implemented as a core AS 7 module, which is a part of the distribution, on the httpd side as a set of libraries installed on the Apache web server.

On the JBoss AS 7 side, you can find already bundled the `mod_cluster` module's subsystem as part of the clustered configuration file. You can locate it either in the `standalone-ha.xml` file or in the `standalone-full-ha.xml` (and of course in the `domain.xml` file) configuration file:

```
<subsystem xmlns="urn:jboss:domain:modcluster:1.0">
    <mod-cluster-config advertise-socket="modcluster"/>
</subsystem>
```

The subsystem contains just a bare-bones configuration that references its socket binding through the `advertise-socket` element:

```
<socket-binding name="modcluster" port="0" multicast-
address="224.0.1.105" multicast-port="23364"/>
```

On the Apache web server side, we have to install the core libraries, which are used to interact with `mod_cluster`. This is a very simple procedure: point the browser to the latest `mod_cluster` release at `http://www.jboss.org/mod_cluster/downloads`.

Once the binaries are downloaded, extract the archive to a folder; then, navigate into the extracted folder. The `mod_cluster` binaries consist essentially of a bundled Apache web server with all required libraries installed.

> The bundled Apache web server configuration, however, requires defining from scratch all the web server key elements, such as server root, binding ports, loaded modules, and directories' configuration. I personally find it much more immediate to use my own Apache web server 2.2 installation; just pick up the modules from the `mod_cluster` bundle, and copy them in the `modules` folder of your Apache web server.

So, whether you choose to use your own Apache web server or the bundled one, you have to load the following libraries into your `httpd.conf` file:

```
LoadModule proxy_module modules/mod_proxy.so
LoadModule proxy_ajp_module modules/mod_proxy_ajp.so
LoadModule slotmem_module modules/mod_slotmem.so
LoadModule manager_module modules/mod_manager.so
LoadModule proxy_cluster_module modules/mod_proxy_cluster.so
LoadModule advertise_module modules/mod_advertise.so
```

Each of these modules covers an important aspect of load balancing, listed as follows:

- `mod_proxy` and `mod_proxy_ajp`: These are the core modules that forward requests to cluster nodes using either the HTTP/HTTPS protocol or the AJP protocol.
- `mod_manager`: This module reads the information from AS 7 and updates the shared memory information in conjunction with `mod_slotmem`. The `mod_proxy_cluster` module is the module that contains the balancer for `mod_proxy`.
- `mod_advertise`: This is an additional module that allows httpd to a advertise via multicast packets—the IP and port—where the `mod_cluster` module is listening.

The next part of the configuration that we need to add is the core load balancing configuration:

```
Listen 192.168.10.1:8888

<VirtualHost 192.168.10.1:8888>
<Location />
    Order deny,allow
    Deny from all
    Allow from 192.168.10.
</Location>
  KeepAliveTimeout 60
  MaxKeepAliveRequests 0
  ManagerBalancerName mycluster
  ServerAdvertise On
</VirtualHost>
```

Basically, you have to replace the `192.168.10.1` IP address with the one where your Apache web server listens for requests, and replace the port value of `8888` with the one you want to use for communicating with JBoss AS.

As it is, the Apache virtual host allows incoming requests from the subnetwork `192.168.10.`

The `KeepAliveTimeout` directive allows reusing the same connection within 60 seconds. The number of requests per connection is unlimited, since we are setting `MaxKeepAliveRequests` to `0`. The `ManagerBalancerName` directive provides the balancer name for your cluster (defaults to `mycluster`).

Most important for us is the `ServerAdvertise` directive, which sets to `On` and uses the advertise mechanism to tell the JBoss AS to whom it should send the cluster information.

Now, restart the Apache web server and the single application server nodes. If you have correctly configured the mode cluster on the httpd side, you will see that each JBoss AS node will start receiving UDP multicast messages from `mod_cluster`.

Clustering your web applications

Clustering web applications requires the least effort for the developer. As we have just discussed, all you need to do to switch on clustering in a web application is to add the following directive in the `web.xml` descriptor:

```
<web-app>
<distributable/>
</web-app>
```

Once your application ships with the distributable stanza in it, the cluster will start, and provided you have correctly designed your session layer, it will be load balanced and fault tolerant.

Programming considerations to achieve HA

In order to support in-memory replication of HTTP session states, all servlets and JSP session data must be serializable.

Serialization is the conversion of an object to a series of bytes so that the object can be easily saved to a persistent storage or streamed across a communication link. The byte stream can then be deserialized, converting the stream into a replica of the original object.

Additionally, in an HTTP servlet that implements `javax.servlet.http.HttpSession`, you need to use the `setAttribute` method to change the attributes in a session object. If you set attributes in a session object with `setAttribute`, by default the object and its attributes are replicated using the Infinispan API. Every time a change is made to an object that is in the session, `setAttribute` should be called to update that object across the cluster.

Likewise, you need to use `removeAttribute` to remove an attribute from a session object.

Achieving HA in JSF applications

In the applications included in this book, we have used JSF and CDI API to manage the web session. In this case, we transparently replicate the other server nodes to the beans, which are marked as `@SessionScoped`.

> Clustering JSF-based applications requires special attention in case you are dealing with both HTTP and EJB sessions created by SFSB. In the earlier servlet-centric frameworks, the usual approach was to store references of Stateful Session Beans in `javax.servlet.http.HttpSession`. When dealing with high-level JSF and CDI Beans, it is vital to provide a `@SessionScoped` controller to your application, which gets injected in the SFSB reference, otherwise you will end up creating a new Stateful Session Beans at each request.

The following is an example of how to adapt your Ticket CDI application (described in *Chapter 4, Learning Context Dependency Injection*) to a clustered environment. At first, as we said, we need to include the distributable stanza in your `web.xml` file to trigger clustering modules:

```
<web-app>
<distributable/>
</web-app>
```

Next, apply the same changes to the `TheatreBox` singleton that we described in the *Turning your cache into a distributed cache* section:

```
@Singleton
@Startup

public class TheatreBox {
    @Resource(lookup="java:jboss/infinispan/container/cluster")
private CacheContainer container;

  // Apply the same changes described in
  // "Turning your Cache into a distributed cache"section
}
```

Since our controller component is bound to a `@SessionScoped` state, you don't need to apply any changes in order to propagate your session across server nodes:

```
@SessionScoped
@Named
public class TheatreBookerBean implements Serializable {
}
```

Finally, remember to include the Infinispan dependency in your `META-INF/MANIFEST.MF`:

```
Dependencies: org.infinispan export
```

Once your application is deployed on both nodes of your cluster, you can test it by hitting the Apache web server (`http://localhost:8888/ticket-agency-cluster` in our example) and start booking tickets:

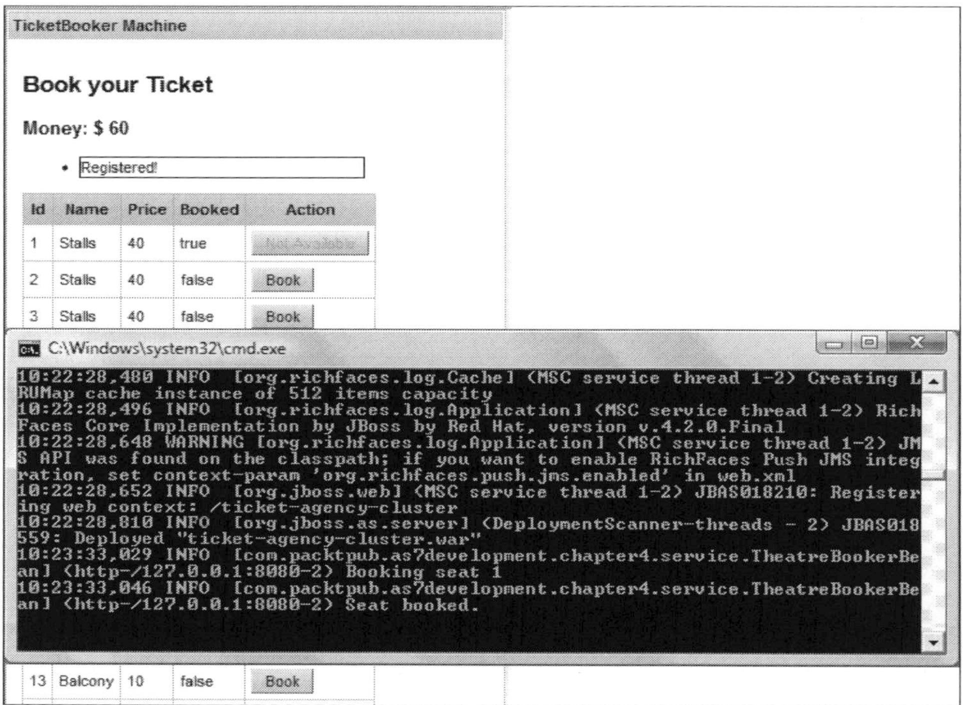

Since the `mod_cluster` subsystem is configured by default to use **sticky web sessions**, all subsequent requests from the same client will be redirected to the same server node. Therefore, by shutting down the sticky server node, you will get evidence that a new cluster view has been created and you can continue shopping on the other server node:

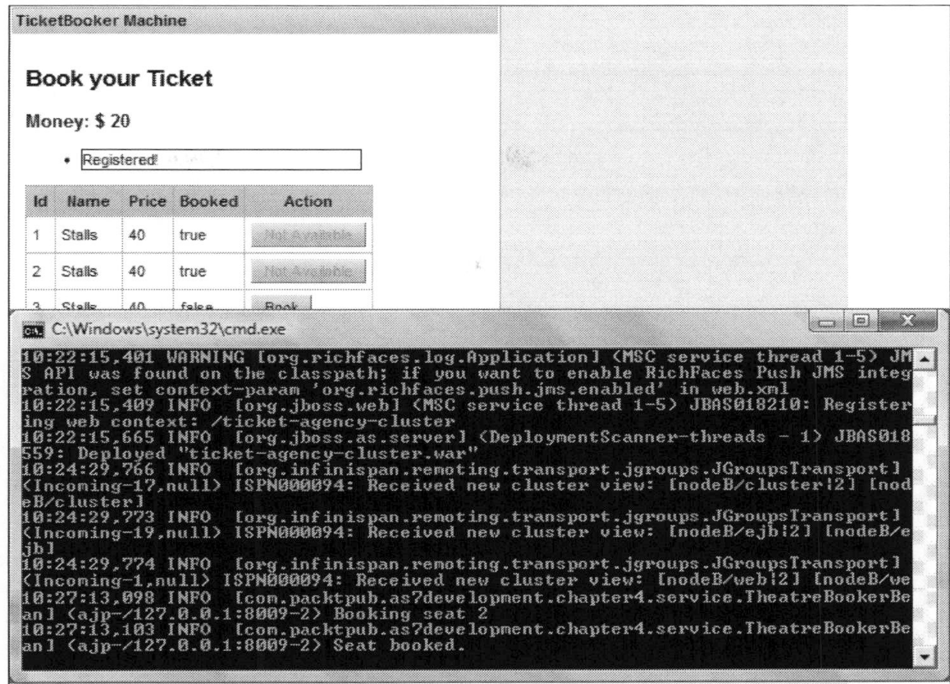

Summary

This chapter was all about the world of clustered applications. Here, we have shown the robust clustering features of JBoss AS and have applied them to some of the examples discussed in this book.

The number of topics related to clustering might be expanded to cover a full book of its own; however, we decided to stress only on some features. In particular, we have learned how to cluster EJBs and how to achieve fault tolerance in case there is a change in the server topology.

Next, we discussed about clustering web applications and the integration with load balancing solutions such as the Apache web server and `mod_cluster`.

In the next chapter, we will add the last piece of the puzzle that's missing in our Enterprise applications: handling security in your applications.

11
Securing JBoss AS 7 Applications

In the previous chapter we have described how to deploy your application in a robust and reliable environment using clustering. The last stop in our journey will be learning about security, which is a key element of any Enterprise application. You must be able to control and restrict who is permitted to access your applications and what operations users may perform.

The Java Enterprise Edition (Java EE) specification defines a simple role-based security model for Enterprise JavaBeans (EJBs) and web components. The implementation of JBoss security is delivered by the **Picketbox** framework (formerly known as JBoss security), which is part of the application server and provides the authentication, authorization, auditing, and mapping capabilities to Java applications.

Here is the specific list of topics we will cover:

- A short introduction to the Java security API
- The foundation of the JBoss AS 7 security subsystem
- Defining and applying login modules for securing Java EE applications
- Using the Secure Sockets Layer (SSL) to encrypt the transport layer

Approaching the Java security API

Java EE security services provide a robust and easily configurable security mechanism for authenticating users and authorizing access to application functions and associated data. To better understand the topics related to security, we should at first give some basic definitions:

- **Authentication**: It is the process by which you can verify who is currently executing an application, regardless of whether it is an EJB or a servlet (and so on). Authentication is usually performed by means of a `Login` module contained in a web/standalone application.
- **Authorization**: It is the process by which you can verify if a user has the right (permission) to access system resources. Authorization, therefore, presupposes that authentication has occurred; it would be impossible to grant any access control if you don't know who the user is first. The difference between authentication and authorization is depicted by the following diagram:

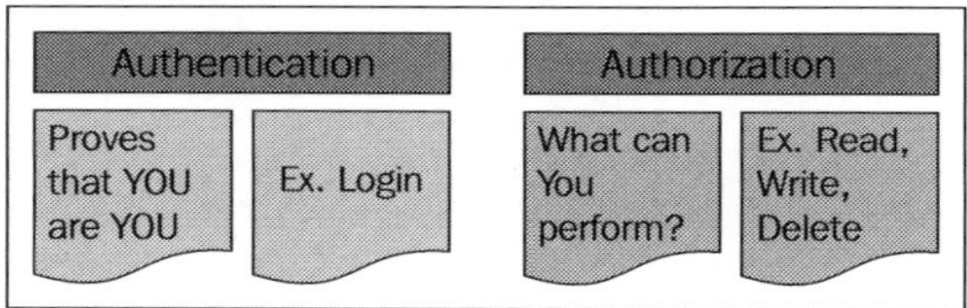

In Java EE, the component containers are responsible for providing application security. A container basically provides two types of security: declarative and programmatic. Let's see them both:

- **Declarative security**: It expresses an application component's security requirements by means of deployment descriptors. Because deployment descriptor information is contained in an external file, it can be changed without the need to modify the source code.

  For example, Enterprise JavaBeans components use an EJB deployment descriptor that must be named `ejb-jar.xml` and placed in the `META-INF` folder of the EJB JAR file.

  Web components use a web application deployment descriptor named `web.xml` located in the `WEB-INF` directory.

Since Java EE 5, you can apply declarative security also by means of annotations just like we have for other key APIs (EJB, web services, and so on). Annotations are specified within a class file and, when the application is deployed, this information is translated internally by the application server.

- **Programmatic security**: It is embedded in an application and is used to make security decisions. It can be used when declarative security alone is not sufficient to express the security model of an application. The Java EE security API allows the developer to test whether or not the current user has access to a specific role, using the following calls:
  - `isUserInRole()` for servlets and JSPs (adopted in `javax.servlet.http.HttpServletRequest`)
  - `isCallerInRole()` for EJBs (adopted in `javax.ejb.SessionContext`)

  Additionally, there are other API calls that provide access to the user's identity:

  - `getUserPrincipal()` for servlets and JSPs (adopted in `javax.servlet.http.HttpServletRequest`)
  - `getCallerPrincipal()` for EJBs (adopted in `javax.ejb.SessionContext`)

  Using these APIs, you can develop arbitrarily complex authorization models.

JBoss AS 7 security subsystem

JBoss security is qualified as an extension to the application server and it is included by default both in standalone servers and in domain servers:

```
<extension module="org.jboss.as.security"/>
```

The following is an extract from the default security subsystem contained in the server configuration file, which contains the `RealmUsersRoles` login module that will be used in the next section to secure the Ticket example application:

```
<subsystem xmlns="urn:jboss:domain:security:1.1">
  <security-domains>
      <security-domain name="other" cache-type="default">
          <authentication>
              <login-module code="Remoting" flag="optional">
                  <module-option name="password-stacking"
                  value="useFirstPass"/>
```

```
                </login-module>
                <login-module code="RealmUsersRoles"
                flag="required">
                    <module-option name="usersProperties"
                    value="${jboss.server.config.dir}/application-
                    users.properties"/>
                    <module-option name="rolesProperties"
                    value="${jboss.server.config.dir}/application-
                    roles.properties"/>
                    <module-option name="realm"
                    value="ApplicationRealm"/>
                    <module-option name="password-stacking"
                    value="useFirstPass"/>
                </login-module>
            </authentication>
        </security-domain>
. . . .
    </security-domains>
</subsystem>
```

As you can see, the configuration is pretty short as it relies largely on default values, especially for high-level structures like the security management area. By defining your own security management options, you could for example, override the default authentication/authorization managers with your implementations. Since it is likely that you will not need to override these interfaces, we will rather concentrate on the `security-domain` element, which is the core aspect of JBoss security.

A security domain can be thought of as a Customs Office for foreigners. Before the request crosses JBoss AS borders, the security domain performs all the required **authorization** and **authentication** checks and eventually notifies if he/she can proceed or not.

Security domains are generally configured at server startup and subsequently bound into the JNDI tree under the key `java:/jaas/`. Within the security domain, you can configure login authentication modules so that you can easily change your authentication provider by simply changing its `login-module`.

There are several login modules implementations available out of the box; there is obviously not enough room here to describe in detail the features of each module, though we will offer a comprehensive description of some popular options, such as:

- The `RealmUsersRoles` login module, which can be used for basic file-based authentication
- The `Database` login module, which checks user credentials against a relational database

Should you need further information about login modules, check out the JBoss AS 7.1 documentation at `https://docs.jboss.org/author/display/AS71/Security+subsystem+configuration`.

Setting up your first login module

In the following section, we will demonstrate how to secure an application using the `RealmUsersRoles` security domain, which has been introduced earlier. The `RealmUserRoles` login module is based on the following two files

- `application-users.properties`: It contains the list of usernames and passwords
- `application-roles.properties`: It contains the mapping between the users and the roles

These files are located in the application server configuration folder and they are updated each time you add a new user via the `add-user.sh`/`add-user.cmd` script. For our purposes, we will create a new application user named `demouser` that belongs to the role `Manager`, as shown in the following screenshot:

```
C:\Windows\system32\cmd.exe
What type of user do you wish to add?
 a) Management User (mgmt-users.properties)
 b) Application User (application-users.properties)
(a): b

Enter the details of the new user to add.
Realm (ApplicationRealm) :
Username : demouser
Password :
Re-enter Password :
What roles do you want this user to belong to? (Please enter a comma separated l
ist, or leave blank for none) : Manager
About to add user 'demouser' for realm 'ApplicationRealm'
Is this correct yes/no? yes
Added user 'demouser' to file 'C:\jboss\jboss-as-7.1.1.Final\standalone\configur
ation\application-users.properties'
Added user 'demouser' to file 'C:\jboss\jboss-as-7.1.1.Final\domain\configuratio
n\application-users.properties'
Added user 'demouser' with roles Manager to file 'C:\jboss\jboss-as-7.1.1.Final\
standalone\configuration\application-roles.properties'
Added user 'demouser' with roles Manager to file 'C:\jboss\jboss-as-7.1.1.Final\
domain\configuration\application-roles.properties'
Press any key to continue . . .
```

Once the user is added, the `application-users.properties` file will contain the username and the MD5 encoding of the password:

```
demouser=290dfdb724ee4ed466b401a22040efd2
```

Conversely, the `application-roles.properties` file will contain the roles granted to the `demouser` username once logged in:

```
demouser=Manager
```

Using the login module in the Ticket web application

We can now apply the `RealmUserRoles` login module into any Ticket web application described in the book. We will show at first how to provide a BASIC web authentication and then we will show a slightly more complex example using FORM-based authentication.

> BASIC-access authentication is the simplest way to provide a username and password when making a request through a browser.
>
> It works by sending an encoded string containing the user credentials. This Base64-encoded string is transmitted and decoded by the receiver, resulting in the colon-separated username and password strings.

Turning on web authentication requires the `security-constraints` element to be defined in the web application configuration file (`web.xml`), as shown in the following code snippet:

```
<web-app>
. . . . . .
<security-constraint>
     <web-resource-collection>
       <web-resource-name>HtmlAuth</web-resource-name>
       <description>application security constraints
       </description>
       <url-pattern>/*</url-pattern>
       <http-method>GET</http-method>
       <http-method>POST</http-method>
     </web-resource-collection>
     <auth-constraint>
       <role-name>Manager</role-name>
     </auth-constraint>
   </security-constraint>
   <login-config>
      <auth-method>BASIC</auth-method>
      <realm-name>file</realm-name>
   </login-config>

   <security-role>
      <role-name>Manager</role-name>
   </security-role>
</web-app>
```

This configuration will add a security constraint on any JSP/servlet of the web application that will restrict access to users authenticated with the role `Manager`. All login modules shown in the earlier section define this role, so you can just use the login module that suits your needs best.

The next configuration tweak needs to be performed on the JBoss web deployment's descriptor, `WEB-INF/jboss-web.xml`. You need to declare the security domain here, which will be used to authenticate the users. Since we are using `RealmUsersRoles`, which is part of the other built-in login module, we will need to include the `java:/jaas/other` context information:

```
<jboss-web>
      <security-domain>java:/jaas/other</security-domain>
</jboss-web>
```

The following diagram illustrates the whole configuration sequence applied to a `Database` login module:

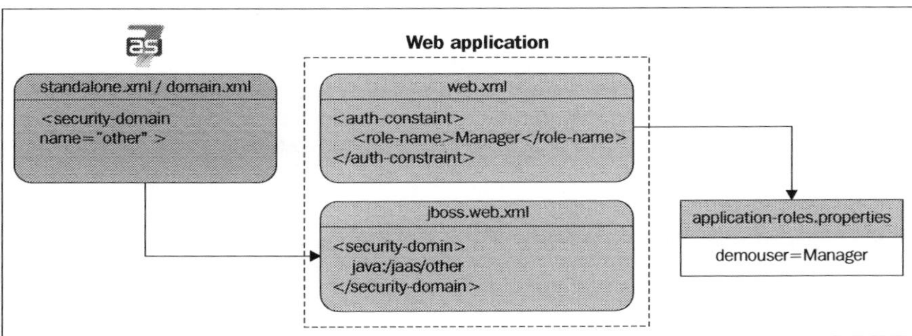

Once you have deployed your application, the outcome should be a blocking pop-up requesting user authentication, as shown in the following screenshot:

Logging in with demouser and the valid password will grant access to the application with the Manager role.

Switching to FORM-based security

FORM-based authentication lets developers customize the authentication user interface, adapting it, for example, to your company's standards. Configuring it in your application requires you to basically modify just the login-config stanza of the security section of your web.xml file. Within it, we will be defining a login landing page (login.jsf) and an error page (error.jsf), in case the login fails. Here is the code snippet for it:

```
<login-config>
    <auth-method>FORM</auth-method>
        <realm-name>file</realm-name>
        <form-login-config>
            <form-login-page>/login.jsf</form-login-page>
            <form-error-page>/error.jsf</form-error-page>
        </form-login-config>
</login-config>
```

The login form must contain fields for entering a username and password. These fields must be named j_username and j_password respectively. The authentication form should post these values to the j_security_check logical name. Here's a simple login.jsf page that can be used for this purpose:

```
<!DOCTYPE html PUBLIC "-//W3C//DTD XHTML 1.0 Transitional//EN"
"http://www.w3.org/TR/xhtml1/DTD/xhtml1-transitional.dtd">
<html xmlns="http://www.w3.org/1999/xhtml"
  xmlns:h="http://java.sun.com/jsf/html">
  <h1>
    Please Login
  </h1>
  <body>
  <form method="post" action="j_security_check"
  name="loginForm">
    <h:panelGrid columns="2">
    <h:outputLabel id="userNameLabel" for="j_username"
    value="Username:"/>
    <h:inputText id="j_username" />
    <h:outputLabel id="passwordLabel" for="j_password"
    value="Password:"/>
    <h:inputSecret id="j_password" />
     <h:panelGroup>
    <h:commandButton type="submit" value="Login"/>
```

```
      </h:panelGroup>
      </h:panelGrid>
    </form>
    </body>
  </html>
```

For the sake of brevity, we won't include the error page, which will simply alert that the user entered an incorrect combination of username and password. The expected outcome is the following login screen, which will intercept all user access to your application and grant access to the default home page if the `username` and `password` credentials are correct.

Please Login

Username:

Password:

Login

Creating a Database login module

The `UserRoles` login module is a good starting point for learning how to put together all the pieces required for securing a web application. In real-world cases, there are better alternatives to protect your applications, such as the `Database` login module. A database security domain follows the same logic exposed in the earlier example; it just stores the credentials within the database. In order to run this example, we will refer to a data source defined in *Chapter 5, Combining Persistence with CDI* (bound at the JNDI name `java:jboss/datasources/jbossas7development`), which needs to be deployed on the application server:

```
<security-domain name="mysqldomain" cache-type="default">
  <authentication>
    <login-module code="Database" flag="required">
      <module-option name="dsJndiName" value="
      java:jboss/datasources/jbossas7development"/>
      <module-option name="principalsQuery" value="select
      passwd from USERS where login=?"/>
      <module-option name="rolesQuery" value="select
      role, 'Roles' from USER_ROLES where login=?"/>
    </login-module>
  </authentication>
</security-domain>
```

In order to get working with this configuration, you have to first create the required tables and insert some sample data in it:

```
CREATE TABLE USERS(login VARCHAR(64) PRIMARY KEY, passwd VARCHAR(64));
CREATE TABLE USER_ROLES(login VARCHAR(64), role VARCHAR(32));
INSERT into USERS values('admin', 'admin');
INSERT into USER_ROLES values('admin', 'Manager');
```

As you can see, the `admin` user will map again to the `Manager` role. One caveat of this configuration is that it uses clear-text passwords in the database; so before rolling this module into production, you should consider adding additional security to your login module. Let's see how in the next section.

Encrypting passwords

Storing passwords in the database as a clear-text string is not considered a good practice; as a matter of fact, a database has even more potential security holes than a regular file system. Imagine, for example, that a DBA added a public synonym for some tables, forgetting that one of those tables was holding sensitive information like application passwords! You then need to be sure that no potential attackers will ever be able to deliver the following query:

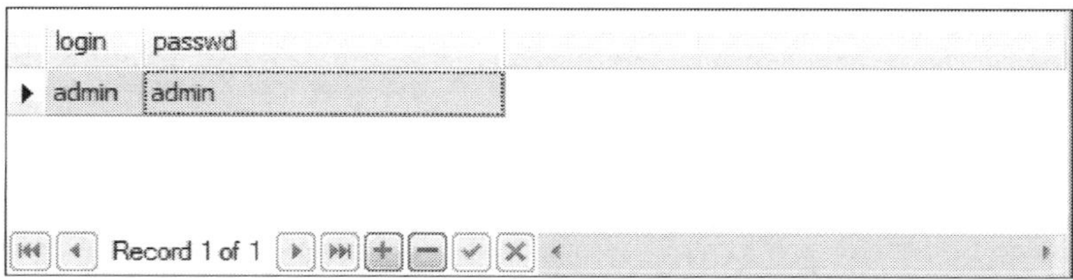

Fortunately, securing application passwords is relatively easy; you can add a few extra options to your Login Module, specifying that the stored passwords are encrypted using a message digest algorithm. For example, in the `mysqlLogin` module, you should add the following highlighted options at the bottom:

```
<login-module code="Database" flag="required">
     <module-option name="dsJndiName" value="java:jboss/datasources/
jbossas7development"/>
     <module-option name="principalsQuery" value="select passwd from
USERS where login=?"/>
     <module-option name="rolesQuery" value="select role, 'Roles' from
USER_ROLES where login=?"/>
     <module-option name="hashAlgorithm" value="MD5"/>
     <module-option name="hashEncoding" value="BASE64"/>
     <module-option name="hashStorePassword" value="true"/>
</login-module>
```

Here we have specified that the password will be hashed against an MD5 hash algorithm; you can alternatively use any other algorithm allowed by your JCA provider, such as SHA.

For an excellent introduction to hashing algorithms, refer to the following link:

http://www.unixwiz.net/techtips/iguide-crypto-hashes.html

For the sake of completeness, we include here a small application, which uses the `java.security.MessageDigest` and `org.jboss.security.Base64Utils` class (contained in the `picketbox-4.0.7.Final.jar` file that is part of the JBoss AS 7 modules), to generate the Base-64 hashed password that is to be inserted in `Database`:

```
public class Hash {

    public static void main(String[] args) throws Exception{
        String password = args[0];
        MessageDigest md = null;
        md = MessageDigest.getInstance("MD5");
        byte[] passwordBytes = password.getBytes();
        byte[] hash = md.digest(passwordBytes);
        String passwordHash =
        org.jboss.security.Base64Utils.tob64(hash);
        System.out.println("password hash: "+passwordHash);
}
```

Running the main program with `admin` as the argument will generate the hash `X8oyfUbUbfqE9IWvAW1/3`. This hash will be your updated password, which needs to be updated in your database as shown in the following screenshot.

```
UPDATE USERS SET PASSWD = 'X8oyfUbUbfqE9IWvAW1/3' WHERE LOGIN =
'admin';
```

You can update it from any SQL client of your liking.

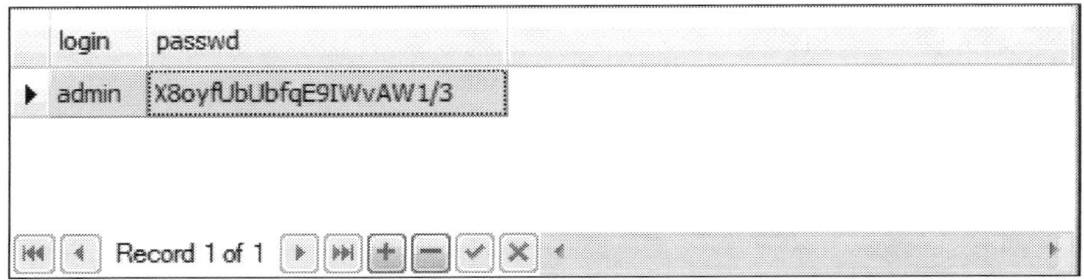

Using the Database login module in your application

Once you are done with the login module configuration, don't forget to reference it through the JBoss web deployment's descriptor, `WEB-INF/jboss-web.xml`.

```
<jboss-web>
      <security-domain>java:/jaas/mysqldomain</security-domain>
</jboss-web>
```

Securing EJBs

Securing applications by means of a web login form is the most frequently used option in Enterprise applications. Nevertheless, the HTTP protocol is not the only choice available to access applications. For example, EJBs can be accessed by remote clients using the RMI-IIOP protocol. In such a case, you should further refine your security policies by restricting access to the EJB components, which are usually involved in the business layer of your applications.

> **How does security work at the EJB level?**
>
> Authentication must be performed before any EJB method is called. Authorization, on the other hand, occurs at the beginning of each EJB method call.

One vast area of improvement introduced in Java EE 5 concerns the use of annotations, which can also be used to perform the basic security checks. There are five available annotations, as follows:

- `@org.jboss.ejb3.annotation.SecurityDomain`: This specifies the security domain that is associated with the class/method.
- `@javax.annotation.security.RolesAllowed`: This specifies the list of roles permitted to access a method(s) in an EJB application.
- `@javax.annotation.security.RunAs`: This assigns a role dynamically to the EJB application during the invocation of the method. It can be used, for example, if we need to temporarily allow a permission to access certain methods.
- `@javax.annotation.security.PermitAll`: This specifies that an EJB application can be invoked by any client. The purpose of this annotation is to widen security access to some methods in situations where you don't exactly know what role will access the EJB application (imagine that some modules have been developed by a third party and they access your EJB application with some roles that are not well-identified).

- `@javax.annotation.security.DenyAll`: This specifies that an EJB application cannot be invoked by external clients. It has the same considerations as those for `@PermitAll`.

Here is an example of how to secure the `TheatreBookerBean` SFSB, which we discussed in *Chapter 4, Learning Context Dependency Injection*:

```
@RolesAllowed("Manager")
@SecurityDomain("mysqldomain")
@Stateful
@Remote(TheatreBooker.class)

public class TheatreBookerBean implements TheatreBooker {

}
```

> Be careful! There is a more than one `SecurityDomain` API available. You have to include `org.jboss.ejb3.annotation.SecurityDomain`. The `@RolesAllowed` annotation, on the other hand, needs importing of `javax.annotation.security.RolesAllowed`.

Annotations can also be applied at the method level; for example, if we want to secure just the `bookSeat` object of the `TheatreBookerBean` class, we would tag the method as follows:

```
@RolesAllowed("Manager")
@SecurityDomain("mysqldomain")
public String bookSeat(int seatId)  throws SeatBookedException {
}
```

What about if you don't want to use annotations for establishing security roles? For example, if you have a security role that is used crosswise by all your EJB applications, perhaps it is simpler to use a plain old XML configuration instead of tagging all EJBs with annotations. In this scenario, you have to declare the security constraints first in the generic `META-INF/ejb-jar.xml` file:

```
<method-permission>
  <role-name>Manager</role-name>
  <method>
   <ejb-name>*</ejb-name>
    <method-name>*</method-name>
  </method>
</method-permission>
```

Then, inside the `META-INF/jboss-ejb3.xml` configuration file, just add a reference to your security domain:

```
<jboss:ejb-jar>
  <assembly-descriptor>
    <s:security>
      <ejb-name>*</ejb-name>
      <s:security-domain>mysqldomain</s:security-domain>
    </s:security>
  </assembly-descriptor>

</jboss:ejb-jar>
```

Here's a snapshot illustrating the EJB-file-based role configuration:

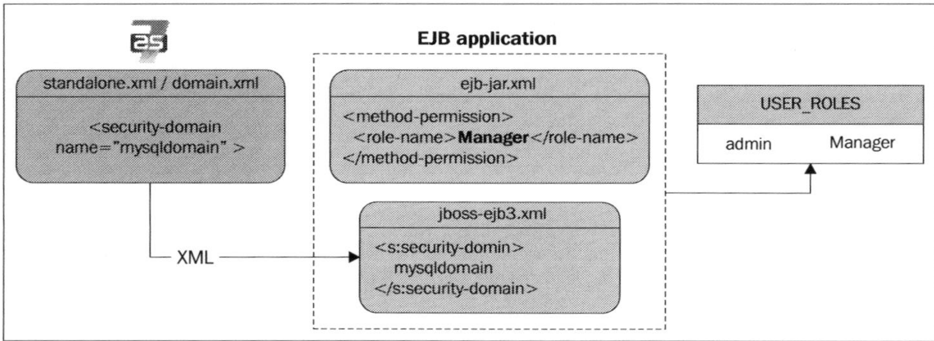

Securing web services

Web service authorization can basically be carried out in two ways, depending on if we are dealing with a POJO-based web service or an EJB-based web service.

Security changes to POJO web services are identical to those we have introduced for servlets/JSP: consistent in defining the `security-constraints` element in `web.xml` and the login modules in `jboss-web.xml`.

If you are using a web client to access your web service, it is all you need to get authenticated. If you are using a standalone client, you will need in turn to specify the credentials to the JAX-WS Factory. Here is an example of accessing the secured `POJOWebService` instance, which was described in *Chapter 8, Adding Web Services to Your Applications*:

```
JaxWsProxyFactoryBean factory = new JaxWsProxyFactoryBean();

factory.getInInterceptors().add(new LoggingInInterceptor());
```

```
factory.getOutInterceptors().add(new LoggingOutInterceptor());

factory.setServiceClass(POJOWebService.class);
factory.setAddress("http://localhost:8080/pojoService");
factory.setUsername("admin");
factory.setPassword("admin");
POJOWebService client = (POJOWebService) factory.create();

client.doSomething();
```

What about EJB-based web services? The configuration is slightly different; since the security domain is not specified into web descriptors, we have to provide it by means of annotations:

```
@Stateless
@WebService(targetNamespace = "http://www.packtpub.com/", serviceName
= "TicketWebService")
@WebContext(authMethod = "BASIC",
            secureWSDLAccess = false)
@SecurityDomain(value = "mysqldomain")

public class TicketSOAPService implements TicketSOAPServiceItf,
Serializable {

   . . . .
}
```

As you can see, the `@org.jboss.ws.api.annotation.Webcontext` annotation basically reflects the same configuration options as that of POJO-based web services, with BASIC authentication and unrestricted WSDL access.

The `@org.jboss.ejb3.annotation.SecurityDomain` annotation should be familiar to you since we have introduced it to illustrate how to secure an EJB. As you can see, it's a replacement for the information contained in the `jboss-web.xml` file, except that the security domain is referenced directly by `mysqldomain` (instead of `java:/jaas/mysqldomain`).

The previous security configuration can also be specified by means of the `META-INF/ejb-jar.xml` and `META-INF/jboss-ejb3.xml` files in case you prefer using standard configuration files.

Securing the transport layer

If you were to create a mission-critical application with just the bare concepts we have learned until now, you are not guaranteed to be shielded from all security threats. For example, if you need to design a payment gateway, where the credit card information is transmitted by means of an EJB or servlet, using just the authorization and authentication stack is really not enough, as the sensitive information is still sent across a network and it could be disclosed by an hacker.

In order to prevent disclosure of critical information to unauthorized individuals or systems, you have to use a protocol that provides encryption of the information. Encryption is the conversion of data into a form that cannot be understood by unauthorized people. Conversely, decryption is the process of converting encrypted data back into its original form so that it can be understood.

The protocols used to secure the communication are SSL and TLS, the latter being considered a replacement for the older SSL.

> The differences between the two protocols are minor and very technical. In short, TLS uses stronger encryption algorithms and has the ability to work on different ports. For the rest of this chapter, we will refer to SSL for both protocols. Check Wikipedia for more information on it: `http://en.wikipedia.org/wiki/Transport_Layer_Security`.

There are two basic techniques for encrypting information: symmetric encryption (also called secret-key encryption) and asymmetric encryption (also called public-key encryption.)

Symmetric encryption is the oldest and best-known technique. It is based on a secret key, which is applied to the text of a message to change the content in a particular way. As long as both sender and recipient know the secret key, they can encrypt and decrypt all messages that use this key. These encryption algorithms typically work fast and are well suited for encrypting blocks of messages at once.

One significant issue with symmetric algorithms is the requirement of a safe administrative organization to distribute keys to users. This generally results in more overhead from the administrative aspect while the keys remain vulnerable to unauthorized disclosure and potential abuse.

For this reason, a mission-critical enterprise system usually relies on the asymmetric encryption algorithms, which tend to be easier to employ, manage, and are ultimately more secure.

Asymmetric cryptography, also known as **public-key cryptography**, is based on the concept that the key used to encrypt is not the same as the key that is used to decrypt the message. In practice, each user holds a couple of keys: the public key that is distributed to other parties and the private key that is kept as secret. Each message is encrypted with the recipient's public key and can only be decrypted (by the recipient) with his private key:

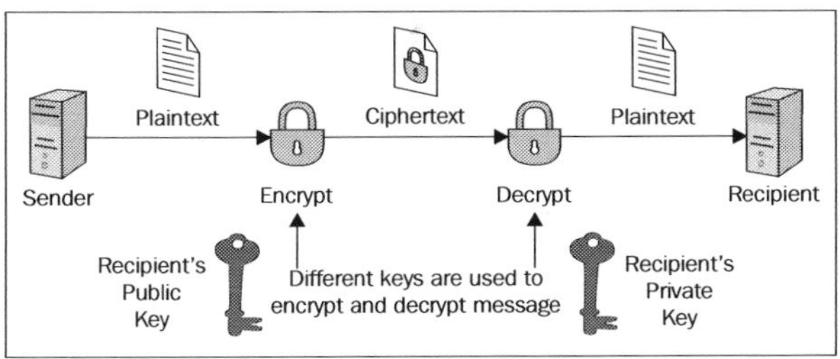

Using asymmetric encryption, you can be sure that your message cannot be disclosed by a third party. However, there is still one vulnerability.

Suppose you want to exchange some valuable information with a business partner and to that end are requesting his public key by telephone or by email. A fraudulent user intercepts your email or simply listens to your conversation and quickly sends you a fake mail with his public key. Now, even if your data transmission will be secured, it will be directed to the wrong person!

In order to solve this issue, we need a document that verifies that the public key belongs to a particular individual. This document is called a **digital certificate** or public key certificate. A digital certificate consists of a formatted block of data that contains the name of the certificate holder (which may be either a user or a system name) and the holder's public key, along with the digital signature of a Certification Authority (CA) for authentication. The certification authority attests that the sender's name is the one associated with the public key in the document:

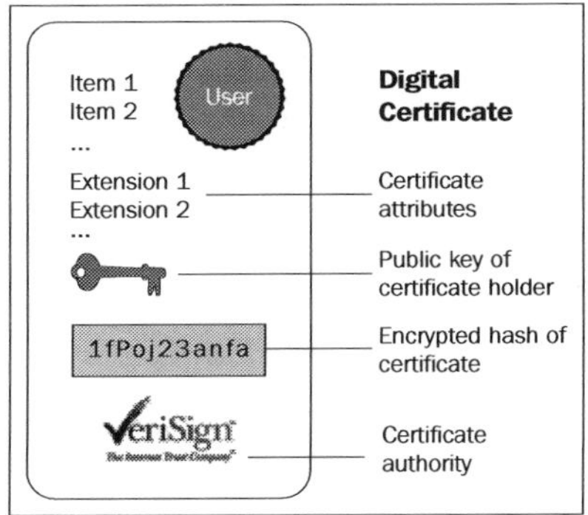

Public key certificates are commonly used for secure interaction with websites. By default, the web browser ships with a set of predefined CAs; they are used to verify that the public certificate served to a browser when you enter a secure site has actually been issued by the owner of the website. In short, if you connect your browser to `https://www.abc.com` and your browser doesn't give any certificate warning, you can safely interact with the entity in charge of the site. That is, unless the site or your browser has been hacked. But this is another story.

> **Simple authentication and client authentication**
>
> In the previous example, we have depicted a simple authentication (also called server authentication). In this scenario, the only party that needs to prove its identity is the server.
>
> SSL however, is able to perform mutual authentication (also called client or two-way authentication); here too the server requests a client certificate during the SSL handshake over the network.
>
> Client authentication requires a client certificate in x.509 format from a CA. The x.509 format is an industry-standard format for SSL certificates. In the next section, we will explore which tools are available to generate digital certificates and how to get your certificates signed by a CA.

Enabling the Secure Socket Layer on JBoss AS

The JBoss AS uses the **Java Secure Socket Extension** (**JSSE**), which is bundled in the J2SE to leverage the SSL/TLS communication.

An Enterprise application can be secured at two different locations: the HTTP level for web applications and the RMI level for applications using EJB. HTTP communication is handled by the web subsystem within the `standalone.xml`/`domain.xml` file. Securing the RMI transport is, on the other hand, not always a compelling requirement of your applications. Actually, in most production environments, JBoss AS is placed behind a firewall.

As you can see from the following diagram, this implies that your EJBs are not directly exposed to untrusted networks, which usually connect through the web server placed in a demilitarized zone:

In order to get started with the JBoss AS and SSL, we need a tool that generates a public/private key pair in the form of an X509 certificate for use by the SSL server sockets. This is covered in the next section.

Certificate management tools

One tool that can be used to set up a digital certificate is **keytool**, a key and certificate management utility that ships with the Java SE. It enables users to administer their own public/private key pairs and associated certificates for use in self-authentication (where the user authenticates himself or herself to other users or services) or data integrity and authentication services, using digital signatures. It also allows users to cache the public keys (in the form of certificates) of their communicating peers.

The keytool stores the keys and certificates in a file termed keystore, a repository of certificates used for identifying a client or server. Typically, a keystore contains one client or server's identity, which is protected by a password. Let's see an example of keystore generation:

```
keytool -genkey -keystore jboss.keystore -storepass mypassword -keypass
mypassword -keyalg RSA -validity 180  -alias as7alias   -dname
"cn=Francesco Marchioni,o=PackPub,c=GB"
```

This command creates the keystore named `jboss.keystore` in the working directory, and assigns it the password `mypassword`. It generates a public/private key pair for the entity whose unique name has the common name `Francesco Marchioni`, organization `PacktPub`, and two-letter country code `GB`.

The result of this action will be a self-signed certificate (using the RSA signature algorithm) that includes the public key and the unique name's information. This certificate will be valid for 180 days, and is associated with the private key in a keystore entry referred to by the alias `as7alias`.

A self-signed certificate is a certificate that has not been verified by a CA and thus leaves you vulnerable to the classic man-in-the-middle attack. A self-signed certificate is only suitable for in-house use or for testing while you wait for your real one to arrive.

Securing the HTTP communication with a self-signed certificate

Now let's see how you can use this keystore file to secure your JBoss web channel. Open your server configuration file and locate the web subsystem.

Within the web subsystem, you have to first change the default `schema` and `socket-binding` to `"https"` and add the `secure` element to it. Next, you have to insert an `ssl` stanza within it, which contains the details of your `keystore` object (in our example, we have dropped the file `jboss.keystore` into the server configuration directory):

```
<subsystem xmlns="urn:jboss:domain:web:1.1" default-virtual-
server="default-host" native="false">
 <connector name="http" protocol="HTTP/1.1" scheme="https" socket-
binding="https" secure="true">

   <ssl key-alias="as7alias" password="mypassword" certificate-key-
file="${jboss.server.config.dir}/jboss.keystore"
  cipher-suite="ALL" protocol="TLS"/>
 </connector>
             . . . . . .
</subsystem>
```

You have to restart the JBoss AS to activate the changes. You should see the following log at the bottom of your console, which informs you about the new HTTPS channel running on port 8443.

INFO [org.apache.coyote.http11.Http11Protocol] (MSC service thread 1-4) Starting Coyote HTTP/1.1 on http--127.0.0.1-8443:

The following screen is what will be displayed by the Internet Explorer browser (the same kind of error message, with a different format, will be displayed by other browsers such as Firefox and Google Chrome) if you try to access the Ticket example using the secured channel (for example, `https://localhost:8443/ticket-agency-cdi`):

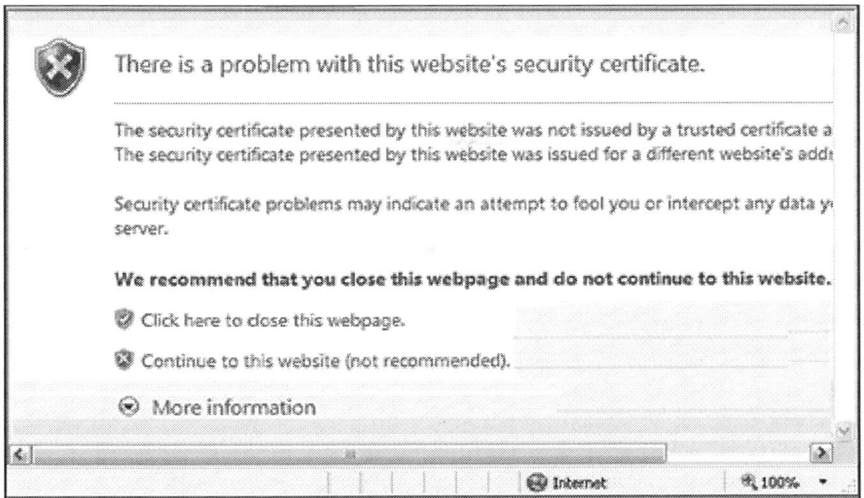

What happened? Once you have established a secure connection with the web server, the server certificate has been sent to the browser. Since the certificate has not been signed by any recognized CA, the browser security sandbox warns the user about the potential security threat.

This is an in-house test so we can safely proceed by choosing **Continue to this website**. That's all you need to do in order to activate the Secure Socket Layer with a self-signed certificate.

Securing HTTP communication with a certificate signed by a CA

Having your certificate signed requires a certificate-signing request (CSR) to be issued to a CA, which will return a signed certificate to be installed on your server. This implies a cost for your organization, which depends on how many certificates you are requesting, the encryption strength, and other factors.

Firstly, generate a CSR using the newly created `keystore` and keyentry:

```
keytool -certreq -keystore jboss.keystore -alias as7alias -storepass
mypassword -keypass mypassword  -keyalg RSA  -file certreq.csr
```

This will create a new certificate request named `certreq.csr`, bearing the following format:

```
-----BEGIN NEW CERTIFICATE REQUEST-----
. . . . . .
-----END NEW CERTIFICATE REQUEST-----
```

The previous certificate needs to be transmitted to the CA. For example, supposing you have chosen **Verisign** as the CA, the following is a screenshot of the request:

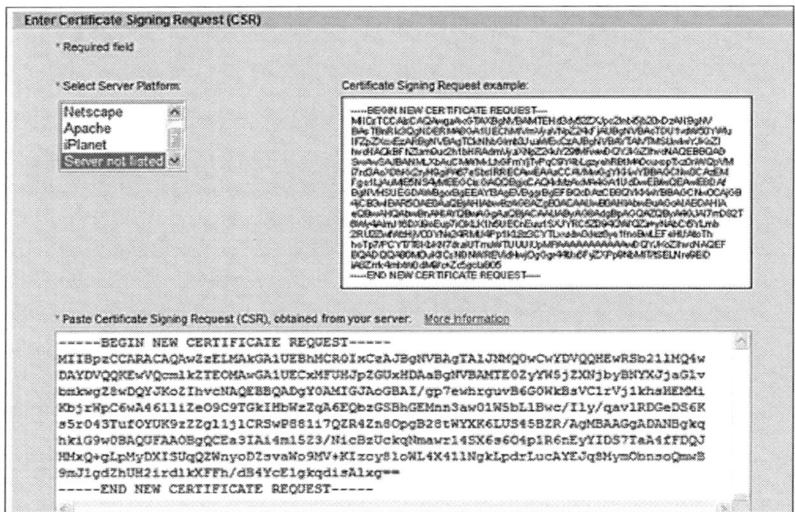

At the end of the enrollment phase, the CA will return a signed certificate that needs to be imported into your keychain. The following code assumes you have saved your CA certificate in a file named `signed_ca.txt`:

```
keytool -import -keystore jboss.keystore -alias testkey1 -storepass
mypassword -keypass mypassword -file signed_ca.txt
```

Now your web browser will recognize your new certificate as being signed by a CA, so it won't complain about not being able to validate the certificate.

Securing EJB communication

EJB clients interact with the Enterprise EJB tier using the RMI-IIOP protocol. The RMI-IIOP protocol has been developed by Sun to combine the RMI programming model with the IIOP underlying transport.

Securing the EJB transport is required for applications having strict secure policies, which cannot be carried out using clear-text transmission. In order to do that, we need to complete the following steps:

1. First generate the SSL certificates and then store the client's public key in the server's `keystore` object and the server's public key on the client's `truststore`.

2. Next, we need to create an SSL-aware security realm that will be used by the `remoting` transport.
3. Finally, we need to apply some changes to our EJB application so that is actually uses the SSL secure channel.

Generating the server and client certificates

Start by generating a public/private key pair for the entity whose unique name has the common name `Francesco Marchioni`, organization `PacktPub`, and two-letter country code `GB`.

```
keytool -genkey -v -alias as7alias -keyalg RSA -keysize 1024 -keystore
jboss.keystore -validity 180 -keypass mypassword -storepass mypassword
-dname "cn=Francesco Marchioni,o=PacktPub,c=GB"
```

Next, export the server's public key into a certificate named `sslPublicKey.cer` that is using the password `mypassword`.

```
keytool -export -keystore jboss.keystore -alias as7alias -file
sslPublicKey.cer -keypass mypassword -storepass mypassword
```

Now we have finished with the server, we will now generate a key pair for the client too. We will do this by using the alias `ejbclientalias` and the same properties as we did for the server's `keystore` object:

```
keytool -genkey -v -alias ejbclientalias -keyalg RSA -keysize 1024
-keystore jbossClient.keystore -validity 180 -keypass clientPassword
-storepass clientPassword -dname "cn=Francesco Marchioni,o=PacktPub,c=GB"
```

The client public key will also be exported into a certificate named `clientPublicKey.cer`.

```
keytool -export -keystore jbossClient.keystore -alias ejbclientalias
-file clientPublicKey.cer -keypass clientPassword -storepass
clientPassword
```

Now, in order to complete the SSL handshake successfully, we need to first import the client's public key into the server's `truststore` object:

```
keytool -import -v -trustcacerts -alias ejbclientalias -file
clientPublicKey.cer -keystore jboss.keystore -keypass mypassword
-storepass mypassword
```

The server certificate also needs to be trusted by the client. You have two available options to solve this issue, as follows:

- Import the server certificate into the client's JDK bundle of certificates
- Create a new repository of certificates trusted by the client (`truststore`)

Importing the server certificate into the client JDK means executing a certificate import into the client's certified authorities.

```
keytool -import -v -trustcacerts -alias as7alias -file sslPublicKey.cer
-keystore C:\Java\jdk1.6.0_31\jre\lib\security\cacerts
```

You have just to replace the path we have used with your actual JDK path and use the client store password in order to complete this operation (default value is `changeit`).

Otherwise, if you want to import the certificate into a newly created `truststore` object, just substitute the `cacerts` destination with your client's `truststore` object.

```
keytool -import -v -trustcacerts -alias as7alias -file sslPublicKey.
cer -keystore jbossClient.keystore -keypass clientPassword -storepass
clientPassword
```

If you choose the latter option, you need to add to your client's JDK arguments the following properties, which will override the default JDK's `truststore` object:

```
java -Djavax.net.ssl.trustStore=<truststorefile>
-Djavax.net.ssl.trustStorePassword=<password>
```

Creating an SSL-aware security realm

Within JBoss AS 7, security realms are used to secure access to the management interfaces and remote JNDI and EJB access. Within a security realm, it is also possible to define an identity for the server; this identity can be used for both inbound connections to the server and outbound connections being established by the server.

Therefore, in order to enable SSL communication for our EJB communication, we will define a security realm (named `EJBRealm`) that is bound to a server identity that references the server's `keystore` object:

```
<security-realm name="EJBRealm">
<server-identities>
      <ssl>
       <keystore path="jboss.keystore" relative-to="jboss.server.
config.dir" keystore-password="mypassword"/>
      </ssl>
   </server-identities>
   <authentication>
        <jaas name="ejb-security-domain"/>
   </authentication>
</security-realm>
```

Besides containing the location where SSL certificates are stored, this security realm also contains the authentication policy used by your EJBs, which is defined by the JAAS's security domain, named `ejb-security-domain`.

The following is a security domain definition that is a simple file-based security domain containing the user credentials and roles in the files `ejb-users.properties` and `ejb-roles.properties` respectively:

```
<security-domain name="ejb-security-domain" cache-type="default">
<authentication>
  <login-module code="Remoting" flag="optional">
    <module-option name="password-stacking" value="useFirstPass"/>
  </login-module>
  <login-module
  code="org.jboss.security.auth.spi.UsersRolesLoginModule"
  flag="required">
    <module-option name="defaultUsersProperties"
    value="${jboss.server.config.dir}/ejb-users.properties"/>
    <module-option name="defaultRolesProperties"
    value="${jboss.server.config.dir}/ejb-roles.properties"/>
    <module-option name="usersProperties"
    value="${jboss.server.config.dir}/ejb-users.properties"/>
    <module-option name="rolesProperties"
    value="${jboss.server.config.dir}/ejb-roles.properties"/>
    <module-option name="password-stacking" value="useFirstPass"/>
  </login-module>
</authentication>
</security-domain>
```

As you can imagine, you need to create the two property files each with some values in them. For example, here's the `ejb-user.properties` file to be placed in the server configuration's folder:

```
adminUser=admin123
```

And this is corresponding `ejb-roles.properties` file that grants the role `ejbRole` to the `adminUser` role:

```
adminUser=ejbRole
```

The last configuration effort would be specifying it in the `security-realm` attribute of your `remoting` connector's element:

```
<subsystem xmlns="urn:jboss:domain:remoting:1.1">
     <connector name="remoting-connector"
      socket-binding="remoting"
      security-realm="EJBRealm"/>
</subsystem>
```

Creating an SSL-aware security realm

As we have learned in *Chapter 3, Beginning Java EE 6 – EJBs*, the RMI-IIOP connection properties are specified in the `jboss-ejb-client.properties` file, which needs to be tweaked a bit to enable SSL connections:

```
remote.connections=node1
remote.connection.node1.host=localhost
remote.connection.node1.port = 4447
remote.connection.node1.username=adminUser
remote.connection.node1.password=admin123
remote.connectionprovider.create.options.org.xnio.Options.SSL_
ENABLED=true
remote.connection.node1.connect.options.org.xnio.Options.SSL_
STARTTLS=true
remote.connection.node1.connect.options.org.xnio.Options.SASL_POLICY_
NOANONYMOUS=true
```

The `SSL_ENABLED` option, when set to `true`, enables the `remoting` connector's SSL communication.

The `STARTTLS` option specifies whether to use **Tunneled Transport Layer Security (TTLS)** mode at startup or when needed.

The `SASL_POLICY_NOANONYMOUS` option specifies whether **Simple Authentication and Security Layer (SASL)** mechanisms, which accept anonymous logins, are permitted.

Finally, since our security realm also included an authentication security domain, we can choose to restrict access to some methods by specifying a `@RolesAllowed` annotation, which requires the role `ejbRole`:

```
@RolesAllowed("ejbRole")
public String bookSeat(int se;atId)  throws SeatBookedException {
  . . . .
}
```

In order to activate the security domain on your EJBs, we need to mention it in the assembly descriptor of your `jboss-ejb3.xml` file:

```
<jboss:ejb-jar>
  <assembly-descriptor>
    <s:security>
      <ejb-name>*</ejb-name>
          <s:security-domain>ejb-security-domain</s:security-domain>
    </s:security>
  </assembly-descriptor>
</jboss:ejb-jar>
```

Now redeploy the Ticket EJB example application, following the directions contained in *Chapter 3, Beginning Java EE 6 – EJBs*, and execute the client.

As you can see from the following screenshot (taken from the **WireShark** network analyzer), the remote handshake is successfully executed using the Secure Sockets Layer:

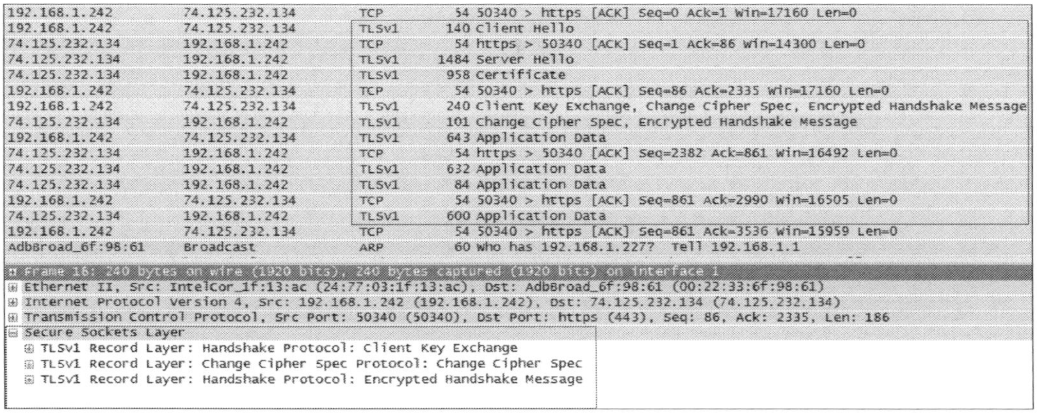

```
192.168.1.242      74.125.232.134     TCP      54 50340 > https [ACK] Seq=0 Ack=1 Win=17160 Len=0
192.168.1.242      74.125.232.134     TLSv1   140 Client Hello
74.125.232.134     192.168.1.242      TCP      54 https > 50340 [ACK] Seq=1 Ack=86 Win=14300 Len=0
74.125.232.134     192.168.1.242      TLSv1  1484 Server Hello
74.125.232.134     192.168.1.242      TLSv1   958 Certificate
192.168.1.242      74.125.232.134     TCP      54 50340 > https [ACK] Seq=86 Ack=2335 Win=17160 Len=0
192.168.1.242      74.125.232.134     TLSv1   240 Client Key Exchange, Change Cipher Spec, Encrypted Handshake Message
74.125.232.134     192.168.1.242      TLSv1   101 Change Cipher Spec, Encrypted Handshake Message
192.168.1.242      74.125.232.134     TLSv1   643 Application Data
74.125.232.134     192.168.1.242      TCP      54 https > 50340 [ACK] Seq=2382 Ack=861 Win=16492 Len=0
74.125.232.134     192.168.1.242      TLSv1   632 Application Data
74.125.232.134     192.168.1.242      TLSv1    84 Application Data
192.168.1.242      74.125.232.134     TCP      54 50340 > https [ACK] Seq=861 Ack=2990 Win=16505 Len=0
74.125.232.134     192.168.1.242      TLSv1   600 Application Data
192.168.1.242      74.125.232.134     TCP      54 50340 > https [ACK] Seq=861 Ack=3536 Win=15959 Len=0
AdbBroad_6f:98:61  Broadcast          ARP      60 Who has 192.168.1.227?  Tell 192.168.1.1

Frame 16: 240 bytes on wire (1920 bits), 240 bytes captured (1920 bits) on interface 1
Ethernet II, Src: IntelCor_1f:13:ac (24:77:03:1f:13:ac), Dst: AdbBroad_6f:98:61 (00:22:33:6f:98:61)
Internet Protocol Version 4, Src: 192.168.1.242 (192.168.1.242), Dst: 74.125.232.134 (74.125.232.134)
Transmission Control Protocol, Src Port: 50340 (50340), Dst Port: https (443), Seq: 86, Ack: 2335, Len: 186
Secure Sockets Layer
  TLSv1 Record Layer: Handshake Protocol: Client Key Exchange
  TLSv1 Record Layer: Change Cipher Spec Protocol: Change Cipher Spec
  TLSv1 Record Layer: Handshake Protocol: Encrypted Handshake Message
```

Summary

We had started this chapter by discussing the basic concepts of security and the difference between authentication and authorization.

JBoss uses the PicketBox framework sitting on top of the **Java Authentication and Authorization Service (JAAS)**, which secures all the Java EE technologies running in the application. The core section of the security subsystem is contained in the security-domain element that performs all the required **authorization** and **authentication** checks.

Then we took a much closer look at the login modules, which are used to store the user credentials and their associated roles. In particular, we learned how to apply the file-based `UserRoles` login module and the `Database` login module. Each login module can be used by Enterprise applications in either a programmatic or declarative way. While programmatic security can provide a fine-grained security model, you should consider using declarative security, which allows a clean separation between the business layer and the security policies.

Finally, in the last section of this chapter, we have covered how to encrypt the communication channel using the Secure Socket Layer and the certificates produced by the `keytool` Java utility.

Rapid Development Using JBoss Forge

In the appendix of this book, we will give you an overview of JBoss Forge, which is a powerful, rapid application development (aimed at Java EE 6) and project comprehension tool. With Forge, you can start a new project from scratch and generate the skeleton for your application just with a few commands. However, it can also be used for incremental enhancements for your existing projects using extra plugins.

Installing Forge

In order to install Forge, you need to perform the following steps:

1. Download and unzip Forge from `http://forge.jboss.org/` into a folder on your hard disk; this folder will be your `FORGE_HOME`.
2. Add `FORGE_HOME/bin` to your path (Windows, Linux, and Mac OSX).

In Unix-based operating systems, this typically means editing your `~/.bashrc` or `~/.profile`; you will need to enter the following code snippet:

```
export FORGE_HOME=~/forge/
export PATH=$PATH:$FORGE_HOME/bin
```

In Windows systems, you will need to open the **Control Panel** window, then click on **System Properties | Advanced | Environment Variables**, and add these two entries visually. It is recommended to set user variables for Forge, unless you have placed the unzipped distribution in a folder where all users can access it.

Starting Forge

In order to start Forge, there is a script named `forge.bat` (or the equivalent `forge.sh` for Unix). Run the following script:

```
forge.bat
```

This will launch the Forge console:

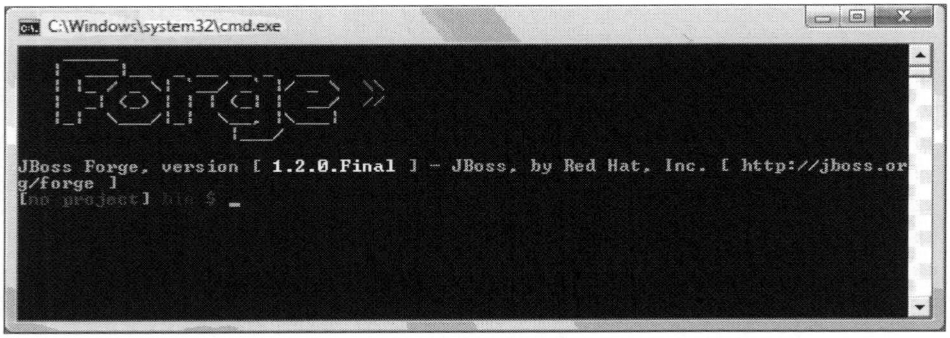

The console accepts a large set of commands, such as commands to navigate and manipulate the filesystems, to create new projects, to operate on the Forge environment and UI generation, and scaffolding commands.

In order to learn all the available commands, you can enter `list-commands` from the shell, as shown in the following screenshot, which enlists all the basic commands you can use in Forge 1.2.0 Final:

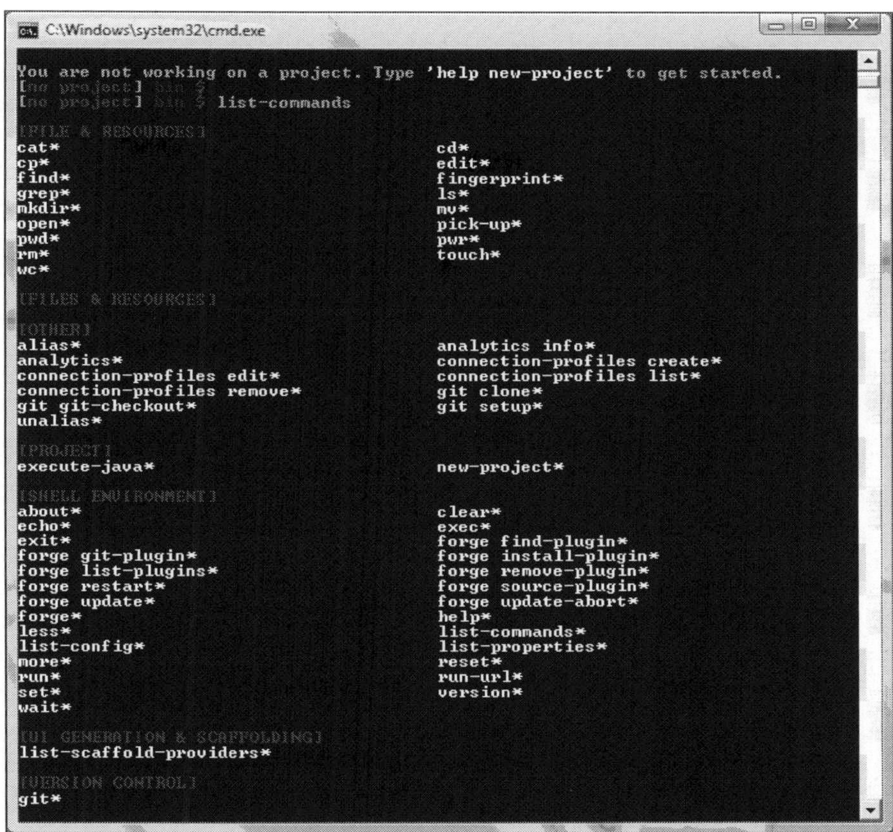

```
You are not working on a project. Type 'help new-project' to get started.
[no project] bin $
[no project] bin $ list-commands
[FILE & RESOURCES]
cat*                                        cd*
cp*                                         edit*
find*                                       fingerprint*
grep*                                       ls*
mkdir*                                      mv*
open*                                       pick-up*
pwd*                                        pwr*
rm*                                         touch*
wc*

[FILES & RESOURCES]

[OTHER]
alias*                                      analytics info*
analytics*                                  connection-profiles create*
connection-profiles edit*                   connection-profiles list*
connection-profiles remove*                 git clone*
git git-checkout*                           git setup*
unalias*

[PROJECT]
execute-java*                               new-project*

[SHELL ENVIRONMENT]
about*                                      clear*
echo*                                       exec*
exit*                                       forge find-plugin*
forge git-plugin*                           forge install-plugin*
forge list-plugins*                         forge remove-plugin*
forge restart*                              forge source-plugin*
forge update*                               forge update-abort*
forge*                                      help*
less*                                       list-commands*
list-config*                                list-properties*
more*                                       reset*
run*                                        run-url*
set*                                        version*
wait*

[UI GENERATION & SCAFFOLDING]
list-scaffold-providers*

[VERSION CONTROL]
git*
```

If you want to learn more about the single commands, you can use `help` followed by the command name:

```
C:\Windows\system32\cmd.exe
(only commands in relevant scope displayed. use --all to see all commands.)
[no project] bin $ help new-project

[new-project] - Create a new project in an empty directory.

[OPTIONS]
        [--named] - The name of the new project - no help text available
        [--topLevelPackage] - The top-level java package for the project [e.g: "
com.example.project"] - no help text available
        [--type] - The project type, defaults to .jar - no help text available
        [--projectFolder] - The folder in which to create this project [e.g: "~/
Desktop/..."] - no help text available
        [--createMain] - Toggle creation of a simple Main() script in the root p
ackage, valid for jar projects only - no help text available
        [--finalName] - The final artifact name of the new project - no help tex
t available

[no project] bin $ _
```

> Besides the standard commands, it is possible to enrich the syntax of the Forge command line with plugins, which add superior capabilities to your project creation. On this link, `http://forge.jboss.org/plugins.html`, you can find a list of available plugins at the time of writing. For example, we are going to use the `hibernate-tools` plugin in order to reverse engineer the database schema into Java entities. We will also use the JBoss AS 7 plugin, which can provide us with seven management capabilities from within the Forge shell.

In the following section, we will demonstrate how to use some of the available commands in order to create a Java EE 6 application.

Creating your first Java EE 6 application with JBoss Forge

So Forge installation is quite easy; however, creating your first Java EE 6 application will be even faster! Although we can create rather advanced applications with Forge, for the purpose of learning we will just use a simple schema that contains a `user` table, which can be built using the following command:

```
CREATE TABLE user (
id int(10) NOT NULL PRIMARY KEY auto_increment,
name varchar(50),
surname varchar(50),
email varchar(50));
```

The first thing we need to do is to create a new project using the `new-project` command. Execute from within the Forge shell the following commands:

```
new-project --named forge-demo --topLevelPackage com.packtpub.
as7development.appendix -projectFolder forge-demo
```

Now you have a new Forge project, which is based on a Maven project structure. Arguably, generating a new project isn't Forge's greatest value—the same could be achieved with Maven archetypes. The sweet part of Forge is that now you have the luxury of defining your own application skeleton interactively after it has already been generated. This means that you can create the project using the Maven archetype first, and then extend it using Forge's intuitive suggestions.

Since we will need to reverse engineer our database table into Java entities, we will install the `hibernate-tools` plugin:

```
forge install-plugin hibernate-tools
```

The next step will be configuring the JPA layer for your application. This application will be based on JBoss' JPA implementation that is based on the Hibernate provider, referencing a database named `MySQL`. This database is reachable at the JNDI named `java:jboss/datasources/MySqlDS`.

```
persistence setup --provider HIBERNATE --container JBOSS_AS7 --database
MYSQL  --jndiDataSource java:jboss/datasources/MySqlDS
```

You will be asked to select which Java EE 6 POM you want to use for your application; you are advised to always use the latest stable version.

You can check the `persistence.xml` file generated by Forge by using the `cat` command:

```
[forge-demo] forge-demo $ cat C:\forge-distribution-
1.1.3.Final\bin\forge-demo\src\main\resources\META-
INF\persistence.xml


<?xml version="1.0" encoding="UTF-8" standalone="no"?>
<persistence xmlns="http://java.sun.com/xml/ns/persistence"
xmlns:xsi="http://www.w3.org/2001/XMLSchema-instance" version="2.0"
xsi:schemaLocation="http://java.sun.com/xml/ns/persistence
http://java.sun.com/xml/ns/persistence/persistence_2_0.xsd">
  <persistence-unit name="forge-default" transaction-type="JTA">
    <description>Forge Persistence Unit</description>
    <provider>org.hibernate.ejb.HibernatePersistence</provider>
    <jta-data-source>java:jboss/datasources/MySqlDS</jta-data-source>
    <exclude-unlisted-classes>false</exclude-unlisted-classes>
    <properties>
      <property name="hibernate.hbm2ddl.auto" value="create-drop"/>
      <property name="hibernate.show_sql" value="true"/>
      <property name="hibernate.format_sql" value="true"/>
      <property name="hibernate.transaction.flush_before_completion"
      value="true"/>
      <property name="hibernate.dialect"
      value="org.hibernate.dialect.MySQLDialect"/>
    </properties>
  </persistence-unit>
</persistence>
```

Next, we will use the `generate-entities` command (from the `hibernate-tools` plugin) in order to generate your `Entity` class. You will need to provide the following JDBC connection information:

- The JDBC URL
- The username and password
- The SQL dialect
- The JDBC Driver class name
- The path in the filesystem where the JDBC driver is located
- The package where the entities will be generated

You can specify all the parameters in a one-line command or complete it interactively as shown in the following transcript:

```
[forge-demo] forge-demo $ generate-entities

 ? Specify the URL for the JDBC connection. jdbc:mysql://localhost/
ticketsystem


 ? Enter the user name for JDBC connection. [null] root

 ? Enter the password for JDBC connection. [ENTER for default] *****


 ? Enter the dialect to use for the datasource. [org.hibernate.dialect.
H2Dialect

] org.hibernate.dialect.MySQLDialect


 ? Specify the class name for the JDBC driver for the datasource. [org.
h2.Driver

] com.mysql.jdbc.Driver


 ? Enter the path in the local file system to the jar file containing
the JDBC driver. [null] C:\forge-distribution-1.1.3.Final\lib\mysql-
connector-java-5.1.18-bin.jar


? In which package you'd like to generate the entities, or enter for
default: [com.packtpub.as7development.appendix.model]

Found 1 tables in datasource

Generated java at C:\forge-distribution-1.1.3.Final\bin\forge-
demo\src\main\java\com\packtpub\as7development\appendix\model\User.java

Generated 1 java files.
```

After completing the persistence layer, we will now create the application GUI using the `scaffold` command, which can be associated with several providers such as the JavaServer Faces provider:

```
[forge-demo] forge-demo $ scaffold setup --scaffoldType faces;
 ? Scaffold provider [faces] is not installed. Install it? [Y/n] Y
 ? Facet [forge.maven.WebResourceFacet] requires packaging type(s) [war],
but is currently [jar]. Update packaging?
(Note: this could deactivate other plugins in your project.) [Y/n] Y
***SUCCESS*** Installed [forge.maven.WebResourceFacet] successfully.
***SUCCESS*** Installed [forge.spec.ejb] successfully.
***SUCCESS*** Installed [forge.spec.cdi] successfully.
***SUCCESS*** Installed [forge.spec.servlet] successfully.
***SUCCESS*** Installed [forge.spec.jsf.api] successfully.
***SUCCESS*** Installed [faces] successfully.
 ? Create scaffold in which sub-directory of web-root? (e.g.
http://localhost:8080/forge-demo/DIR) [/] view
```

As you can see from the previous transcript, the `scaffold` command will need to update the project packaging format (from `jar` to `war`) and request a folder to use for storing scaffolding data.

Now we will generate a **CRUD (create, read, update, and delete)** view of your entities using the `scaffold from-entity` command:

```
scaffold from-entity com.packtpub.as7development.appendix.model.*
--overwrite;
***INFO*** Using currently installed scaffold [faces]
***SUCCESS*** Generated UI for [com.packtpub.as7development.appendix.
model.User]
```

Please verify if the user's ID type matches with the corresponding UserBean ID type at the time of writing.

Building and deploying the application

Now it is time to build your application using the `build` command, which will compile and package your application in a web application archive (`forge-demo.war`).

```
[forge-demo] forge-demo $ build
[INFO] Scanning for projects...
[INFO]
```

```
[INFO] ------------------------------------------------------------
[INFO] Building forge-demo 1.0.0-SNAPSHOT
[INFO] ------------------------------------------------------------
. . . . . . . . . .
[INFO] Packaging webapp
[INFO] Assembling webapp [forge-demo] in [C:\forge-distribution-
1.1.3.Final\bin\forge-demo\target\forge-demo]
[INFO] Processing war project
[INFO] Copying webapp resources [C:\forge-distribution-1.1.3.Final\bin\
forge-demo\src\main\webapp]
[INFO] Webapp assembled in [740 msecs]
[INFO] Building war: C:\forge-distribution-1.1.3.Final\bin\forge-demo\
target\forge-demo.war
[INFO] -----------------------------------------------------------
[INFO] BUILD SUCCESS
[INFO] ------------------------------------------------------------
[INFO] Total time: 12.830s
[INFO] Finished at: Sat Feb 23 19:59:47 CET 2013
[INFO] Final Memory: 7M/18M
```

The Maven `build` command has been created for the artifact `forge-demo.war` in the `target` folder of your project. You can now either manually copy the archive into the `deployments` folder of your application server (or alternatively use the management interfaces) or install the AS 7 Forge plugin by typing the following command:

```
[forge-demo] forge install-plugin jboss-as-7
```

Once you install the AS 7 plugin, you need to set up some configuration parameters (it is suggested that you leave the default values and just override the `As7` folder, unless you want to let Forge download it for you).

```
[forge-demo] forge-demo $ as7 setup
 ? The Java Home 'C:\Java\jdk1.6.0_31' is already set, would you like to
override it? [y/N]
 ? A default version of 7.1.3.Final is already set, would you like to
override it? [y/N]
 ? Enter path for JBoss AS or leave blank to download: C:\jboss-as-
7.1.1.Final
***SUCCESS*** Installed [AS7ServerFacet] successfully.
```

Now you can deploy your application using the `as7 deploy` command:

```
[forge-demo] forge-demo $ as7 deploy
```

```
The deployment operation (FORCE_DEPLOY) was successful.
```

If, later on you want to undeploy the application from JBoss, you can use the corresponding command, which will remove your application from the available applications:

```
[forge-demo] forge-demo $ as7 undeploy
```

Your forge-demo application in action

You can access your application at the default URL, `http://localhost:8080/forge-demo/`.

The main application screen will contain the list of users that have been added, a **Search** button which can be used to filter across the users, and a **Create New** button, which obviously will insert some data:

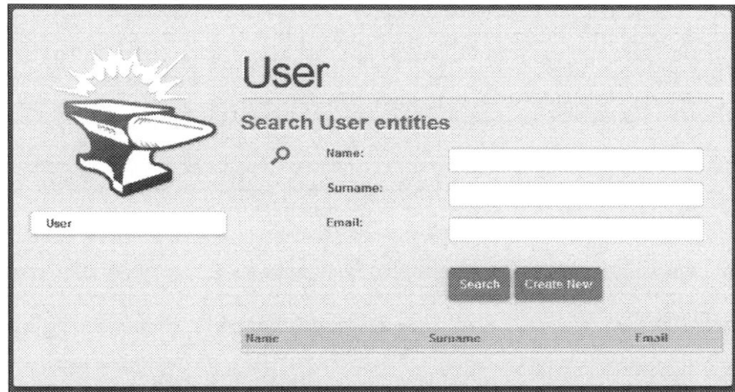

By clicking on the **Create New** button, you will be taken to the screen that allows the insertion of a new user in to the database (remember we have configured this application to run against a MySQL database):

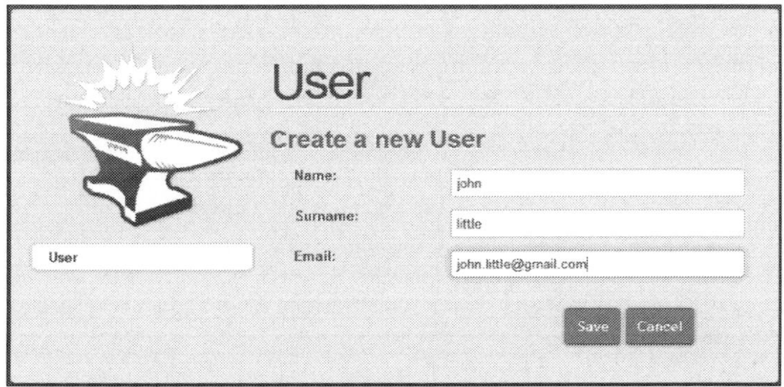

Once saved, the data will be available in the main screen window:

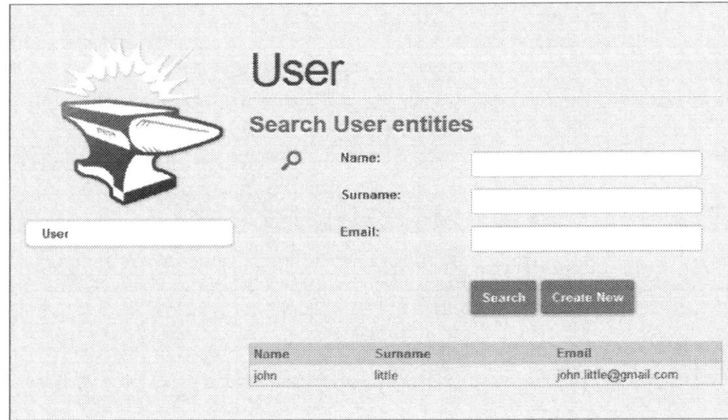

For the sake of completeness, we will mention that an edit/update view of the application will be available when you click on the list of users contained in the data table:

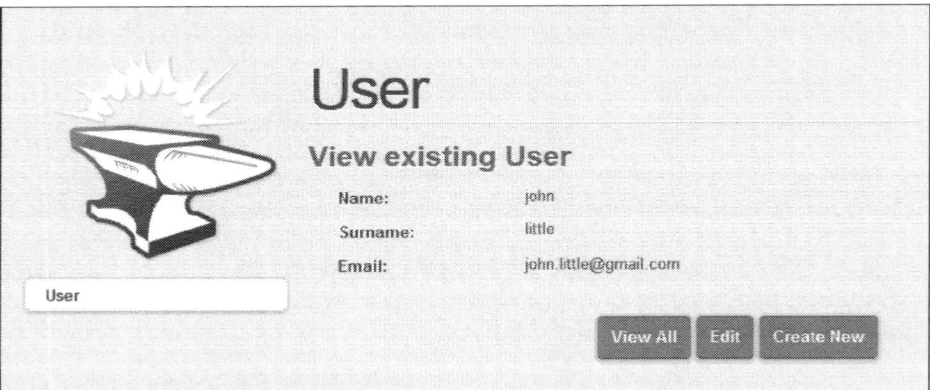

Index

Symbols

A

B

E

F

G

H

I

J

K

L

M

N

O

P

Q

R

S

T

U

W

X

Thank you for buying

JBoss AS 7 Development

About Packt Publishing

Packt, pronounced 'packed', published its first book "*Mastering phpMyAdmin for Effective MySQL Management*" in April 2004 and subsequently continued to specialize in publishing highly focused books on specific technologies and solutions.

Our books and publications share the experiences of your fellow IT professionals in adapting and customizing today's systems, applications, and frameworks. Our solution based books give you the knowledge and power to customize the software and technologies you're using to get the job done. Packt books are more specific and less general than the IT books you have seen in the past. Our unique business model allows us to bring you more focused information, giving you more of what you need to know, and less of what you don't.

Packt is a modern, yet unique publishing company, which focuses on producing quality, cutting-edge books for communities of developers, administrators, and newbies alike. For more information, please visit our website: `www.packtpub.com`.

About Packt Open Source

In 2010, Packt launched two new brands, Packt Open Source and Packt Enterprise, in order to continue its focus on specialization. This book is part of the Packt Open Source brand, home to books published on software built around Open Source licences, and offering information to anybody from advanced developers to budding web designers. The Open Source brand also runs Packt's Open Source Royalty Scheme, by which Packt gives a royalty to each Open Source project about whose software a book is sold.

Writing for Packt

We welcome all inquiries from people who are interested in authoring. Book proposals should be sent to author@packtpub.com. If your book idea is still at an early stage and you would like to discuss it first before writing a formal book proposal, contact us; one of our commissioning editors will get in touch with you.

We're not just looking for published authors; if you have strong technical skills but no writing experience, our experienced editors can help you develop a writing career, or simply get some additional reward for your expertise.

[PACKT] open source
community experience distilled
PUBLISHING

JBoss AS 7 Configuration, Deployment and Administration

ISBN: 978-184951-678-5 Paperback: 380 pages

Build a fully-functional, effecient application server using JBoss AS

1. Covers all JBoss AS 7 administration topics in a concise, practical, and understandable manner, along with detailed explanations and lots of screenshots
2. Uncover the advanced features of JBoss AS, including High Availability and clustering, integration with other frameworks, and creating complex AS domain configurations
3. Discover the new features of JBoss AS 7, which has made quite a departure from previous versions

---

HornetQ Messaging Developer's Guide

ISBN: 978-1-84951-840-6 Paperback: 250 pages

Avoid being stung by JBoss HornetQ messaging service whether you're an existing user or a newcomer with this agile, fast-paced, example-rich guide

1. Rethink the way you process messages in a stable, powerful and adaptive way, using the JBoss HornetQ messaging system.
2. Learn how to set up and code real-world, high performance message applications.
3. Real-world advanced medical scenario features as the main example that will lead you from the basics of enterprise messaging to the advanced features

Please check **www.PacktPub.com** for information on our titles

[PACKT] open source
PUBLISHING
community experience distilled

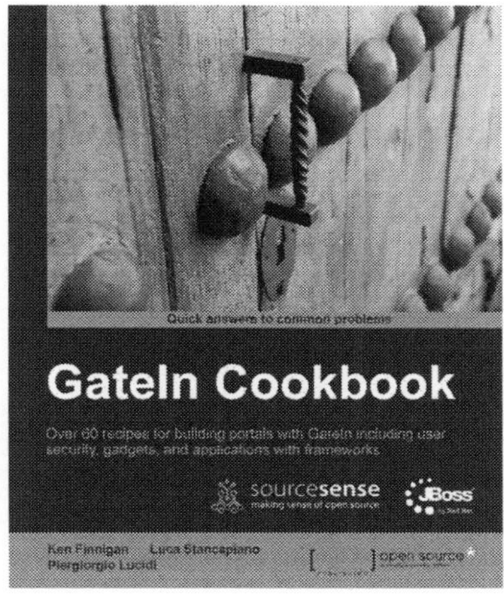

GateIn Cookbook

ISBN: 978-1-84951-8-628 Paperback: 392 pages

Over 60 recipes for building portals with GateIn including user security gadget, and applications with frameworks

1. All you need to develop and manage a GateIn portal and all available portlets
2. Thorough detail on the internal architecture needed to use the components
3. Manage portal resources on a command line; choose the authentication system, configure users and groups and migrate portlets from other portals

---

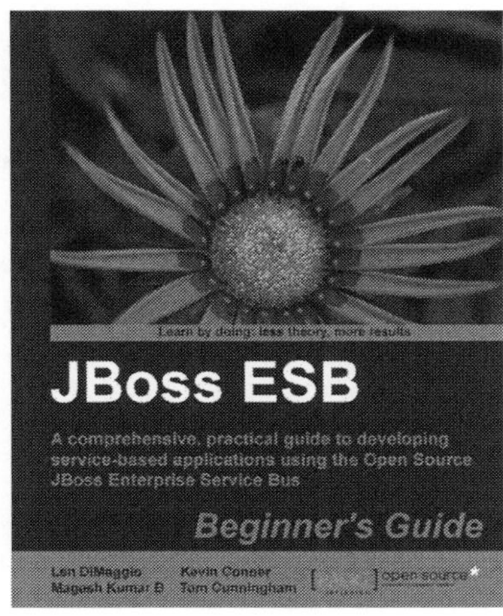

JBoss ESB Beginner's Guide

ISBN: 978-1-84951-658-7 Paperback: 320 pages

A comerhensive, practical guide to developing service-based applications using the Open Source JBoss Enterprise Service Bus

1. Develop your own service-based applications, from simple deployments through to complex legacy integrations
2. Learn how services can communicate with each other and the benefits to be gained from loose coupling
3. Contains clear, practical instructions for service development, highlighted through the use of numerous working examples

Please check **www.PacktPub.com** for information on our titles

4606330R00181

Printed in Great Britain
by Amazon.co.uk, Ltd.,
Marston Gate.